The End

of

"CHRISTIAN PSYCHOLOGY"

The End

of

"CHRISTIAN PSYCHOLOGY"

Martin & Deidre Bobgan

EastGate Publishers
Santa Barbara, CA 93110

Scripture quotations are taken from the Authorized
King James Version of the Holy Bible.

THE END OF "CHRISTIAN PSYCHOLOGY"

Copyright © 1997 Martin and Deidre Bobgan
Published by EastGate Publishers
Santa Barbara, California

Library of Congress Catalog Card Number 97-94482
ISBN 0-941717-12-7

Printed in the United States of America

For other foundation can no man lay than that is laid, which is Jesus Christ. 1 Corinthians 3:11

In whom all the building fitly framed together groweth unto an holy temple in the Lord: in whom ye also are builded together for an habitation of God through the Spirit. Ephesians 2:21-22

As ye have therefore received Christ Jesus the Lord, so walk ye in him: rooted and built up in him, and stablished in the faith, as ye have been taught, abounding therein with thanksgiving. Beware lest any man spoil you through philosophy and vain deceit, after the tradition of men, after the rudiments of the world, and not after Christ. For in him dwelleth all the fulness of the Godhead bodily. And ye are complete in him, which is the head of all principality and power. Colossians 2:6-10

CONTENTS

1

The End of "Christian Psychology"

We begin by explaining the title of this book. Quotes around *Christian psychology* indicate that there is really no "Christian psychology." What is called "Christian psychology" is comprised of the same confusion of contradictory theories and techniques as secular psychology. Professional psychologists and psychiatrists who profess Christianity have simply borrowed the theories and techniques from secular psychology. They practice what they consider a perfect blend of psychology and Christianity. However, they use the same psychology as non-Christian psychologists and psychiatrists. They use theories and techniques contrived by such men as Freud, Jung, Adler, Fromm, Maslow, Rogers, Ellis, Glasser, Harris, Janov, all of whom we critique in this present volume and none of

3

whom embraced Christianity or developed a psychological system from the Word of God.

The Christian Association for Psychological Studies (CAPS) is an organization of psychologists who are professing Christians. The following was admitted at one of their meetings:

> We are often asked if we are "Christian psychologists" and find it difficult to answer since we don't know what the question implies. We are Christians who are psychologists but at the present time there is no acceptable Christian psychology that is markedly different from non-Christian psychology. It is difficult to imply that we function in a manner that is fundamentally distinct from our non-Christian colleagues . . . as yet there is not an acceptable theory, mode of research or treatment methodology that is distinctly Christian.[1]

When we use the words *Christian psychology* and other similar phrases, let it be understood that there is no such practice or person in the sense that the practice or the person is performing a specifically Christian activity. Also, when we use the word *Christian* in reference to various mental health professionals, it does not necessarily mean that the person is a true believer.

Christian psychology depends on psychology itself. Because psychology is such a broad field, we want to make it clear that when we use the word *psychology*, we are referring to psychotherapy and its underlying psychologies.

Since Christian psychology depends on secular psychology, the bulk of this book will be directed at scientifically and biblically exposing the myths surrounding such psychology. If secular psychology falls under such scrutiny, then the domino effect should topple Christian psychology as well.

A Questionable, Detrimental Counterfeit?

Professional psychotherapy with its underlying psychologies is questionable at best, detrimental at worst, and a spiritual counterfeit at least. The purpose of this book is to demonstrate the truth of that statement and to raise the challenge of purging the church of all evidences of this scourge. On the one hand there is enough biblical and scientific evidence to shut down the secular Psychology Industry and with it the Christian Psychology Industry. On the other hand, we are not naive enough to believe that the overwhelming evidence supporting its demise will be heeded by the majority of Christians.

Many will not be interested in reading about the biblical and scientific evidence, because it will contradict their established assumptions about the psychological way. Most therapeutic practitioners, who rely on income produced by their therapeutically oriented clients, will not even read about the research condemning professional psychotherapy, which is presented in this book. And, Christian therapists will resist the potential demise of their therapeutically produced income and will pay little, if any, attention to the research results and criticisms of how contrary to Scripture are their wares. One professional psychotherapy organization reveals:

> It is no secret that therapists are rarely swayed by research findings. . . . once in practice, most clinicians are far more influenced by the last workshop they went to or how their clients respond to a given intervention than by anything published in the scholarly journals.[2]

First, we will deal with the overall picture of the psychological way and its false promises. Then we will reveal the fallacies of various biblical justifications for using psychology. There are no valid scientific reasons for using professional psychotherapy by either believers or unbelievers, but the psychological way should be doubly condemned and rejected by Christians. First, the psychological way should be condemned and rejected because of the lack of research support for the use of professional psychological counseling and its underlying psychologies. Second, the psychological way of understanding and changing people is condemned by the very Word of God. There is a psychological way and a biblical way to understand human nature and to transform the lives of people. The psychological way is the way of psychotherapy, which is simply the treatment of problems of living by psychological, man-made means. By applying techniques and methodologies based on psychological theories, a psychologically trained counselor attempts to assist an individual to change attitudes, feelings, perceptions, values, and behavior.

Psychotherapists are those who are trained and licensed to perform a wide variety of therapies. They include psychiatrists, psychoanalysts, clinical psychologists, marriage and family counselors, some social workers, and many who call themselves Christian psychologists, Christian counselors, and even biblical counselors. In addition, many individuals practice psychotherapy without a license and many of the self-help systems are psychotherapies in practice without being named as such.

Furthermore, the psychological way encompasses all the psychological ways of understanding the human condition, why people act the way they do, and how they change. These teachings have become so prevalent in secular schools, books, magazines and other media that they permeate the thinking of most people. Worse yet, these teachings have become so accepted in Christian schools, seminaries, churches, missionary organizations, books, radio and other media that many Christians assume such psychological ideas are true and even biblical. Thus, the tentacles of the psychological way have a global, gargantuan, gridiron grasp on the thinking of many Christians.

The pure biblical way, on the other hand, is based on God's Word rather than on human wisdom. Instead of using psychological theories, Christians are to minister God's grace through biblical means. They are to help one another identify with Christ in them and live according to His life, increasing in Christlike attitudes, thoughts, words and actions. Although the biblical way has existed for thousands of years, the psychological way is relatively new. It has only been during the twentieth century that Christians began to trust psychology more than the Bible in dealing with problems of living. As a result, psychology has displaced much of Christianity. Even for those who are Christians, psychotherapy and its underlying psychologies have contaminated the pure ministry of the Word of God and the life of Christ in the believer. Today people wholeheartedly believe that psychological counseling theories, dressed in a wide variety of styles and shades, contain the secrets and answers for helping troubled souls. Their confidence in the curative power of psychotherapy has increased in spite of the absence of substantial proof of any great degree of effectiveness.[3] Persuaded by the claims of psychotherapists, they fail to question the validity of its claims, refuse to examine research, and blindly believe popular myths about psychotherapy.

Those who must accept the most responsibility for the church's capitulation to psychotherapy are not the psychotherapists for offering their services, but rather the Bible colleges, seminaries, and churches where psychology is either promoted or permitted. Those teachers and pastors who are recommending and referring to this pseudo-scientific substitute for the true cure of souls should be denounced and renounced; but those leaders who have simply permitted the rise of this heresy without a word of warning to the sheep are also culpable.

Contrary to what most people think, psychotherapy is a belief system similar to that of a religion. Psychotherapeutic beliefs and religious beliefs both rely on faith. We will be examining some of the psychotherapeutic faith systems and consider the following questions: Does psychotherapy really work? Can psychotherapy harm? Is psychotherapy based on observable, verifiable fact or on subjective theories and interpretations? To what extent is psychotherapy medicine, philosophy, or religion? On what ideologies are the various psychotherapeutic systems founded? Are Christianity and psychotherapy truly compatible? In addition, the question of Christians ministering to one another will be examined and a challenge given to the church to restore the original practice of ministering to troubled souls.

Most Christians agree that the Bible is the basis for living the Christian life, but very few seem to believe that the Bible is sufficient to deal with **all** problems of living, which include those nonorganically caused categories of behavior that now carry psychiatric and psychological diagnostic labels. Many in the church believe that the Bible provides preventative principles for mental-emotional-behavioral well-being but hesitate to accept that the Bible contains restorative power. We maintain that God and His Word provide a completely sufficient foundation for living the Christian life, which would include mental-emotional-behavioral health. We further maintain that the Bible contains the healing balm for all nonorganically based problems of living that might be labeled as mental-emotional-behavioral disorders.

The Bible should also be used to minister to the souls of those who are suffering from biological diseases, even though they are under the care of a medical doctor. To substantiate this position, we expose the weaknesses of psychotherapy in contrast to biblical means of living a life pleasing to God and facing the challenges of life in the midst of trials and affliction.

Our concern in this book has to do with the doctrines and methods of psychotherapy and its underlying psychologies, and not the numerous other fields of psychology. We believe that all problems of living, including nonorganically related mental-emotional-behavioral disorders have a spiritual, Christ-centered solution rather than a psychological, self-centered solution. However, because psychotherapy has been embraced and promoted by seminary and Bible college professors, pastors, and other Christian leaders, this position may evoke an extreme reaction from many, including those who, through training or current professional involvement, have vested interests and commitments in the Psychology Industry.

Nevertheless, we pray that this book will encourage believers that they do not have to turn to the wisdom of men in their search for "the way, the truth, and the life." Indeed, this is Jesus' place in the believer. He is, indeed, "the way, the truth, and the life," and He Himself is in the believer. Thus every true Christian has been given "all things pertaining to life and godliness, through the knowledge of Him" (2 Peter 1:3).

The Word of God, the Holy Spirit, and the very life of Christ in the believer are more than sufficient for dealing with the most difficult problems of living, including those that have been given psychiatric and psychological labels, as well as meeting the ordinary challenges of life. We also pray that this book will encourage believers to take confidence in God's way of meeting life's challenges and of ministering to one another in the Body of Christ according to the life of Christ in each believer.

The Popularity of the Psychological Way

Modern psychotherapy is less than one hundred years old, but during this period of time it has influenced and changed modern man's way of thinking about himself and about the very meaning of life. Many have been trained through these years to have great confidence in psychology for healing mental, emotional, behavioral and other such personal and relational problems. Besides having unquestioned confidence in it, many have come to believe that if anyone doubts, questions, or contradicts psychology, there must be something wrong with that person. Many have been led to believe that only nonthinking, naive individuals have such reservations and that any intelligent, informed person must accept psychotherapy as the healing "balm of Gilead."

In the early years of psychotherapy, medical doctors, ministers, and many others questioned and even ridiculed its theories and practice. But now, after years of effective propaganda, this craze has so influenced every walk of life that to doubt or disagree is to be narrow-minded, nonintelligent, or maybe even neurotic. After all, who would criticize or contradict something so seemingly caring and helpful as psychology?

Since the beginning of psychotherapy at the turn of the century, psychological definitions, diagnoses, and labels of mental-emotional-behavioral disorders have progressively expanded to include a vast array of both mild and severe problems of living. The number of people considered needing help has dramatically increased.

In her book *Manufacturing Victims*, Dr. Tana Dineen says, "Over ten million Americans seek the services of the Psychology Industry each year."[4]

In documenting the growth of psychotherapy, Dineen says:

> In the early 1960's, 14% of the U.S. population (25 million of a total 180 million) had ever received psychological services. By 1976, that number had risen to 26%. However by 1990, at least 33% (65 million of 250 million) have been psychological users at some point in their lives and in 1995, the American Psychological Association stated that 46% of the U.S. population (128 million) had seen a mental health professional. Some even predict that by the year 2000 users will be the majority—constituting 80% of the population.[5]

Along with this exploding population of psychotherapy users, there is an exploding population of providers. According to Dr. Robyn Dawes, the number of licensed professional psychologists is doubling every ten years.[6] One prediction indicated a 64% increase in the number of psychologists in the next ten years.[7] These psychologists represent only one of a number of licensed professional groups providing psychotherapy.

This expansion includes those operating under the "Christian" label. The American Association of Christian Counselors has over 17,500 members. The Christian psychological counseling market includes many individuals, small counseling centers, and also large conglomerates with radio programs that entice Christians into therapy programs. In 1996, the Minirth Meier New Life Clinic was reported as having 25 inpatient units, 55 outpatient units, and over 600 employees. That clinic alone reported 500 inpatient admissions and 7,600 outpatient clinic visits just during the month of June 1996. Rapha, another mental health provider, has 63 programs, "has a network of 3,500 churches in its RaphaCare program," and "has doubled in size in the last 18 months."[8]

In terms of costs throughout the field, Dawes estimates that in 1990 the costs of office-based, licensed clinical psychologists, psychiatrists, and other licensed professionals exceeded 12 billion dollars.[9] Putting these figures together with an earlier total cost of mental health services (17 billion dollars in the late seventies[10]), it would not be unreasonable to estimate that the total cost of mental health in America exceeds 24 billion dollars. Researcher Dr. Jerome Frank has commented about the burgeoning business of psychotherapy as follows:

> The demand for psychotherapy keeps pace with the supply, and at times one has the uneasy feeling that the supply may be creating the demand. . . . Psychotherapy is the only form of treatment which, at least to some extent, appears to create the illness it treats.[11]

Psychotherapy in its various forms is frantically being sought by the worried well, who are looking for a psychological solution for an internal anxiety that often has no real external justification. Myriads of people are going to therapists for an ever-expanding variety of discomforts that merely represent one form of anxiety or another. Some even seek psychological counseling because they suspect that there must be more to life than what they are presently experiencing. Frank concludes:

> Too many people today have too much money and not enough to do, and they turn to psychotherapy to combat the resulting boredom. . . . Today hosts of persons seek psychotherapy for discomforts that a less affluent society would regard as trivial.[12]

Psychological providers, in turn, are eager to deal with these discomforts. According to the Ralph Nader research group, "A distressingly large number of mental health professionals take the position that everyone who walks into their offices needs therapy, frequently long-term therapy, which often stretches for several years to the tune of thousands of dollars."[13]

Frank notes: "Our psychotherapeutic literature has contained precious little on the redemptive power of suffering, acceptance of one's lot in life, filial piety, adherence to tradition, self-restraint and moderation."[14]

Leo Rosten says:

> As recently as 30 years ago, no one questioned your right to be unhappy. Happiness was considered a blessing, not a guarantee. You were permitted to suffer pain, or fall into moods, or seek solitude without being analyzed, interpreted and discussed.[15]

George Albee, a past president of the American Psychological Association says:

> The old conventional sources of explaining the mysteries of human existence, such as religion and science, no longer hold much water for a lot of people. So people have turned largely to psychology as one field which attempts to answer questions about the meaning of life.[16]

Alan Stone observes:

> The psychologizing of the American public has created an expanding market. . . . As a result of the psychologizing of the American public, people who

have marital problems, sex problems, problems with their children, who are having psychological "discomfort" increasingly look for psychological help. It is an infinitely expanding market.[17]

Many people look to psychotherapy to make them happy, to escape the pain of living, and to find fulfillment and satisfaction. As long as they look to psychotherapy with hope and expectancy, the popularity of psychology will continue to soar.

The Psychotherapeutic Marketplace

In the psychotherapeutic marketplace it has been estimated that there are over 400 different therapeutic approaches and more than 10,000 specific techniques available to the consumer.[18] Dr. Morris Parloff reports:

New schools emerge constantly, heralded by claims that they provide better treatment, amelioration, or management of the problems and neuroses of the day. No school has ever withdrawn from the field for failure to live up to its claims, and as a consequence all continue to co-exist.[19]

All continue to exist and all claim success in spite of the fact that the various techniques, as well as the theories on which they rest, often contradict each other. For instance, one therapeutic technique may encourage freedom from responsibility while another may place a high value on personal responsibility. Through popular articles, advertising, and word of mouth, the consumer is led to the conclusion that any kind of therapy may work, no matter how silly or satanic it may be. However, people generally improve without any therapy at all.

The number of therapies has proliferated greatly, so much so that it would be difficult to imagine a form of psychotherapy that has not already been conceived and practiced. Such forms of psychotherapy range all the way from very simple ones, which may include lying to the client by telling him that he is getting better (even when the therapist knows he is not getting better), to physically active ones, which require the client to perform specified acts whether he wants to or not. We have jokingly suggested that we could contrive a theory and give it either a simple title, such as "Theory X," or some esoteric title that no one understands, such as "Osmotic Therapy." To make it saleable, we could select several available concepts from any psychology text. Then to make it particularly appealing, we could add some trinitarian structure similar to Freud's id, ego, and superego; or Harris's Parent, Adult, and Child; or Sullivan's good-me, bad-me, and not-me; or Glasser's reality, responsibility, and right-and-wrong.

Next we would need to write a simple book about it that could be easily understood by the general public, set up an institute (preferably in Los Angeles or New York) and hire a staff. Then, after the initial "success," we would contact the media and tell the world about our unrivaled triumphs, ignore or conceal our failures, and promise unsurpassed miracles of happiness, adjustment, solutions to personal problems, and even physical healing. We would attempt to have several psychology magazines write articles about our new therapy. Then we would provide seminars to train therapists in our new psychotherapy. Finally, we would have to make room for the lonely, bored, frustrated, and anxiety-ridden masses who have tried the other brands of psychotherapy to no avail.

We are not accusing all psychotherapists of being dishonest or merely fabricating therapies out of whole cloth. However, when people feel desperate, they are vulnerable to the psychological promises of relief, and, because they are uninformed about the kind of treatment they will receive, they enroll hoping for relief.

Manufacturing Victims

Dineen, a licensed psychologist, has abandoned her clinical practice and written a book titled *Manufacturing Victims: What the Psychology Industry is Doing to People.*

Dineen's book is the result of her extensive knowledge of the research in psychotherapy as well as her own practical experience in the field. Dineen uses the expression "Psychology Industry" to include a number of individuals. She names "traditional mental health professions of psychology, psychiatry, psychoanalysis and clinical social work" as well as "psychotherapy." She says:

> No longer can clear distinctions be made between them; so, what I call the Psychology Industry comprises all five of these and it encompasses, as well, the ever expanding array of psychotherapists: the counsellors and advisors of all persuasions, whether licensed, credentialed, proclaimed, or self-proclaimed.[20]

Dineen's main thesis for which she provides extensive support is this:

> With degrees in psychology, medicine, social work, nursing or with no academic qualifications at all, the expanding work force of the Psychology Industry relies for its survival and growth on its ability to manufacture victims.[21]

Dineen relates in detail how the psychological manufacturing of victims takes place. She differentiates between real victims and the ones manufactured by the Psychology Industry, which involves a blurring between the two and spreads a net to include virtually everyone. She concludes her book by saying:

> The Psychology Industry can neither reform itself from within nor should it be allowed to try. It should be stopped from doing what it is doing to people, from manufacturing victims. And while the Psychology Industry is being dismantled, people can boycott psychological treatment, protest the influence of the Psychology Industry and resist being manufactured into victims.[22]

Manufacturing Victims is a blunt but honest appraisal of what the Psychology Industry is doing to people and will continue to do unless a miracle puts a stop to it. While Christians may describe this book as a "secular book," for a "secular audience," it is even more important for those in the church to read it. The author has accurately described "The Psychology Industry with its false explanations of cause, false statements of fact, false reports of cure and false claims of authority."[23] Christians need to know the information in Dineen's book, because the church has been overrun with the theories and therapies of the Psychology Industry, which has tentacles into almost every facet of the church through some of the most popular Christian writers.

The Death Knell of Psychotherapy?

Because of all the research on the effectiveness of psychotherapy and for numerous other reasons related to the practice of psychotherapy, such as the use of mental health professionals as experts in court and other realms of life, people are becoming concerned. One person who is both knowledgeable and concerned is R. Christopher Barden, Ph.D., J.D., who has proposed a bill for federal and state legislation. Barden's proposed bill, titled "The Truth and Responsibility in Mental Health Practices Act," reads:

> To reform the mental health system; to restrict federal and state health care reimbursements to those mental health treatments proven reasonably safe and effective by reliable scientific methods; to require states receiving federal health care funding to limit state health care reimbursements to those mental health treatments proven reasonably safe and effective by reliable scientific methods; to require mental health practitioners to truthfully inform patients, clients and insurance systems of known and reasonably foreseeable benefits, risks, hazards and alternative mental health treatments

as demonstrated by reliable scientific research methods; to protect the integrity of the legal system and the rights of citizens from unscientific and reckless expert testimony in courts of law; and other reforms.[24]

A version of the bill called the "Barden Letter" has been signed by a number of distinguished professionals in the mental health field. We believe that fair minded and thinking individuals will support this bill; but we know that politics often prevail rather than common sense and justice for all.

It may be years before such a bill is passed by the National Congress. However, in the meantime, Indiana became the first state to adopt a consumer protection law for mental health practices. A press release from Barden's office states:

> Importantly, the new law requires that "a mental health provider shall inform each patient . . . of the reasonably foreseeable risks and relative benefits of proposed treatments and alternative treatments." National experts in law and psychology called this a landmark in the history of the mental health system.
>
> "The mental health system will never be the same again," said R. Christopher Barden, a psychologist, lawyer and President of the National Association for Consumer Protection in Mental Health Practices. **"It is indeed shocking that many, if not most forms of psychotherapy currently offered to consumers are not supported by credible scientific evidence."**[25] (Bold added.)

This act, if adopted throughout America, may bring the mental health industry to its knees. Barden says, "Too many Americans do not realize that much of the mental health industry is little more than a national consumer fraud."[26] Christians should not be so naive as to believe that Christian psychologists are not involved in such fraudulent practices.

Regardless of the passage, implementation, and policing of the Barden bill, we believe there is no psychotherapy to which Christians should submit themselves. We present both research and biblical reasons in this book, as well as in our other books.[27]

False Assumptions about Psychotherapy

A first step away from being intimidated or infatuated with psychology would be to look seriously at some of psychology's false assumptions. People who believe these popular assumptions about psychology often do not know where these notions originated or that these ideas are merely human opinions. Then, when these ideas are combined with Scripture, people wrongly assume they are biblical. The following are some **false assumptions that have no biblical or scientific basis**.

1. The id, ego, and superego are actual parts of the human psyche.

2. A person's unconscious mind drives behavior more than his conscious mind chooses behavior.

3. Dreams are keys to understanding the unconscious and thus the person.

4. Present behavior is determined by unresolved conflicts from childhood.

5. Many people are in denial because they have repressed unpleasant memories into the unconscious.

6. Parents are to blame for most people's problems.

7. People need insight into their past to make significant changes in thoughts, attitudes and actions.

8. Children must successfully pass through their "psychosexual stages" of development or they will suffer from neurosis later on.

9. If I am to experience significant change, I must remember and re-experience painful incidents in my past.

10. The first five years of life determine what a person will be like when he grows up.

11. Everything that has ever happened to me is located in my unconscious mind.

12. People use unconscious defense mechanisms to cope with life.

13. People need to attribute worth to themselves.

14. People need positive self-regard.

15. Most problems are because of low self-esteem.

16. People need high self-esteem. They need to feel good about themselves.

17. God's main purpose is to meet peoples' felt needs.

18. Christians can learn much about themselves through studying psychological theorists, such as Sigmund Freud, Carl Jung, Alfred Adler, Carl Rogers, and Albert Ellis.

19. Christians need to be trained in psychology to really help people.

20. People need training in biblical counseling, because just knowing the Bible is not enough for helping people with serious problems.

21. The best counselor uses both psychology and the Bible.

22. Alcoholics Anonymous was started by Christians and is based on Christian principles.

23. Alcoholics Anonymous and other recovery groups are necessary for Christians to overcome addictions.

24. Learning about temperament types and tests can help Christians understand one another.

25. Professional psychologists and therapists are better than amateurs in dealing with mental-emotional-behavioral problems.

26. People must pay money to obtain the best help for mental-emotional-behavioral problems.

27. Paying for professional counseling effectively motivates people to improve.

28. A psychotherapist's training, credentials, and experience are all important ingredients for effectively helping others with problems of living.[28]

These false assumptions pervade the church and even permeate missionary efforts throughout the world. How many Christians can read through such a list of false assumptions without thinking we are "throwing the baby out with the bath water"? We declare that we are **not** throwing the baby out with the bath water. Those who are drowning the church in psychology, need to get rid of the contaminated water. If the baby represents the babe in Christ or the whole Body of Christ and the bath water is what contains the contamination of the world, the babe in Christ or the Body of Christ can only be clean if the bath water is thrown out. Throughout this book and in our other writings we provide documentation demonstrating that the false assumptions listed above have no biblical or scientific support.

2

Science

or

Pseudoscience?

Through study and imagination, psychologists have been pursuing the dream of discovering scientific methods of observing, explaining, and transforming human behavior. This dream of developing a scientific study of human nature and a scientific method of treating problems of living is very alluring. Such a hoped-for science of behavior promises much to those who struggle to unravel the vast complexities of individual personalities in equally complex circumstances. However, this hoped-for scientific status of psychology has not yet been realized, especially in psychotherapy.

While some psychology utilizes the scientific method, the one part of the total discipline of psychology that is riddled with pseudoscience is that of psychotherapy. The dictionary defines *pseudoscience* as "a system of theories,

21

assumptions, and methods erroneously regarded as scientific."[1] Pseudoscience or pseudoscientism uses the scientific label to protect and promote opinions that are neither provable nor refutable.

If psychotherapy had established itself as a science, there would be some consensus in the field regarding mental-emotional-behavioral problems and how to treat them. Instead, the field continues to expand with contradictory theories and techniques, all of which communicate confusion rather than anything approximating scientific order.

Psychotherapy continues to proliferate with its growing number of conflicting explanations of human beings and their behavior. Psychologist Roger Mills, in his article "Psychology Goes Insane, Botches Role as Science," says:

> The field of psychology today is literally a mess. There are as many techniques, methods and theories around as there are researchers and therapists. I have personally seen therapists convince their clients that all of their problems come from their mothers, the stars, their bio-chemical make-up, their diet, their life-style and even the "kharma" from their past lives.[2]

Instead of knowledge being added to knowledge with more recent discoveries resting on a body of solid information, one system contradicts another, one set of opinions is exchanged for another, and one set of techniques replaces another.

Psychotherapy changes along with current cultural trends. An accumulation of over 400 separate systems, each claiming superiority, should discourage anyone from thinking that so many diverse opinions could be scientific or even factual. **Psychotherapy and its underlying psychologies are amassed in confusion, with their pseudoknowledge and pseudotheories resulting in pseudoscience.**

Pseudoscience?

Psychotherapists claim to provide advantageous behavioral patterns for daily living, new awareness of the possibilities for selfhood, and adjustment to life and circumstances. They address both internal phenomena, such as thoughts, fears, and anxiety, and outward behavior, such as social interaction, withdrawal, and aggression. However, in attempting to assess and change internal and external behavior, psychotherapy is swathed in subjectivity. Nevertheless, its proponents call it scientific and dress it in professional jargon. Then, staged as a science and costumed in professional-sounding vocabulary, psychotherapy unabashedly performs according to personal opinion, influenced by the many, often conflicting theoretical systems.

Is psychotherapy science or superstition? Is it objective or subjective? Is it fact or fabrication? Such questions are important because we have learned to trust almost anything labeled science. Our society has a penchant for science, for it has lifted us out of the ordinary, taken us to the moon, and helped us explore the distant planets and the inner workings of the brain. We have been impressed, surprised, and even awed by the wonders of science. Science and its accompanying technology have propelled us towards a more comfortable way of life, although not necessarily towards a peaceful state of mind.

Science has made us feel knowledgeable, for it has enabled us to discover and describe many of the natural, physical laws of the universe. Likewise, we are anxious to have similar laws to describe human nature. Therefore, because psychotherapy has identified itself with science and has been labeled a *behavioral* science, many consider it scientific in describing, analyzing and treating the human condition.

Although many disciplines outside the realm of science may be fascinating and attractive, they do not command confidence the way science does. People tend to equate the word *scientific* with such concepts as truthfulness, accuracy, and reliability. If, indeed, psychotherapy and its underlying psychologies are scientific, they may command our respect and attention. However, if they are not, we have reason to question and to doubt their bold assertions and methods.

Since psychotherapy is based on psychological theories, it would be reasonable to ask if these psychological theories can be considered science. Attempting to evaluate the status of psychology, the American Psychological Association appointed Dr. Sigmund Koch to plan and direct a study which was subsidized by the National Science Foundation. This study involved eighty eminent scholars assessing the facts, theories, and methods of psychology. The results of this extensive endeavor were published in a seven-volume series entitled *Psychology: A Study of a Science*.[3]

Examining the results, Koch qualifies his concerns by saying, "I am *not* saying that no subfields of psychology can be regarded as parts of science."[4] However, psychotherapy would be one of Koch's primary targets when he says, "I think it by this time utterly and finally clear that *psychology cannot be a coherent science*."[5] (Italics in original, bold added.) Koch suggests, "As the beginning of a therapeutic humility, we might re-christen *psychology* and speak instead of *the psychological studies*."[6] (Italics in original.)

Koch would certainly criticize psychotherapy for living under "the delusion that it already *is* a science" when it is not.[7] And, he would certainly confirm that psychotherapy "cannot be a coherent science." One reason why psychotherapy cannot legitimately be called a coherent science is because it attempts to deal with human complexities that cannot be directly observed or consistently predicted. Furthermore, the therapist and client are each individually unique and their interaction lends an additional dimension of variability. When one adds time and changing circumstances, it is no wonder that the therapeutic relationship escapes the rigors of science.

In considering the dilemma between science and personal individuality, Dr. Gordon Allport says:

The individual, whatever else he may be, is an internally consistent and unique organization of bodily and mental processes. But since he is unique, science finds him an embarrassment. Science, it is said, deals only with broad, preferably universal, laws. . . . Individuality cannot be studied by science, but only by history, art, or biography.[8]

We could add, the individual not only escapes the formulas of science, but also defies the descriptions of literature. Nevertheless, if one must choose between the two, it appears that literature has more ably revealed human beings. Language describes the complexities of individuality far better than formulas. Language and literature, rather than personality theories and psychotherapy, best portray human nature and provide a glimpse into the depths of the soul.

Does Research Make Psychotherapy a Science?

Further confusion about psychotherapy and science concerns the use of scientific research methods to investigate the success or failure of a given theory or treatment procedure. We will be quoting much research that questions the usefulness of professional psychotherapy, in which scientific methods were used, including the use of meta-analysis, which is a statistical technique. Some people assume that, because such scientific methods are used, psychotherapy is a science. While it is true that research employs scientific methods, it does not follow that whatever is being investigated is scientific. Many nonscientific and even questionable practices, such as E.S.P., biorhythms, fingertip reading, and psychic phenomena, have been investigated by scientific research procedures. The scientific method has been used to investigate everything from art to Zen and from prayer to politics. We certainly would not call all of these "science."

Theory and Fact

Bertrand Russell once said, "Science, ever since the time of the Arabs, has had two functions: (1) to enable us to know things, and (2) to enable us to do things."[9] Can psychotherapy qualify as a science in terms of what it does? Does psychotherapy enable us to know and to do? If we translate "knowing" into facts and "doing" into treatment, we can evaluate the scientific status of psychotherapy. The effectiveness of psychotherapeutic treatment will be discussed later. Here we will look at the facts and theories of psychotherapy.

One major distinction between psychotherapy and science is the development and support of their respective theories. Scientific theories arrange observable, objective, verifiable facts into causal relationships.[10] Psychotherapeutic theories and personality theories, on the other hand, organize and suggest causal relationships of subjective ideas, insights, and intuition.

This question of scientific and pseudoscientific theories intrigued Sir Karl Popper, who is considered one of the greatest philosophers of science. As Popper investigated the differences between physical theories, such as Newton's theory of gravity and Einstein's theory of relativity, and theories about human behavior, he began to suspect that the psychologies underlying the psychotherapies could not truly be considered scientific.[11]

Although such theories **seem** to be able to explain or interpret behavior, they rely on subjective interpretations. Even the claims of clinical observation cannot be considered objective or scientific, because they are merely interpretations based on the theories familiar to the observer.[12] These theories depend upon confirmation rather than testability. If one is looking for verifications or confirmations, they can be found with every psychotherapeutic theory. But, the person who is trying to test a theory will try to disprove it.

Popper says: "Every genuine *test* of a theory is an attempt to falsify it, or to refute it"[13] (italics in original); and, "Confirming evidence should not count *except when it is the result of a genuine test of the theory.*[14] (Italics in original.) Furthermore, Popper declares that psychological theories formulated by Freud, Adler, and others, **"though posing as sciences, had in fact more in common with primitive myths than with science; that they resembled astrology rather than astronomy."**[15] (Bold added.) He also says, "These theories describe some facts, but in the manner of myths. They contain most interesting psychological suggestions, but not in a testable form."[16]

Other researchers echo the same conclusions. Jerome Frank refers to psychotherapies as psychotherapeutic myths because "they are not subject to disproof."[17]

Research psychiatrist E. Fuller Torrey, in his book *The Mind Game*, says, "The techniques used by Western psychiatrists are, with few exceptions, on exactly the same scientific plane as the techniques used by witchdoctors."[18]

Dr. Adolf Grünbaum, a distinguished professor of philosophy and research, levels extensive criticism at *The Foundations of Psychoanalysis*, which is the title of his book. Based on his writings, it is obvious he would condemn the psychological foundations of psychotherapy and would not regard them as scientific theories.[19]

The idea that psychotherapists know a lot about human behavior is also a myth. To be perfectly honest, they know very little and have proved even less. Psychologist Robert Rosenthal says, "But for all the centuries of effort, there is no compelling evidence to convince us that we do understand human behavior very well."[20] Explanations of human behavior include almost entirely unverifiable theories based upon introspection, interpretation, and imagination.

Psychologists have developed numerous subjective theories with very little factual support. The varieties of these theories include the analytic, psychoanalytic, social psychological, constitutional, self, field psychology, and so forth. Within these theories are other theories about such themes as infantile sexuality, the unconscious, dreams, and motivation. One might think that these theories would constitute a body of knowledge. However, personality theories and their psychotherapeutic counterparts do not fit together, for they often conflict with one another in both principle and application, as well as in terminology.

Koch contends that much of psychology is not a cumulative or progressive discipline in which knowledge is added to knowledge. Rather, what is discovered by one generation "typically disenfranchises the theoretical fictions of the past." Instead of refining and specifying larger generalizations of the past, psychologists are busy replacing them. Koch declares, **"Throughout psychology's history as 'science,' the *hard* knowledge it has deposited has been uniformly negative."**[21] (Italics in original, bold added.)

Other Philosophical Voices

Numerous other voices have entered into the discussion of science versus pseudoscience. Many of them attack the very idea that there is such a thing as objectivity and truth. What is science and scientific, and can both physics and psychotherapy claim those labels? Many books have been written on this subject and the philosophy of science is a specialty within the field of philosophy. Some philosophers speak of "soft sciences" and "hard sciences." Others would rather use the terms *acceptable* and *unacceptable*. Still others would distinguish their understandings of *science* and *scientific* through using a subjective consensus or objective approach. All approaches to what is and what is not science have their critics. However, some people do not even accept the possibility of there even being universal laws regarding an orderly created universe that man can strive to discover.

One such person is Dr. Thomas S. Kuhn, a science historian, who wrote a book titled *The Structure of Scientific Revolutions*, which was published in 1962. This book became a best seller and as a result many people began using the expression "paradigm shift." Kuhn's idea of a paradigm shift is based on his theory of how scientific revolutions occur. He describes how one fundamental theory in science is replaced by another. Kuhn explicitly denies that successive physics theories "grow ever closer to, or approximate more and more closely to, the truth."[22] A number of physicists, as well as philosophers of science, have shown that Kuhn's theory is **not** confirmed when one looks at the history of scientific models, such as the Standard Model of particle physics, which by 1980 had swept away all previous theories of particle physics, but not in a manner postulated by Kuhn.

The reason we mention Kuhn is because many Christians have naively used Kuhn's ideas to establish psychology as a science, little wondering how Kuhn's view compares with a biblical view of God, the Creator of an orderly universe, and of man, by God's permission the discoverer of God's orderly universal laws.

Kuhn believed that scientists do not discover anything that is really true. According to Kuhn, all scientific paradigms will eventually be replaced by new paradigms. Kuhn believes that the choice of one paradigm over another is not based solely on objective grounds. Two physicists describe Kuhn's position this way:

> So according to Kuhn, the business of science is not about truth and reality; rather it is about transient vogues—ephemeral and disposable paradigms.[23]

These writers state that, according to Kuhn's ideas, "if the scientific establishment decrees that 'fairies exist,' then this would be scientific indeed."

One writer, critical of Kuhn, says:

> If Kuhn is correct, then it is largely irrelevant whether or not there exist laws of Nature, what forms they take if they do, for science is entirely human activity that cannot find them out. Kuhnian science is the scientist looking in a partially reflecting mirror. Whereas Popper would be willing to concede that we will almost certainly never discover *the* laws of Nature, because they are buried so deep in

reality, none the less, unique and universal laws do exist. Kuhn, by contrast, regards laws of Nature as an ever-changing creation of the scientist's mind, part of the symbiotic psychological relationship between the observed and the observer. This is the most radical and general view that one could take about the subjectivity that is introduced into our study of Nature by our human intellectual tendencies: having recognized that there is a sociology of science it concludes that there is nothing more to science than its sociology.[24] (Italics in original.)

Many Christians elevate psychology to the level of science through Kuhn's view of science. Yet, Kuhn's view seems to ignore a universe created by God with universal laws of His making and with permission given to man, through common grace and general revelation, to investigate and learn more about the universe, which is an expression of God Himself. Kuhn appears to reduce science to human perception rather than man's attempt to know and understand a universe that has laws established by the Creator.

Another popular voice involved in the discussion of what is and what is not science is Paul Feyerabend. According to Feyerabend, "There is only one principle that can be defended under all circumstances and in all stages of human development. It is the principle: Anything goes."[25] For Feyerabend, "Freud is God" is as scientific as "There are two hydrogen atoms in one water molecule." In a *Science* article Feyerabend was quoted as saying that "normal science is a fairy tale" and that "equal time should be given to competing avenues of knowledge such as astrology, acupuncture, and witchcraft."[26]

While the average person would not understand much of the philosophizing going on in the area of what constitutes science, it is obvious that fairy tales and physics do not both deserve the label "science." It should be equally clear that psychotherapy and surgery are not synonymous.

Personal Opinion Offered as Science

Creators of these theoretical, psychological explanations have become infatuated and puffed up with their innovative schemes as if their theories constitute reality, when, in fact, each theory only constitutes one man's impression of reality, which others have accepted. These theories only amount to ideas and beliefs about reality rather than to reality itself. They are only imaginative suppositions, not proven facts.

It is important to note that the originators of the psychological systems, which are taught and used by Christians, were not believers. The originators of these often competing systems did not begin with Scripture; nor is there any indication that they compared what they concluded with Scripture. They devised their systems out of their own fallen opinions about the human condition.

In her article "Theory as Self-Portrait and the Ideal of Objectivity," Dr. Linda Riebel clearly shows that "theories of human nature reflect the theorist's personality as he or she externalizes it or projects it onto humanity at large." She says that "the theory of human nature is a self-portrait of the theorist . . . emphasizing what the theorist needs" and that theories of personality and psychotherapy "cannot transcend the individual personality engaged in that act."[27]

Dr. Harvey Mindess has written a book titled *Makers of Psychology: The Personal Factor*. He says:

> It is my intention to show how the leaders of the field portray humanity in their own image and how each one's theories and techniques are a means of validating his own identity.[28]

> The only target I wish to attack is the delusion that psychologists' judgments are objective, their pronouncements unbiased, their methods based more upon external evidence than personal need. Even the greatest geniuses are human beings, limited by the time and place of their existence and, above all, limited by their personal characteristics.

Their outlooks are shaped by who they are. There is
no shame in that, but it is a crime against truth to
deny it.[29]

The field as a whole, taking direction as it does from
the standpoints of its leaders—which, as I will
demonstrate, are *always* personally motivated—
may be regarded as a set of distorting mirrors, each
one reflecting human nature in a somewhat lopsided
way, with no guarantee that all of them put together
add up to a rounded portrait.[30] (Italics in original.)

The enigma of human nature, we may say, is like a
giant Rorschach blot onto which each personality
theorist projects his own personality characteristics.[31]

The conclusions we should reach about the field as a
whole, however, must begin with a recognition of the
subjective element in all personality theories, the
limited applicability of all therapeutic techniques,
and proceed to the relativity of psychological
truth.[32]

Learning theories about human behavior and personality is vastly different from knowing facts. For too long
too many have believed these theories to be factual. They
would do well to stay out of the morass of opinions,
contradictions, and unproven conceptions; stop speaking
of these theories as if they represent reality and, worse
yet, acting as if they are true; and recognize that there is
much subjectivity, sentimentality, superstition, and even
shamanism within these theoretical sand castles.

Take any text on behavior or personality or psychotherapy and examine it to see how much is subjective
theory and how little is objective fact. Then remove all
the pages that contain unprovable theories and see what
remains. In most cases there would be almost nothing
left. We are not saying that psychotherapeutic theories
are intentionally dishonest, deceitful, or untruthful; we
are merely pointing out a common error in thinking.

Psychotherapy is not a coherent science, but rather a discipline based upon many unscientific theories and few verifiable facts. Besides the confusion between theory and fact, notice that psychotherapeutic theories invariably cover the deepest and most profound levels of human behavior, while psychotherapeutic facts reveal the most superficial. Verifiable facts are not only few and far between; they cover only the most obvious aspects of man. Often they sound a little ridiculous. For example, a fact of human behavior would be something like this: people communicate with one another through language.

The deeper a person plunges into the psyche of man, the more theoretical he becomes. In order to explain these deep levels, the psychologist uses a mumbo jumbo of jargon and metaphors, of psychological language and symbols. People gain comfort and confidence with personality theories, because they seem to explain or categorize behavior. But, just because one feels comfortable does not mean that the theories are verifiable through objective, scientific testing.

Perhaps people like theories because they help organize attitudes and easily explain away individual complexity. Being confronted by human behavior without a frame of reference makes one feel insecure. Frank points out, "The first step to gaining control of any phenomenon is to give it a name."[33] He also says that we "need to master some conceptual framework to enable us to . . . maintain our own confidence."[34] People seek names, words and thoughts. They look for a Rosetta Stone to decipher the mysterious symbols and actions of the human psyche.

Without psychological theories people may feel weak, ineffective, and impotent; but with such theories they sense stability, direction, and power. Theories, whether true or false, do seem to fulfill a need to grasp and make sense out of what people see and experience. Thus, humans invent and manipulate symbols for their own security and then believe and act upon them as though they were reality, even when they are not.

Naming, describing, and categorizing human behavior does not necessarily bring knowledge and understanding. There is a great gulf between describing human behavior and truly understanding it, and also between talking about human behavior and changing it. Psychotherapeutic theory is merely a combination of subjective, yet scientific-sounding words. Yet, many are seduced by a scientific-sounding psychological system that is sometimes just "a tale told by an idiot, full of sound and fury, signifying nothing" *(Macbeth,* Act V, Scene V).

The Medical Model and Mental Illness

If you go to a doctor when you're physically sick, what's wrong with seeing a psychologist for mental-emotional-behavioral problems? That question is asked by those who confuse the use of medicine with the practice of psychotherapy. Individuals making such an error assume that the medical and the mental can be thought of and talked about in the same manner and with the same terms. This error is one of using the medical model to justify the use of psychotherapy.

In the field of logic this is known as a *false analogy.* One logic text explains:

> An argument from analogy draws a conclusion about something on the basis of an analogy with or resemblance to some other thing. The assumption is that if two or more things are alike in some respects, they are alike in some other respect.[35]

In regard to a false analogy the text says:

> To recognize the fallacy of false analogy, look for an argument that draws a conclusion about one thing, event, or practice on the basis of its analogy or resemblance to others. The fallacy occurs when the analogy or resemblance is not sufficient to warrant the conclusion.[36]

In the medical model physical symptoms are caused by some pathogenic agent. For example, a fever may be caused by viruses; remove the pathogenic agent and you remove the symptom. Or, a person may have a broken leg; set the leg properly and the leg will heal. People have confidence in the medical model because it has worked well in the treatment of physical ailments. With the easy transfer of the model from medicine to psychotherapy, many people erroneously believe that mental problems can be thought of in the same way as physical problems.

Applying the medical model to psychotherapy and its underlying psychologies came from the relationship between psychiatry and medicine. Since psychiatrists are medical doctors and since psychiatry is a medical specialty, many think that the medical model applies to psychiatry just as it does to medicine. Furthermore, psychiatry is draped with such medical trimmings as offices in medical clinics, hospitalization of patients, diagnostic services, prescription drugs, and therapeutic treatment. The very word *therapy* implies medical treatment. Further expansion of the use of the medical model to all of psychotherapy was easy after that.

The practice of medicine deals with the physical, biological aspects of a person; psychotherapy deals with the mental, emotional, and behavioral aspects. Whereas medical doctors attempt to heal the body, psychotherapists attempt to alleviate or cure mental, emotional, behavioral, and even spiritual suffering and to establish new patterns of thought and behavior. In spite of such differences, the medical model continues to be called upon to support the activities of the psychotherapist.

Additionally, the medical model supports the idea that a person with mental, emotional, or behavioral problems is ill. And with much sympathy we label people *mentally ill*, and we often categorize mental problems under the key term *mental illness*. Dr. Thomas Szasz adroitly explains it this way:

> If we now classify certain forms of personal conduct as illness, it is because most people believe that the

best way to deal with them is by responding to them as if they were medical diseases.[37]

Psychotherapy deals with thoughts, emotions, and behavior, but not with the brain itself. Psychotherapy does not deal with the brain's biology, but with the mind's activity and the individual's social behavior. In medicine we understand what a diseased body is, but what is a parallel in psychotherapy? It is obvious that in psychotherapy mental illness does not mean brain disease. If brain disease were the case, the person would be a *medical* patient, not a *mental* patient.

Szasz very sharply refers to the "psychiatric impostor" who "supports a common, culturally shared desire to equate and confuse brain and mind, nerves and nervousness."[38]

The assumption that medical illness and mental illness are alike is further dealt with by Szasz in his book *The Myth of Mental Illness*. He says:

> It is customary to define psychiatry as a medical specialty concerned with the study, diagnosis, and treatment of mental illnesses. This is a worthless and misleading definition. Mental illness is a myth.[39]

He continues:

> I have argued that, today, the notion of a person "having a mental illness" is scientifically crippling. It provides professional assent to a popular rationalization—namely, that problems in living experienced and expressed in terms of so-called psychiatric symptoms are basically similar to bodily diseases.[40]

Although one may result from the other, *medical illness* and *mental illness* are simply not the same. *Biological* and *psychological* are not synonymous. One has to do with the organic processes and the other with the thought and emotional life. We should have rejected the word *illness* after the word *mental* from the very beginning.

Dr. Ronald Leifer, in his book *In the Name of Mental Health*, says:

> If we grant that in . . . medicine the term "disease" refers to the body, to modify it with the word "mental" is at worst a mixture of logical levels called a category error, and at best it is a radical redefinition of the word "disease." **A category error is an error in the use of language that, in turn, produces errors in thinking.** . . . Whatever the mind may be, it is not a thing like muscles, bones, and blood.[41] (Bold added.)

Leifer discusses the arguments for the medical model and then the defects of such arguments. He concludes by saying:

> The principal advantages of this argument are therefore neither scientific nor intellectual. They are social. They prejudice the lay public to see psychiatric practices as more like medical treatment than like social control, socialization, education, and religious consolation. It bids them to presume that the psychiatrist, like other physicians, always serves the individual in his pursuit of life, health, and happiness.[42]

The use of the medical model in psychotherapy does not reveal truth; instead it merely disguises psychotherapy with the mask of medical terminology and ends up confusing everyone. Research psychiatrist Torrey says:

> The medical model of human behavior, when carried to its logical conclusions, is both nonsensical and nonfunctional. It doesn't answer the questions which are asked of it, it doesn't provide good service, and it leads to a stream of absurdities worthy of a Roman circus.[43]

Using the medical model of human behavior and confusing *medical* with *mental* through a false analogy can lead to justifying support for ESP, past lives, UFOs,

Eastern religions, and the occult. Transpersonal or religious psychologies are being supported through such false analogies and usage of the medical model.

Through such transpersonal psychotherapies, various forms of Eastern religion are creeping into Western life. Psychologist Daniel Goleman quotes Chogyam Trungpa as saying, "Buddhism will come to the West as psychology." Goleman points out that Asian religions "seem to be making gradual headway as psychologies, not as religions."[44]

Dr. Jacob Needleman says:

A large and growing number of psychotherapists are now convinced that the Eastern religions offer an understanding of the mind far more complete than anything yet envisaged by Western science. At the same time, the leaders of the new religions themselves—numberless gurus and spiritual teachers now in the West—are reformulating and adapting the traditional systems according to the language and atmosphere of modern psychology.[45]

Needleman also says:

With all these disparate movements, it is no wonder that thousands of troubled men and women throughout America no longer know whether they need psychological or spiritual help. The line is blurred that divides the therapist from the spiritual guide.[46]

Related to this inclusion of the *spiritual* into the *mental*, which is erroneously confused with the *medical*, is a new category of "mental illness" in the fourth edition of the *Diagnostic and Statistical Manual of Mental Disorders*. The new category has to do with spiritual and religious problems.[47]

The error of applying medical terminology to mental life causes erroneous thinking and responding. The very word *medical* carries with it the suggested treatment, for if we are dealing with an illness, medical treatment is implied. Therefore, whenever someone suggests that you should believe in psychotherapy because you believe in medicine, remember that *medical* and *mental* are **not** the same. **It is a false analogy and a false application of the medical model.** Using false analogies and misapplying the medical model to the mind could even lead one to ask, "If you go to a medical doctor when you're sick, what's wrong with seeing a witch doctor?"

Psychology grew out of philosophy. Each theory behind each therapy provides a philosophy of life and a theology of man—why we are the way we are and how we change. In fact, psychotherapy resembles religion more than it resembles medicine. After all, the word *psychology* comes from two words meaning the study of the soul. However, many psychotherapists and their advocates misuse the medical model to support psychotherapy. They continue to make this false analogy to their own shame and to the detriment of others.

Conclusion

Instead of recognizing the fallacies of psychotherapy, many people have hailed it as a science and have trusted its conclusions, theories, and methods of diagnosis. Although it purports to be a science and attempts to align itself as such, it falls short of the objectivity and testability of science. Although it claims to dispense knowledge about the human condition, it has revealed few hard facts and has filled the vacuum with a collage of theories. Psychotherapy is not a coherent science in principle or in theory, diagnosis, or treatment.

3

Integration
or
Separation?

Psychoheresy is the integration of secular psychological counseling theories and therapies with the Bible. Psychoheresy is also the intrusion of such theories into the preaching and practice of Christianity, especially when they contradict or compromise biblical Christianity in terms of the nature of man, how he is to live, and how he changes. We coined the word *psychoheresy* in our book by that name, because heresy is a departure from the fundamental truth of the Gospel, and psychotherapy and its underlying psychologies constitute a broad road of departure.

Psychoheresy has been of grave concern to us for more than twenty years. During that time we have watched the proliferation of Christians who have attempted to integrate psychology with the Bible in their counseling, teaching, and preaching. We have grieved over those multitudes of Christians who have turned to the wisdom of men in the midst of their problems instead of solely relying on God and His provisions. We want to encourage Christians to find Jesus Christ and the Word of God sufficient for matters of life and conduct. We yearn for believers to rely on the Bible for understanding themselves and others and to learn to walk according to the Spirit, grow in Christian maturity, and confront problems of living.

A very telling graphic titled "The Roots and Shoots of Christian Psychology" shows a tree with branches bearing the names of some of the well-known psychological integrationists situated on branches labeled "Spiritual Seekers," "Family/Marriage," "Clinical Care," "Dissociative Disorders," "Self-Esteem," and "Pastoral Counseling."[1] The roots, labeled "Secular & Humanistic Pioneers," include Carl Rogers, Carl Jung, Sigmund Freud, Abraham Maslow, B. F. Skinner, and Virginia Satir, all of whom opposed Christianity, with at least the first three involved in blatant occult practices. Each of these "roots" had strong metaphysical beliefs that comprised their unbiblical, anti-Christian belief systems.

What kind of tree is this, with occult and secular humanistic religious roots? It is clear that the roots are ungodly. Is this a tree from which Christians should eat? Or, does it more resemble "the tree of knowledge of good and evil" (Genesis 2:9)? Jesus said:

> Beware of false prophets, which come to you in sheep's clothing, but inwardly they are ravening wolves. Ye shall know them by their fruits. Do men gather grapes of thorns, or figs of thistles? Even so every good tree bringeth forth good fruit; but a corrupt tree bringeth forth evil fruit. A good tree cannot bring forth evil fruit, neither can a corrupt tree bring forth good fruit. Every tree that bringeth not forth good fruit is hewn down, and cast into the fire (Matthew 7:15-19).

We contend that the tree of "Christian psychology" should be hewn down right at its base. While this tree has names of professing Christians on every branch, the roots are clearly secular and the sap that flows through its veins is made up of the opinions of agnostics, atheists, and occultists. The psychotherapies that Christians dispense and use were not invented by Christians but by those who have denied the God of the Bible. Psychoheresy is not just a minor diversion from sound biblical doctrine. It is one of the most subtle means of undermining the faith. It is also one of the most rapidly expanding features of the Christian community. In spite of a growing public awareness of problems in the Psychology Industry, the Christian counseling business continues to flourish. An ever increasing number of Christians are becoming professional dispensers of psychotherapy and an equally expanding Christian clientele seeks their services.[2]

In light of the unbiblical roots of psychotherapy and its underlying psychologies, what, if any, might be the justification for Christians to promote, dispense, use and condone psychotherapy? How did this kind of psychology become so accepted and popular in the church? Why did the church move, during the past fifty years, from an almost complete rejection of psychology to its wholehearted embracing of it? The reasons given by many have to do with what they believe is included in common grace, God's truth, and God's general revelation to man.

Common Grace and Psychotherapy

One way Christians accept psychological therapies and their underlying psychologies is through the theological concept of *common grace*. Common grace is that grace given by God to all humanity whereby natural man has an innate moral sense and can observe, think, reason, evaluate, and come to conclusions. God's grace is undeserved kindness; common grace includes all good gifts to men. One example of His kindness to all is found in Matthew 5:45, "for he maketh his sun to rise on the evil and on the good, and sendeth rain on the just and on the unjust."

Common grace explains why unbelievers may exhibit moral behavior and concern for other humans and why they are able to pursue and excel in both art and science. One Scripture that supports the idea of common grace is Romans 2:14-16.

> For when the Gentiles, which have not the law, do by nature the things contained in the law, these, having not the law, are a law unto themselves: Which show the work of the law written in their hearts, their conscience also bearing witness, and their thoughts the mean while accusing or else excusing one another.

The Gentiles did not have the Law (special revelation), but they did have a "law written in their hearts." This common grace of a "law written in their hearts" serves to restrain evil and leads to a measure of morality and social welfare. However, this gift common to all also makes all responsible, and, because all sin, all end up under the condemnation of God and are in desperate need of God's special grace, which is communicated through special revelation. In other words, "For all have sinned, and come short of the glory of God" (Romans 3:23), are under God's condemnation, and are in need of salvation. Common grace both restrains and reveals sin. Common grace therefore allows for moral behavior and social responsibility, but it is not saving grace.

The natural heart is depraved in spite of the moral law etched upon it. Only God's special grace can redeem the human heart and lead an individual along the path of sanctification and unto glorification. Psychotherapy and its underlying psychologies cannot help you to "put off concerning the former conversation the old man, which is corrupt according to the deceitful lusts," "be renewed in the spirit of your mind," or "put on the new man, which after God is created in righteousness and true holiness" (Ephesians 4:22-24). Psychotherapy and its underlying psychologies cannot save or sanctify and thus have nothing to offer a Christian for understanding the soul, overcoming problems of living, or knowing how to live.

Is All Truth God's Truth?

Individuals who want to make psychological theories and therapies available to Christians and who attempt to integrate such theories and techniques with Scripture justify these practices by saying, "All truth is God's truth." At first such a statement sounds plausible and even true. However, we need to look at what might be included on each side of the equation of "all truth = God's truth."

First of all, what is *truth*? While there are several definitions of *truth*, one generally assumes that truth represents that which is true, real, and actual. Truth is the perfect expression of that which is. If what is put into the category of "all truth" is limited to "the perfect expression of that which is," then that would be "God's truth." However, the assortment of ideas, opinions, and even apparent facts under the designation of "all truth" reduces *truth* to meaning "imperfect human perception of that which is."

The broad field of psychology at best involves human observation and interpretation of Creation and therefore is subject to human error and the blindness of the unregenerate heart as described in Ephesians 4:18, "Having the understanding darkened, being alienated from the life of God through the ignorance that is in them, because of the blindness of their heart."

Psychotherapy and its underlying psychologies have the further problem of subjective imagination also proceeding from unregenerate individuals. They represent a further departure from expressing that which truly is. Instead, they present some subjective observation, reasoned analysis, creative imagination, and much distortion. If these ideas are included under the declaration, "All truth is God's truth," one must conclude that those who use the expression have greatly misunderstood the nature of truth, let alone God's truth.

In raising human observation, interpretation, and opinions to the same level and authority as God's truth revealed through Jesus and in the written Word of God, those who promote psychology among Christians demonstrate their high view of human opinion and their low view of Scripture.

In his discussion of "all truth is God's truth," John Moffat says, "I think that, in many ways, this slogan is the verbal equivalent of a graven image; something that appears to represent truth but does not."[3] He explains:

> None of the people that use this "all truth" expression actually say that they consider man's thoughts equal to God's revealed Word, it just happens to work that way in practice; just as at first the graven images were not meant to replace God, only to represent Him.[4]

Then to show where "all truth is God's truth" thinking can lead a person, Moffat says:

> I can imagine Nadab and Abihu talking before the early worship service in the wilderness. One says to the other, "All fire is God's fire. God made all fire; therefore it is all of him." Or while Moses was up on Mount Sinai, the children of Israel could have said to Aaron, "All worship of God is God's worship." These analogies have the same deceptive sound of being logical at first glance, but they are full of the same ambiguity and deceit as the expression "all truth is God's truth."[5]

In contrast to the broad category labeled "all truth" by those who want to include what humans perceive through their senses, achieve through their reason, conceive in their minds, receive from one another, and interweave with Scripture, the specific category of "God's truth" includes only what is perfectly and flawlessly true. God Himself is true and He has made known His truth through His Son, who referred to Himself as *the truth* (John 14:6); through His written Word, which perfectly states what is true (John 17:17); and through the Holy Spirit, who is called the Spirit of Truth who will guide believers into all truth (John 16:13). With all that God has provided in His Son, His Word, and His Holy Spirit, one wonders why people are so enamored with the psychological opinions of men.

All humans have partial perception, fragmentary knowledge, and incomplete morality through common grace and general revelation. While these are gifts common to all mankind, they are contaminated by human depravity. Whatever truth people have perceived is contaminated by their unrighteousness. Apart from special revelation and special grace, all stand guilty before God, because they hold whatever truth they have gained through general revelation or common grace in a state of unrighteousness (Romans 1:18). Do such people appear to be reliable sources for Christians to seek counsel for godly living? Indeed, general revelation and common grace serve as very weak and even dangerous justifications for dipping into psychotherapy and its underlying psychologies, all of which were conceived and developed by unredeemed minds.

General Revelation and Psychotherapy

As theologians have considered how God reveals Himself to humanity, they have noted that God reveals Himself through *general revelation* and *special revelation*. In their book on theology, Bruce Demarest and Gordon Lewis define these two kinds of revelation:

> *General revelation* refers to the disclosure of God in nature, in providential history, and in the moral law within the heart, whereby all persons at all times and places gain a rudimentary understanding of the Creator and his moral demands. *Special revelation* refers to God's self-disclosure through signs and miracles, the utterances of prophets and apostles,

and the deeds and words of Jesus Christ, whereby specific people at particular times and places gain further understanding of God's character and a knowledge of his saving purpose in his Son.[6]

This special revelation is recorded in the Bible, God's Holy, inerrant Word.

While the justifiers of psychology may attempt to support their theories from Scripture (special revelation), they primarily appeal to general revelation to justify the use the various psychotherapies and their underlying psychologies. They argue that God has left the door open to psychological knowledge about man by general revelation. However, God's general revelation does not leave the door open for humanity to know about the depths of the soul (psyche). **God through special revelation (His Word) has already provided people the truth about themselves that psychology pretends to know**.

The primary text regarding general revelation that is used to justify the use of extrabiblical material in understanding the nature of man, how he is to live and how he changes is Romans 1. Here we see what God has revealed about Himself to all mankind apart from the special revelation of Scripture.

> Because that which may be known of God is manifest in them; for God hath shewed it unto them. For the invisible things of him from the creation of the world are clearly seen, being understood by the things that are made, even his eternal power and Godhead; so that they are without excuse: Because that, when they knew God, they glorified him not as God, neither were thankful; but became vain in their imaginations, and their foolish heart was darkened (Romans 1:19-21).

To examine whether Romans 1 allows for the intrusion of psychotherapeutic theories and therapies, we need to consider what it says and what it does not say. Demarest notes three important truths that come from this text on general revelation. He says:

Surely the *locus classicus* [authoritative passage] for God's self-disclosure in nature is Paul's discussion in Romans 1:18-21. Here the apostle explicates most completely the relationship between natural [general] revelation and man's knowledge of God. In this key text, Paul makes at least three important assertions.

The first is that *mankind properly perceives truth about God from nature* (vv. 19-21). . . .

The second important assertion Paul makes in this Romans 1 text is that *knowledge of God is mediated by natural revelation* (v. 20). . . .

The third assertion that Paul makes in the Romans 1 text is that *man consistently suppresses all forms of general revelation* (vv. 21-32).[7] (Italics in original.)

Books on general revelation discuss the various understandings of what, in general, God has revealed. Demarest discusses the various historical views of Augustine, Anselm, Aquinas, Luther, Calvin, the Puritans and others. In a section on John Calvin, Demarest says:

. . . the burden of Calvin's teaching is that when natural man acquired natural knowledge of God, he immediately moved to suppress that knowledge. Instead of cultivating the fundamental knowledge of God given in His works and humbly looking to God for additional light, man in the deceitfulness of his heart trampled the remembrance of God underfoot and asserted his own autonomy.[8]

One can see a difference between Calvin's position regarding general revelation and the Puritans' position, as presented by Demarest:

Thus from the evident magnitude, precision, and beauty of the universe, rational men rightly ought to conclude both *that* God is and *what* God is. The data of Creation cogently point not only to God's existence but also to His unity, eternity, power, wisdom, goodness, and holiness.[9] (Italics in original.)

Romans 1 deals primarily with God's revelation of Himself. But does knowing the "invisible things of him from the creation of the world" reveal much about humans? Does knowing the character of God, his "eternal power and Godhead," reveal the depths of knowledge about humanity? We answer *no* to both questions for a variety of reasons. While the human being was created in the image of God, God and man have only some—not all— characteristics in common.

God always existed but human beings are born, grow, develop, and have a variety of developmental experiences. Finite human beings are distinctly different from the eternal, infinite God. Also, those who do not glorify God as God or thank Him become "vain in their imaginations" and do not see God accurately. Their vision is so distorted that they worship the creature rather than the Creator. How can they have an accurate understanding of God or of man created in the image of God? While certain things about God can be seen through Creation, sin and rebellion distort the vision so that human beings must have special revelation to see general revelation clearly.

It is difficult to justify the idea that those who rejected the very existence of God can know either the character of God or the human soul through general revelation. Cornelius Van Til put it this way:

> After sin has entered the world, no one of himself knows nature aright, and no one knows the souls of man aright. How then could man reason from nature to nature's God and get anything but a distorted notion of God? The sort of natural theology that the sinner who does not recognize himself as a sinner makes is portrayed to us in the first chapter of Romans.[10]

Notice the indictment on mankind found in Romans 1. After properly perceiving truth about God through nature, people consistently suppress that truth. Therefore, one wonders how psychological theorists, such as Freud, Jung, Maslow, Rogers, and Ellis, who have suppressed the truth about God can now dip into general revelation about humans, who were created in the image of God. Romans 1 clearly states that those who rejected God "became vain in their imaginations, and their foolish heart was darkened. Professing themselves to be wise, they became fools." By rejecting God's revelation of Himself they have forfeited the ability to gain accurate self-knowledge or a true understanding of the inner person through such general revelation.

God has revealed His "eternal power and Godhead" through Creation, but to truly know Him one must have His special revelation. Human beings cannot know the "breadth, and length, and depth, and height" (Ephesians 3:18) or "know the love of Christ, which passeth knowledge" (Ephesians 3:19) without God's special revelation. God has already revealed in His Word who man is and how God is known and how man is to grow in the spirit. "All scripture is given by inspiration of God, and is profitable for doctrine, for reproof, for correction, for instruction in righteousness: That the man of God may be perfect, thoroughly furnished unto all good works" (2 Timothy 3:16,17). There is no psychotherapeutic system that can even approach that goal.

While general revelation gives general knowledge about God, those who want to justify using psychology see Scripture as giving only general ideas about man and thus needing to be supplemented with specifics. Consequently, they appeal to what they think is included in general revelation to discover specific details about the human mind, will, emotions, and behavior to fill in what they believe is missing from the Bible. They trust the opinions of unsaved individuals to explain the details of the soul on the basis of their view of general revelation.

God in His grace and mercy does allow unbelievers to investigate His universe and discover physical laws. But there is a huge difference between understanding aerodynamics, for instance, and the complexities of the human soul. While superficialities can be observed about mankind, the depths of human nature elude scientific investigation and morality is beyond its comprehension. Natural reason can draw some conclusions from observation, but these again are at the superficial level and subject to human distortion. Anything beyond the superficial ends up being speculation and opinion.

Scripture is clear about who is able to know and understand the inner man. "The heart is deceitful above all things, and desperately wicked: who can know it? I the LORD search the heart, I try the reins, even to give every man according to his ways, and according to the fruit of his doings" (Jeremiah 17:9). Knowing the inner workings of the human heart, soul, mind, and spirit is God's domain. Because He is the primary Person molding each of His children who have been born again by His Spirit, this is His prerogative to know and to reveal.

While people may learn very general things about human nature through general revelation, it is presumptuous to assume specificities gleaned from such psychotherapeutic theorists as Freud, Jung, Maslow, Rogers, Ellis, and others were revealed by God. Natural man can only know about the most superficial aspects of man. The deeper one plunges into man, the more he needs God's special revelation about the inner man. Psychology cannot deal with man's sinful nature or God's remedy for sin and provision for spiritual growth. At best, psychology can only give wild guesses about the most important aspects of man. It is here where only God's Word can be trusted.

Just as general revelation does not show the way of salvation, general revelation cannot give any information about the new life in Christ or about sanctification or Christian growth. At best, psychological theories and therapies are limited to helping the old nature or flesh. They cannot touch the "new man, which after God is created in righteousness and true holiness" (Ephesians 4:24). Scripture is clear about unbelievers having their "understanding darkened, being alienated from the life of

God through the ignorance that is in them, because of the blindness of their heart" (Ephesians 4:18). Therefore it is pointless for Christians to attempt to improve their psyche (soul) through psychology or to look to the wisdom of men for how to live.

The "wisdom of psychology" is the very wisdom of men about which God warns: "That your faith should not stand in the wisdom of men, but in the power of God" (1 Corinthians 2:5). Those of us who believe Christians should not integrate secular counseling psychologies with the Bible are often dismissed with such shibboleths as "all truth is God's truth," when, in fact, the kind of psychology we are opposed to is made up of opinions and myths, rather than truth. Which of the more than 400 different psychotherapeutic systems (which disenfranchise each other to at least some extent) or the 10,000-plus techniques (many of which contradict each other) can be considered to be God's truth as revealed through general revelation? These do not constitute God's truth. They are "science falsely so called." Christians should follow Paul's admonition to Timothy: "O Timothy, keep that which is committed to thy trust, avoiding profane and vain babblings, and oppositions of science falsely so called: Which some professing have erred concerning the faith" (1 Timothy 6:20,21).

When one considers all the admonitions in Scripture regarding foolish speculations, why would God give special insights regarding the innermost mysteries of the soul to those who have denied Him? Paul clearly presented God's position regarding the wisdom of men:

> For it is written, I will destroy the wisdom of the wise, and will bring to nothing the understanding of the prudent. Where is the wise? where is the scribe? where is the disputer of this world? hath not God made foolish the wisdom of this world? . . . Because the foolishness of God is wiser than men; and the weakness of God is stronger than men. . . . But God hath chosen the foolish things of the world to confound the wise. . . . That no flesh should glory in

his presence. But of him are ye in Christ Jesus, who of God is made unto us wisdom, and righteousness, and sanctification, and redemption (1 Corinthians 1:19,20,25,27,29,30).

But the natural man receiveth not the things of the Spirit of God: for they are foolishness unto him: neither can he know them, because they are spiritually discerned. But he that is spiritual judgeth all things, yet he himself is judged of no man. For who hath known the mind of the Lord, that he may instruct him? But we have the mind of Christ (1 Corinthians 2:14-16).

Paul further warned the Colossians: "Beware lest any man spoil you through philosophy and vain deceit, after the tradition of men, after the rudiments of the world, and not after Christ" (Colossians 2:8).

As we have already demonstrated, psychological theories that purport to understand and explain the human condition and that develop methods for change are created out of the theorists' own subjectivity and speculation. Such theories are **opinions**, not truth. Such theories are not truth discovered from general revelation, but rather personal belief systems created from the theorists' imagination.

Because they are belief systems, they have more in common with religion than science. Each is based on faith and includes an extrabiblical world view; an extrabiblical understanding of the nature of the human condition; an extrabiblical theory about the mind, will, emotions, and behavior; an extrabiblical explanation about why people behave the way they do; and an extrabiblical direction for change. We contend that these extrabiblical gleanings did not come from God's general revelation to mankind. They more likely came from the ruler of darkness, even as he may appear as an angel of light.

Rather than psychotherapy being a blessing of God given to men through general revelation, we believe that it is a counterfeit that competes with true Christianity.

While there may be some similarities between the counterfeit and the true, the person who follows the counterfeit is like an idolater. Just as the Israelites sought to gain from idolatry in addition to worshiping Jehovah, today Christians seek to gain from psychotherapy and its underlying psychologies in addition to going to church, reading the Bible, worshiping, and praying.

Special Revelation and Psychotherapy

We have already discussed some justifications for our contention that professional psychotherapy is questionable at best, detrimental at worst, and a spiritual counterfeit at least. Another reason why Christians are seduced by psychotherapy is the way they use special revelation to support it. They believe that there is a way to check out this type of psychology with Scripture (special revelation) to determine its acceptability.

Christians who practice and promote psychotherapy agree that some theories and some techniques are unbiblical. They, however, are confident that what they personally have gleaned from psychotherapy and its underlying psychologies meets one of three criteria: (1) already in Scripture, (2) not in Scripture, (3) not contradicted by Scripture. They contend that they can use the Bible to sift through the theories and therapies and thereby end up with a biblically acceptable psychology.

The fallacy of supposing that a biblical psychology can be developed out of the wisdom of men can readily be seen when one considers that there are more than 400 psychotherapeutic systems with their underlying psychologies and 10,000-plus techniques. Various proponents of this fallacy have attempted to find biblical support for their particular combinations of therapies and techniques. However, considering that almost all of these systems, psychologies, and techniques are used by Christians, one must conclude that various people are passing them through their own subjective view of Scripture. With so many subjective grids, almost none of the psychotherapies would be excluded.

In fact, take any new talk therapy or invent one of your liking and it is almost certain to be found by some therapists to be in Scripture, neutral because it is not in Scripture, or not contradicted by Scripture. The technique used to find these psychological notions in Scripture is called *eisegesis*, which is reading one's own ideas and beliefs into Scripture. In contrast, *exegesis* is drawing out the meaning of Scripture from what is actually there.

Eisegesis obviously permits great latitude in what can be confirmed by Scripture. If some of the most visible Christian psychotherapists can justify using the Oedipus complex and use the Bible in this manner to support the use of the Freudian ego defense mechanisms, then it seems that almost any psychotherapeutic system or technique can pass the test through *eisegesis*. For instance, one therapist announced on a nationwide radio broadcast that "there are forty defense mechanisms that we know about and nearly all of these are described in Scripture as well as in the psychiatric research."[11]

Christian psychotherapists have very imaginatively used Scripture to find psychological theories and techniques there. They find any number of conceivable psychotherapeutic theories and techniques in Scripture, and for the many not mentioned in Scripture they label them as neutral or find no contradiction. They wrongly assume that if something is missing from Scripture, it must be neutral, and, if there is no direct contradiction, it must be biblical. According to this erroneous method of determining what is biblical, one must accept a huge amount of contradictory opinions and techniques as being biblical.

If these theories and therapies were truly biblical, there would be some consensus among those Christians who dispense psychotherapy as to which of the therapies and techniques are biblical. But, there is no such consensus. Those in the Christian Psychology Industry do not agree among themselves. What one ends up with is a conglomeration of systems and techniques with each therapist picking and choosing what supposedly is in Scripture or not contradicted by Scripture. Each one forms an eclectic combination that is different from the combinations of other Christian therapists.

In the midst of writing an earlier book about psychotherapy and Christianity, we asked ourselves and then others, "What types of psychotherapeutic approaches most influence the Christian psychotherapist?" No one we contacted was able to answer that question. Therefore, we devised a simple, easy-to-answer survey form comprised of a list of ten major psychotherapies. The survey was administered to members of the Christian Association for Psychological Studies (CAPS). Each respondent was asked to rank one or more of these psychotherapeutic approaches that influenced his professional practice. Additional space was provided for participants to add other psychotherapies before ranking.

The results of the survey indicate that Christian psychotherapists or counselors are eclectic in that they are influenced by and use a variety of psychological approaches rather than just one or two. In other words, there is not just one Christian psychotherapeutic way. A great variety of approaches influence the clinical practice of CAPS members. This survey demonstrated that, while some psychotherapies are more influential than others in the practice of Christian counseling, in general the Christian psychotherapist is both independent and eclectic in his/her approach to counseling.

The Best of Both Worlds?

Those who attempt to integrate psychology and Christianity hope to bring together the best of both. Their faith rests in a combination of one or more of the many psychological systems along with some form of Christianity. Dr. Gary Collins is president of the American Association of Christian Counselors, which is probably the largest of the Christian counseling organizations. Collins says that Christian therapists have goals that are different from secular therapists.[12] Nevertheless they use theories and methods borrowed directly from approaches devised by secular psychologists whose systems have underlying presuppositions that are antithetical to the Bible.

Collins admits that Christians cannot trust all of psychology. However, in answer to the question, "Can you trust psychology?" Collins says, "It all depends on the psychology and the psychologist."[13] Then he gives his criteria of acceptance, which would be widely endorsed among Christian psychotherapists. He says:

> When a psychologist seeks to be guided by the Holy Spirit, is committed to serving Christ faithfully, is growing in his or her knowledge of the Scriptures, is well aware of the facts and conclusions of psychology, and is willing to evaluate psychological ideas in the light of biblical teaching—then you can trust the psychologist, even though he or she at times will make mistakes, as we all do. If the psychology or psychological technique is not at odds with scriptural teaching, then it is likely to be trustworthy, especially if it also is supported by scientific data.[14]

If one were to ask the numerous Christian psychologists if they met Collins' criteria, they would all say they do. But then we have to ask why it is that these numerous Christian psychologists who would say that they meet Collins' criteria come to contradictory conclusions about what therapeutic systems to use and which techniques to apply. There must be a lot of proof-texting, to say the least.

Collins accuses Christians who say they use only the Bible of also using a variety of biblical approaches. However, the basis for biblical ministry should be the truth revealed by God, while the basis for psychological counseling is merely a collection of human opinions. No matter how much one attempts to biblicize psychology or use only what appears to be neutral or safe because it does not seem to contradict Scripture, one still ends up with mere human opinion. Even after supposedly finding a certain psychology in Scripture or failing to find it contradicted in Scripture, it is still opinion. It would be difficult to think of one of the more than 400 approaches to psychotherapy or one of its underlying psychologies that cannot somehow be rationalized biblically. But rationalizing it biblically does not make it biblical or raise it above subjective opinion.

One Christian psychologist will depend on Carl Rogers' nondirective approach; another on the Freudian unconscious determinants of behavior; another on William Glasser's reality, responsibility, and right-and-wrong; and another on Albert Ellis's Rational Emotive Behavioral Therapy. Numerous other Christian psychologists, all "willing to evaluate psychological ideas in the light of biblical teaching," will use other mutually conflicting systems and multifarious contradictory techniques.

The results of a study of 177 articles having to do with integration indicated that most Christians practicing psychology do not use theology as a filter to retain only that which is biblical.[15] Approximately one third use a form of integration which stresses compatibility. However, the researchers are quick to add:

> Psychological and theological facts may appear on the surface to be saying the same thing, but a more comprehensive understanding of each may prove that there are significant differences between the secular and Christian concepts identified as parallel.[16]

The predominant mode was that of "active reconstruction and relabeling," either by "reinterpreting psychological facts from the perspective of theological facts" or "reinterpreting theological facts from the perspective of psychological facts."[17]

The integration approach, while complimentary of psychology, often ends up being derogatory of the Bible. As we have shown, it gives psychology a status not confirmed by philosophers of science and other experts on the subject. Thereby it denigrates the Bible in a subtle, yet definite way. According to a study conducted by E. E.

Griffith, the psychological counseling done by those who describe themselves as operating within a "Christian framework" actually consists mostly of secularly derived techniques.[18]

To confuse matters even more, Christian critics of psychology also claim to meet Collins' criteria. We will substitute in Collins' criteria the words "critic of psychology" for the word "psychologist" as follows: "When a [critic of psychology] seeks to be guided by the Holy Spirit, is committed to serving Christ faithfully, is growing in his or her knowledge of the Scriptures, is well aware of the facts and conclusions of psychology, and is willing to evaluate psychological ideas in the light of biblical teaching—then you can trust the [critic of psychology], even though he or she at times will make mistakes, as we all do." Or, is Collins suggesting that the critics are not "guided by the Holy Spirit," etc.?

What is a Christian to do? The psychologists claim to be following God; critics of psychology claim to be following God. The psychologists who claim to follow God often use contradictory systems; the critics of psychology may appear to be using different systems. However, the critics of psychology use the Bible as their first source, while the psychologists use psychology as their first source.

Remember that the originators of these psychological systems were not Christians. The originators of these often competing systems did not begin with Scripture; nor did they evaluate what they concluded with Scripture. They devised their systems out of their own fallen opinions about man.

This is truly a case of the opinions of nonbelieving psychologists being used by Christian psychologists on the basis of whether these opinions **seem** biblical. Is it not strange that conflicting personal opinions by these non-Christians are to be evaluated on the basis of the testimony of Christians who claim to fulfill Collins' criteria?

Collins says, "If the psychology or psychological technique is not at odds with scriptural teaching, then it is likely to be trustworthy, especially if it also is supported by scientific data." The criteria of "not at odds with scriptural teaching" as a means of being "trustworthy" is strange. Apparently the psychologist who meets Collins' criteria up to this point only needs to make sure the psychology used is "not at odds with scriptural teaching." However, the intent and purpose of Scripture is not to serve as a support or framework for worldly wisdom regarding who man is and how he should live. Of course all must be evaluated in terms of Scripture, but that does not mean that a theory or opinion that is not in Scripture is therefore "not at odds with scriptural teaching" simply because it is not mentioned. Anyone who seeks to evaluate the wisdom of men in the light of Scripture must immerse himself more in the Bible than in the wisdom of men. There should be a biblical bias rather than a psychological bias.

How about using another criteria such as "only if it is not at odds with other psychological systems"? (Of course that would eliminate all of them.) Or, "only if it is not addressing problems already addressed in Scripture?" The "not at odds with scriptural teaching" criteria is open to individual interpretation and this is why so many Christian psychologists use so many different, often contradictory systems. In addition, does this criteria for psychology not open a hopeless facsimile of Pandora's box? For examples, graphology, use of the Hindu chakras, hypnosis, and levitation could all be rationalized to be "not at odds with scriptural teachings" by some Christians (not us!). But should a Christian use them? The last part of the sentence "especially if it also is supported by scientific data" should, in all fairness, read "**only** if it also is supported by scientific data." Why would anyone want to use an unproved and unsupported psychology or psychological technique?

Which Way Pleases the Father?

Problems can motivate a person to move closer to God and find Him sufficient, or they can tempt a person to move away from God and to look for answers in the world. Psychological theories and therapies could very well lead a person further out of the will of God. The point is not which way works. The point must be: Which way pleases the Father?

We receive much information from individuals who have been therapized by Christian professionals, from Christians who have left the profession, and from numerous others about whether or not Collins' theme is played out in practice. In addition, the Christian therapists who participated in our survey of CAPS, described earlier, would certainly believe that they are being led by the Holy Spirit, in spite of the fact that they follow a widely divergent variety of theories and practices. There is about as much agreement among them as among their secular counterparts. In fact, some who claim to be led by the Holy Spirit even use techniques from Eastern therapies with their emphasis on visualization and spirit guides. There are also no consistent and dependable differences between Christian therapists and secular therapists. The picture of Holy Spirit-led therapists coming to conclusions and having practices much different from their secular counterparts is inaccurate.

The great difference between those who minister biblically and those who integrate with psychology is whether the reliance is solely on the Word of God and the work of the Holy Spirit or on a combination of human opinions and elements of the Christian faith. Think of all the psychological theorists, such as Freud, Jung, Adler, Rogers, Ellis, et cetera. Do you know of any major psychological theorist who is a Christian? In contrast to this, the Bible provides the complete and only unchanging explanations and answers from God about humans; whereas psychology is a constantly changing chameleon-like catechism of cure. Dr. Charles Tart, a prolific speaker and writer in the field of psychology, admits that the prevailing popular psychotherapeutic systems merely reflect the current culture.[19] We know that the truths of Scripture are eternal, but which psychological "truths" are eternal?

How dangerous is this growth of Christian psychology in the church? We believe it is a diabolical means of infusing the church with the world's ways and ideas. It takes the eyes off Christ and onto self. It substitutes the Word of God with the wisdom of men and it replaces the work of the Holy Spirit with human ingenuity. It feeds the flesh and hinders spiritual growth.

God's Word is His revelation to mankind about Himself and about the nature of humanity, how people are to live, and how they change. Jesus died to give brand new life to those who are born again through faith in Him, and the Holy Spirit enables believers to live according to God's Word.

Jesus did not call people to an external methodology, but to a relationship that affects every aspect of a person's life and operates every moment of the day or night. Nor did Jesus call people to live in and for themselves, but rather in and for Him and with other believers. Therefore, He compared His relationship to believers with a vine and its branches (John 15) and with a shepherd and his sheep (John 10). It is a relationship of profound love and intimacy. It is the oneness Jesus expressed in His high priestly prayer in John 17, when he prayed:

> Neither pray I for these alone, but for them also which shall believe on me through their word; that they all may be one; as thou, Father, art in me, and I in thee, that they also may be one in us: that the world may believe that thou hast sent me. . . . that the love wherewith thou has loved me may be in them, and I in them (20-21, 26).

What offering of psychology can compare with this opulent treasure of relationship with the Father and the Son? Even a brief moment of awareness of this awesome truth is far more glorious than all psychology can offer.

Those who have been devastated by disappointment, who have suffered pain inflicted by sinful humanity, and who seek an end to suffering will find balm for their souls in Jesus. Why ply them with psychological theories and therapies?

Those who have been in bondage to sin can only be set free through Jesus. All other methods of overcoming sin are superficial and temporary. Why mix and blend the systems of the world with the promises in the Word? Such freedom does not come from a magical combination of psychology and Christianity, but rather through faith in the finished work of Jesus Christ, with his life infusing the believer. Those indwelt by Jesus can walk by His life and His Word rather than by the psychological works of the flesh.

4

Does Psychotherapy Work?

What does research say about professional psychotherapy and why should it be rejected by both Christians and non-Christians? We want to make it clear that, for both biblical and scientific reasons, we are opposed to professional (services for pay) psychotherapy for both believers and unbelievers. This statement is based on the truth of Scripture and on the available research that would lead one to this conclusion. Since we live in a free society, anyone has the right to seek professional psychological counseling (psychotherapy) or other similar means of help for pay. However, the pay required contradicts the research results.

While research does not justify the costs of psychotherapy for anyone, Christians have greater reasons to reject psychological counseling. When one looks at research and knows the available resources God has given in His Word, empowered by the Holy Spirit and ministered from one believer to another, it is tragic that Christians would use such an ungodly and unsatisfactory system as psychotherapy with its underlying psychologies.

We will present the beginnings of serious research about psychotherapy. Next, we will present psychotherapy in the most positive light that research permits. Then we will add the research details of the broader picture of the various facets of it. **We will demonstrate that, if one is honest and fair about the research results, one will at minimum question the use of professional psychotherapy, if not reject it altogether.**

Could Psychotherapy Be Harmful?

Before discussing the question of positive results of psychotherapy, we need to consider the problem of possible negative effects. Some people think of psychotherapy in a manner similar to the way they think about vitamin supplements: may be helpful, but at least not harmful. This seems to be the prevailing attitude towards psychotherapy: it can be helpful, but at least it can't hurt anyone. Research reveals that view is false.

In medical literature the word *iatrogenic* refers to unexpected detrimental effects of taking medicine or receiving other medical treatment. For example, a person may come to a medical doctor with a cold, receive antibiotics, and then suffer negative reactions to the antibiotics. This negative effect is called an *iatrogenic effect*. It is an adverse, though unexpected result of treatment.

Research shows that a similar effect occurs in psychotherapy. While improvement may occur under treatment, a patient may also get worse or deteriorate as a result. Psychotherapy may be helpful to an individual, but it may also be harmful.

The *Handbook of Psychotherapy and Behavior Change* says the following in the section on "Deterioration, Negative Effects, and Estimates of Therapeutic Change":

> . . . research suggests that some patients are worse as a result of psychotherapy. . . . Many more recent studies continue to document rates of deterioration in patients, even in those who participate in carefully controlled research protocols. . . . After reviewing the empirical literature and the critiques of the evidence accumulated, **it is our view that psychotherapy can and does harm a portion of those it is intended to help.**[1]

One group of researchers surveyed 150 "expert clinicians, theoreticians, and researchers" on the negative effects of psychotherapy. They received seventy responses, which they say "represent a spectrum of contemporary thinking of some of the best minds in the field of psychotherapy."[2] The researchers conclude:

> It is clear that negative effects of psychotherapy are overwhelmingly regarded by experts in the field as a significant problem requiring the attention and concern of practitioners and researchers alike.[3]

At the end of his book on therapy, Dr. Jeffrey Masson, former Projects Director of the Sigmund Freud Archives, says:

> Everybody should know, then, that to step into the office of a psychotherapist, regardless of the latter's persuasion, is to enter a world where great harm is possible.[4]

We will not attempt to dramatize the iatrogenic effects of psychotherapy by quoting numerous studies' percentages. Important here is the fact that most people never suspected such an effect from psychotherapy until researchers brought the possibility to the public's attention. After all, how could talking and listening hurt anyone?

There is disagreement about the amount of harm that may occur in psychotherapy, but there is no question that deterioration can and does occur. Researchers do not fully understand why and how deterioration happens in therapy, but they know that negative effects happen.

Dr. Terence Campbell has written a book warning the public about the "talking cure." He says, "too often, psychotherapy severely damages people."[5] The subtitle of his book is *Psychotherapy May Be Hazardous To Your Mental Health*. This warning should be on every psychotherapist's door.

Beginnings of Serious Research

In 1952 Dr. Hans Eysenck, an eminent English scholar, published a monograph that evaluated the effectiveness of psychotherapy. From his research, Eysenck concluded, "roughly two-thirds of a group of neurotic patients will recover or improve to a marked extent within about two years of the onset of their illness, whether they are treated by means of psychotherapy or not."[6] Fifteen years later Eysenck reported:

> To date, then, there is no real evidence for the effectiveness of psychotherapy—as is now admitted even by leading psychoanalysts and psychotherapists—though with further search such evidence might be uncovered.[7]

Two other researchers at the time, Truax and Carkhuff, agreed:

> . . . after a careful review of the relevant research literature, it now appears that Eysenck was essentially correct in saying that average counseling and psychotherapy as it is currently practiced does not result in average client improvement greater than that observed in clients who receive no special counseling or psychotherapeutic treatment.[8]

During the years that followed, more research was conducted and many books were written criticizing psychotherapy. The following books are just a few of the many that were published criticizing psychotherapy:

> *The Death of Psychiatry* by E. Fuller Torrey
> *The Psychological Society* by Martin Gross
> *The Myth of Psychotherapy* by Thomas Szasz
> *The Shrinking of America* by Bernie Zilbergeld
> *The Myth of Neurosis* by Garth Wood
> *House of Cards* by Robyn Dawes
> *Manufacturing Victims* by Tana Dineen

Psychotherapy At Its Best

The most positive research reveals that psychotherapy appears to work. However, adding the complete details of the research findings will eclipse the positive results.

A research group summed up the evidence on psychotherapy's effectiveness by referring to the dodo bird in *Alice in Wonderland*. On one occasion in the story, all the animals were wet and the dodo bird suggested that a "caucus-race" would be the best way to get dry. The dodo bird marked out a race course "in a sort of circle." The animals could start anywhere or stop and start when and where they wanted during the race. A "half or hour or so" after the race started, it was obvious that the animals were all dry. Then the dodo bird called out, "The race is over!" The animals then wanted to know who had won the race. After some thought, the dodo bird announced, "*Everybody* has won, and *all* must have prizes."[9]

This anecdote has often been used throughout the psychotherapy literature to illustrate what the research indicates about the effectiveness of psychotherapy.[10] There are more than 400 different approaches to psychotherapy. Not all have been tested, but of those that have, the overwhelming conclusion is "*Everybody* has won, and *all* must have prizes." In other words, all psychotherapies appear to work. One additional finding is that all psychotherapies seem to work equally well. With certain exceptions, the research findings add up to the idea that **all psychotherapies work and all seem to work equally well.** This result is known in the research literature as the **"equal outcomes phenomenon."**[11]

It is obvious that neither physics nor chemistry is plagued with the equal outcomes results of psychotherapy. Think about it. Do all natural science theories lead to equal outcomes as with psychotherapy?

This equal outcomes phenomenon has been a consistent finding over a number of years. Dr. Morris Parloff refers to the "disconcerting finding that all forms of psychotherapy are effective and that all forms of psychotherapy appear to be equally effective."[12] He says:

> No consistent differences are found among different forms of therapy in terms of type or degree of benefit with comparable patients.[13]

Parloff also says:

> Nearly 500 rigorously controlled studies have shown with almost monotonous regularity that all forms of psychological treatment . . . are comparably effective.[14]

The *Handbook of Psychotherapy and Behavior Change* (hereafter referred to only as the *Handbook*) is known as the "bible" of outcome research in psychotherapy. The most recent edition of the *Handbook* states:

> . . . meta-analytic methods [a statistical procedure] have now been extensively applied to large groups of comparative studies, and these reviews generally offer similar conclusions (i.e., little or no difference between therapies).[15]

It may appear that we are making a case for psychotherapy rather than against it. But, is the equal outcomes result evidence in favor of or against psychotherapy? If one uses the dodo bird, the equal outcomes result, to support the use of professional psychotherapy, that would be a dodo (i.e., foolish or stupid) conclusion. Why? Because, what works is common to all.

The *Handbook*'s "Summation" makes the point of equal outcomes even more powerful by stating:

> With some exceptions, which we will consider, **there is massive evidence that psychotherapeutic techniques do not have specific effects**; yet there is tremendous resistance to accepting this finding as a legitimate one.[16] (Bold added.)

Dr. Morris Parloff and Dr. Irene Elkin say:

> The specificity hypothesis would lead one to expect that specific benefits are associated with the application of specific strategies, procedures, techniques and experience. The failure to find empirical support for such expectations provoked the formulation of the nonspecificity or common factors hypothesis.[17]

Psychiatrist Jerome Frank says that from the therapists' view, "little glory derives from showing that the particular method one has mastered with so much effort may be indistinguishable from other methods in its effects."[18] The fact that there are more than 400 different, often-conflicting psychological counseling approaches and 10,000-plus not-often-compatible techniques with various incompatible underlying psychological theories must raise a huge question mark over why they all seem to work equally well.

One rather interesting sidelight is that ethnic groups do not utilize psychotherapy the way others do. The *Handbook* reveals that "there is limited research on ethnic minority groups" and admits that "many researchers and practitioners believe that psychotherapy is ineffective with members of ethnic minority groups."[19] The huge question mark over the effectiveness of therapy would need to have an exclamation mark next to it for ethnic minorities.

The equal outcomes conclusion has led to a search to find factors that are common to all therapeutic approaches, since no therapeutic approach stood out above the rest. The result of that search revealed some very interesting and condemning information about psychotherapy. However, before discussing those common factors, we will look at some possible reasons for the apparent change in research results.

What Caused the Change in Outcomes?

The current conclusion that all psychotherapies work and all seem to work equally well obviously contradicts the earlier reported conclusions from Eysenck and others. What caused the change from questioning, criticizing and even condemning psychotherapy to complimenting it? How did the results of psychotherapy research move from questionable to positive? We believe two major ingredients in the change involve both the therapists used and the population therapized.

The Therapists Used

Studies determining the effectiveness of psychotherapy are usually based on the use of the best therapists. When conducting a study, a select group of therapists is generally used. Therapists are chosen because they are known to be good therapists or else the therapists agree to participate because they are confident in their counseling abilities. In reference to the positive results that they have found, Dr. Allen Bergin and Dr. Michael Lambert say:

> . . . we believe that a major contributor to these newer findings is that more experienced and competent therapists have been used in recent studies.[20]

Bergin later confirmed that this continues to be true.[21] The use of above-average therapists would tend to inflate outcome results greatly.

Bergin reports how outcome studies depend on the use of good therapists and not those who are average or below.[22] This raises several questions research does not answer. First: "Does the use of average psychotherapists yield better results on treated patients than no treatment at all?" Second: "How much more harm occurs with average or below-average psychotherapists?" And, finally: "How many good therapists are there?" No one really knows how many good therapists there are. Nor does anyone know whether no treatment would yield better results than the use of average or below-average therapists. Furthermore, no one knows how high the harm rate is with average or below-average therapists.

However, there is some doubt as to whether there are many good therapists. Researchers Truax and Mitchell say, "From existing data it would appear that only one out of three people entering professional training has the requisite interpersonal skills to prove helpful to patients."[23] Two other researchers estimate that only one-fifth of the therapists are competent.[24] On top of this, some studies have indicated that while "warmth and empathy are highly important variables in determining client benefit . . . graduate programs do not help students to greatly increase their interpersonal skills."[25] The authors of *Psychotherapy for Better or Worse* note that "the therapist himself was one of the most often cited sources of negative effects in psychotherapy."[26]

The research studies are not only based on the use of above average psychotherapists. Studies use almost exclusively other-than-private-practice therapists. One psychotherapy research review revealed only fifteen private-practice studies were done during a twenty-five-year period of time. There are few such studies because private-practice psychotherapists are reluctant to participate.[27]

Expanded Population

From the psychotherapeutic enterprise's beginning until now the population being therapized has expanded in numbers and particularly in who is regarded as needing psychological therapy. For psychiatrists the official "bible" for identifying and categorizing mental disorders is the *Diagnostic and Statistical Manual of Mental Disorders (DSM)*. In 1952 the *DSM-I* "contained 106 different diagnostic categories."[28] The 1994 manual, *DSM-IV*, includes 340 different psychiatric conditions.[29] The figures reported earlier, with the skyrocketing percentage of the American population in psychotherapy between 1960 to 1995, reveal more people receiving therapy than ever before and, more importantly, for far more trivial matters than ever before.

It is clear and should be obvious that **psychotherapy works best for those who need it least**. Over the years more and more people with fewer and fewer psychotherapeutic needs are being therapized. These less needy, more therapized groups would naturally have better results with psychotherapy on the average in comparison with fewer people with greater needs. And, as we pointed out earlier, almost any kind of therapy will work for the worried well.

Common Factors

The *Handbook* refers to the "general finding of no-difference in the outcome of therapy for clients who have participated in highly diverse therapies" and then offers three possible explanations. The research literature repeatedly gives the following explanation:

> Different therapies embody common factors that are curative although not emphasized by the theory of change central to a particular school.[30]

The equal outcomes result (all therapies work and all seem to work equally well) naturally raises the question of what factors are common to all therapies. **What are some common factors that would, on the average, give all therapies and therapists positive results?** Therapy consists of a client, a counselor (therapist), and the conversation, which is the medium through which therapy methodology moves. Thus, the client, counselor, and conversation are the three most obvious factors to

investigate to find what might be common to all therapies. Of these three, and far more important than the
other two, is the client, the person being therapized. As a
matter of fact, it would be quite appropriate to say that
the client is not only the most important factor in therapy, but is also the one factor that eclipses all the others.

The Client

The *Handbook* makes it clear that client characteristics make a big difference with respect to outcomes in
therapy. The *Handbook*'s "Summation" states:

> . . . it is the client more than the therapist who
> implements the change process. If the client does
> not absorb, utilize, and follow through on the facili-
> tative efforts of the therapist, then nothing happens.
> Rather than argue over whether or not "therapy
> works," we could address ourselves to the question
> of whether or not "the client works"![31]

Clients motivated to change who are therapized by a variety of therapies and therapists will certainly result in far
greater positive change than clients who do not wish to
change being therapized by whatever therapies and therapists.

Besides what the client brings to the therapeutic
experience, there are some factors that influence the
client as he participates. **Four of the many factors
that influence the client, which are mostly independent of the therapies and therapists used, are
technically termed** *regression effect, illusion of efficacy, placebo effect,* **and** *expectancy arousal.*

Dr. Robyn Dawes explains one of these factors as follows:

> Because most people enter therapy when they are
> extremely unhappy, they are less likely to be as
> unhappy later, independent of the effects of therapy
> itself. Hence, this "regression effect" can create the
> illusion that the therapy has helped to alleviate
> their unhappiness, whether it has or not.[32]

Dr. David Myers, in his book *The Inflated Self,* indicates that there is an "illusion of efficacy" which often occurs when people go for psychotherapy. The illusion of efficacy is a deceptive belief about causation.[33] Testimonies are given about self-improvement after various workshops, therapy, and therapeutic activities. There seems to be a cause and effect here: a workshop or other therapeutic experience is followed by an improvement. Therefore the person concludes that the therapeutic experience must have caused it, whether there was any connection or not. Psychotherapist Allen Fromme claims that any change will usually result in improvement, no matter what it is.[34] Myers explains:

> The principle of "regression toward the average" also contributes to the illusion of efficacy. Since people tend to seek help when things have hit bottom, any activity that is then undertaken may seem to be effective—to both the client and the therapist.[35]

Dr. Arthur Shapiro, clinical professor of psychiatry at Mount Sinai School of Medicine, suggests that the power of psychological counseling may be the effect of a placebo. The placebo effect takes place when one has faith in a pill, a person, a process or procedure, and it is this faith that brings about the healing. The pill, person, process, or procedure may all be fake, but the result is real. Shapiro says:

> Just as bloodletting was perhaps the massive placebo technique of the past, so psychoanalysis— and its dozens of psychotherapy offshoots—is the most used placebo of our time.[36]

If one out of three individuals finds relief through the use of a medical placebo, what percent of the individuals who see a psychotherapist receive similar relief through a type of mental placebo? A group of researchers at Wesleyan University compared the benefits of psychotherapy with those of placebo treatments. The placebo treatments were activities (such as discussion of current events, group play reading, and listening to records) that attempted to help individuals without the use of psychotherapeutic techniques. The researchers concluded:

> . . . after about 500 outcome studies have been reviewed we are still not aware of a single convincing demonstration that the benefits of psychotherapy exceed those of placebos for real patients.[37]

Shapiro criticized his professional colleagues at an annual meeting of the American Psychopathological Association for ignoring placebo effects and therefore skewing the results of their research.[38] He believes that if placebo effects were considered, "there would be no difference between psychotherapy and placebo."[39]

Eysenck has said:

> The general tenor of the evidence produced in recent years seems to be that the conclusion of my 1952 article is still valid: psychotherapy works, as far as it does, by means of non-specific or placebo effects.[40]

The placebo not only affects the individual, but it affects those who come in contact with the individual. Everyone tends to feel and believe that progress will be made because something is being done. The placebo effect, along with other factors just mentioned, greatly diminishes the authority of any positive results reported for professional psychotherapy itself. While some researchers criticize this idea, it has not been given its fair testing, as we shall note later when we offer a challenge to professional psychotherapy.

Dr. David Shapiro has proposed an idea that would be a common factor that could lead to success for therapies. He calls this idea the "expectancy arousal hypothesis," which he explains this way: "treatments differ in effectiveness only to the extent that they arouse in clients differing degrees of expectation of benefit."[41] According to this hypothesis, as the conversation or therapy proceeds and there is an arousal of positive expectancy in the client, then improvement will occur. Thus, according to Shapiro, as the therapist uses any one of a number of therapeutic conversations, the effectiveness will be related to the client's own expectancy of benefit. Therefore, the specific therapeutic conversation would not matter, but rather the client's expectancy of benefit. Again, it's what the client brings to the therapy rather than therapy itself.

The regression effect, illusion of efficacy, placebo effect and expectancy arousal are four common effects that occur when a client enters therapy. Therapies and therapists that can enhance these four common effects available to all therapies and therapists may lead to positive results irrespective of specific therapies used by individual therapists.

The Counselor

Of the three common factors, being the client, counselor and conversation, the second in importance is the counselor. **Researchers are aware that the interpersonal qualities of the counselor far outweigh his training and techniques.** Research psychiatrist E. Fuller Torrey reports:

> The research shows that certain personal qualities of the therapist—accurate empathy, non-possessive warmth, and genuineness—are of crucial importance in producing effective psychotherapy.

He notes that "therapists who possess these qualities consistently and convincingly get better therapeutic results than those who do not possess them."[42]

Frank reports:

> Anyone with a modicum of human warmth, common sense, some sensitivity to human problems, and a desire to help can benefit many candidates for psychotherapy.[43]

Bergin says that "change appears to be a function of common human interactions, including personal and belief factors."[44] Dr. Lewis Thomas says, "Most psychiatrists of my acquaintance are skilled in therapy, but the therapy, when it works, is really plain friendship."[45]

Research examining common factors of the counselor or therapist, regardless of the therapy used, has found that "consistent evidence exists to support the assertion (now nearly a 'truism') that a warm and supportive therapeutic relationship facilitates therapeutic success."[46]

Conversation (Therapy)

Aside from the presence of two or more people in a therapeutic setting, the most prominent, but least important factor is the aspect of the conversation that is based on models and methodologies of psychological theories. Psychological theories and techniques that come through conversation comprise the third and least important factor compared to the client and the counselor. We want to make it clear that it is the specificity from theories and techniques undergirding the conversation that are the least important components regarding change, **not** the fact of the conversation itself. **The psychological type of conversation or therapy yields equal outcomes, but the fact of conversation is common to the more than 400 different types of therapy.**

Dr. Joseph Wortis clarifies this. He says, "The proposition of whether psychotherapy can be beneficial can be reduced to its simplest terms of whether talk is very helpful." He continues, "And that doesn't need to be researched. It is self evident that talk can be helpful."[47]

But, how does a therapist establish what the *Handbook* refers to as "a warm and supportive therapeutic relationship"?[48] Primarily through conversation. Conversation is the glue that can hold a counselor and client together or the wedge that can drive them apart. It is through conversation that one can motivate, confirm, engender faith, encourage hope, and express love. But no one therapy has the market on these active therapeutic ingredients. It is common to all talk therapies. The *Handbook* indicates that "therapist empathy was most predictive of being an effective or ineffective therapist."[49]

The *Handbook* "Summation" suggests that the equal outcomes phenomenon result is due to a "a caring relationship characterized by warmth, support, attention, understanding, and acceptance."[50] Again, this is communicated mostly through the common denominator of conversation regardless of the psychological type of conversation or therapy. **Thus, the *caring* communicated through the conversation, rather than the specific theoretical or methodological content of communication, is the common factor.**

Common factors that appear to give the positive outcomes to therapy are not dependent on the professional therapeutic process. Common factors regarding the client are the regression effect, illusion of efficacy, placebo effect, and expectancy arousal. Common factors regarding the therapist are interpersonal qualities, such as warmth, empathy, and genuineness. And, the common factor of the conversation is the caring relationship that comes through talking.

Professional Versus Nonprofessionals

From the previous research provided, one can guess what the results would be in comparing the effectiveness of professional therapists and nonprofessionals used as therapists. Researchers Strupp and Howard say:

> The controversy between "unique" and "common" factors in the therapeutic influence has had other implications. With respect to the training of therapists, it has been argued that if professionals essentially use "common factors" in their work, what is unique about their expertise? Furthermore, might not naturally talented and intuitive people, without prolonged and thorough training, be able to function as effectively in the therapist role?[51]

As we said earlier, we are opposed to professional psychotherapy. We will now bring together additional research and comments to support our opposition to professional psychotherapy. Here it is important to note that the most serious problems with psychotherapy involve the therapist. While there are many variables related to the professional therapist, we will first consider three of them together and then consider a fourth variable.

Three Variables

The three variables related to the therapist are: the professional therapists' training, credentials, and experience. Dawes refers to a famous 1977 research article written by psychological researchers Mary Smith and Gene Glass in the *American Psychologist*.[52] Through a technique known as meta-analysis, Smith and Glass summarized and compared the results from a variety of research studies.

In discussing Smith and Glass's meta-analytic findings, Dawes says "the therapists' credentials—Ph.D., M.D., or no advanced degree—and experience were unrelated to the effectiveness of therapy."[53] Dawes later declares:

> But we do know that the training, credentials, and experience of psychotherapist are irrelevant, or at least that is what all the evidence indicates.[54]

Related to the above conclusion, Dawes says:

> . . . one's effectiveness as a therapist was unrelated to *any* professional training.[55] (Italics in original.)

> . . . *the credentials and experience of the psychotherapists are unrelated to patient outcomes*.[56] (Italics in original.)

> There is no reason, however, to seek out a highly paid, experienced therapist with a lot of credentials.[57]

Dawes reports:

> In the years after the Smith and Glass article was published, many attempts were made to disprove their finding that the training, credentials, and

experience of therapists are irrelevant. These attempts failed.[58]

Dawes notes that "professional psychologists and other mental health professionals . . . are no better as psychotherapists than are others of comparable intelligence who are minimally trained."[59] The *Handbook* states the following:

> Most meta-analytic reviews suggest that length of therapist experience by itself is neither a strong nor a significant predictor of amount of improvement.[60]

Because of the results of the various studies on training, credentials and experience of professional psychologists and mental health professionals, the future of the highly trained, credentialed, experienced professional is questionable. Dr. Keith Humphreys, in an *American Psychologist* article titled "Clinical Psychologists as Psychotherapists," says:

> As managed care and other cost-containment strategies become central features of the American health care system, doctoral-level clinical psychologists will be increasingly supplanted in the role of psychotherapist by lower cost providers such as social workers, marriage and family counselors, and masters-level psychologists.[61]

One would naturally believe that training, credentials, and experience would make a difference. Aren't these some of the major reasons why people pay professionals? But we repeat, "**Training, credentials, and experience of psychotherapists are irrelevant.**"

Prediction: A Fourth Variable

One of the main failures of psychotherapy as a science is in the area of prediction. In physics and chemistry one can predict what will happen under given circumstances. One can even talk about the probability of certain events occurring. However, in psychotherapy the system breaks down at the level of prediction. No one knows why some people get better and some worse; and no one can even predict which ones will get better and which ones will deteriorate.

Much research on clinical judgment and decision-making reveals that the experts lack substantially in the ability to predict. Hillel Einhorn and Robin Hogarth say, "It is apparent that neither the extent of professional training and experience nor the amount of information available to clinicians necessarily increases predictive accuracy."[62] Dawes says:

> No one has yet devised a method for determining who will change, or how or when. Professional psychologists cannot predict that. (If any have been able to do so, it has been kept secret from the research literature.)[63]

Dawes also says:

> It's not that people don't change—they do, sometimes profoundly. Rather, no personal skill has yet been developed—or assessment instrument devised—that allows us to predict who will change, when, and how.[64]

The American Psychiatric Association admits that psychiatrists cannot even predict future dangerous activities of their patients. In a court case involving a person who committed murder shortly after having seen a psychiatrist, the APA presented an *amicus curiae* brief, which stated that research studies show that psychiatrists are unable to predict future potential dangerous behavior of a patient.[65]

Psychotherapy is based on psychological theories that purport to understand why people are the way they are and why they do what they do. Theories that claim to understand and facilitate change should also be able to predict. The very fact that they cannot predict greatly undermines any psychotherapeutic system. Based on evidence that psychotherapists cannot predict behavior, Dawes makes an accusation:

The inability to predict implies a lack of understanding—not because understanding and prediction are synonymous, but because a claim to understanding implies an ability to predict.[66]

The shocking thing about all this, the researchers point out, is that in spite of the great fallibility in professional judgment people seem to have unshakable confidence in it.

To circumvent this problem of prediction, some have called psychotherapy a *postdictive science* rather than a *predictive science*. One psychologist admits, "Since the days of Freud, we have had to rely on postdictive theories—that is, we have used our theoretical systems to explain or rationalize what has gone on before."[67] Thus, psychotherapists cannot predict the future mental-emotional-behavioral health of their clients with any confidence. They can merely look into a person's past and guess how he got that way. Psychotherapy should not even be labeled *postdictive* because the explanation of behavior and its relationship to the past is subjective and interpretive rather than objective and reliable.

Added to the fact that the training, credentials and experience of the psychotherapists are irrelevant is the fact that their failure at prediction about their clients implies a lack of understanding. This adds another exclamation point to the question mark about professional psychotherapy.

More Research and a Challenge

It would be easy to provide a list of studies indicating the effectiveness of nonprofessional therapists. For example, the *Handbook* reports:

In a meta-analytic review of studies that address level of training, Berman and Norton (1985) concluded that professionally trained therapists had no systematic advantage over nonprofessional therapists in evoking treatment gains.[68]

Dawes says:

> **Evaluating the efficacy of psychotherapy has led us to conclude that professional psychologists are no better psychotherapists than anyone else with minimal training—sometimes those without any training at all; the professionals are merely more expensive.**[69] (Bold added.)

Numerous other studies could be used to support the effectiveness of nonprofessionals.

Frank once referred to the shocking fact of "the inability of scientific research to demonstrate conclusively that professional psychotherapists produce results sufficiently better than those of nonprofessionals.[70]

The best possible test comparing professionals and nonprofessionals could not be conducted because it would involve deception. The best comparison would involve giving the nonprofessionals titles, degrees, credentials, etc., equivalent to the professionals. Eysenck makes a point about placebo treatments that usually involve amateurs and are used in comparison to professional psychotherapeutic treatment. He says:

> Nothing is said about the *quality* of the placebos used. To be effective, placebos should contain all the theoretically effective elements of the treatment that is being tested; that means equal duration, equal attention, and **equal belief in effectiveness on the part of the patient**. I have never seen a study that even approximated, let alone reached, such a degree of equivalence.[71] (Italics in original, bold added.)

The same criticism applies to the use of nonprofessionals. To overcome this criticism, we suggest that the professionals be stripped of their titles, degrees, credentials, etc. For a fair comparison, the therapy clients should not know the backgrounds of either the nonprofessionals or the professionals. The reason for this is obvious. If the professionals are presented with all of their titles, etc. they would have all the culturally sanctioned assets accruing to other professionals in our society.

One additional ingredient needed to create as much equivalency as possible is to use individuals from other people-oriented professions who have not been psychotherapeutically trained. For example, one could select teachers, nurses, medical doctors, clergy, and other such professionals to serve as the nonprofessional therapists.

An excellent example of how culturally-sanctioned assets influence the outcome can be seen in the following description of findings reported in *Psychotherapy Research: Methodological and Efficacy Issues*, published by the American Psychiatric Association:

> An experiment at the All-India Institute of Mental Health in Bangalore found that Western-trained psychiatrists and native healers had a comparable recovery rate. The most notable difference was that the so-called "witch doctors" released their patients sooner.[72]

A study of professional and nonprofessional therapists by Strupp at Vanderbilt University compared the mental-emotional improvement of two groups of male college students. Two groups of "therapists" were set up to provide two groups of students with "therapy." The two student groups were equated on the basis of mental-emotional distress as much as possible. The first group of therapists consisted of five psychiatrists and psychologists. "The five professional therapists participating in the study were selected on the basis of their reputation in the professional and academic community for clinical expertise. Their average length of experience was 23 years."

The second group of "therapists" consisted of seven college professors from a variety of fields, but without therapeutic training. Each untrained "therapist" used his own personal manner of care, and each trained therapist used his own brand of therapy. The students seen by the professors showed as much improvement as those seen by the highly experienced and specially trained therapists.[73]

An important ingredient here is the fact that the professors, though amateurs at therapy, had the necessary culturally sanctioned assets equivalent to those of the professional therapists.[74]

While on the one hand we do not recommend Alcoholics Anonymous, on the other hand the *Consumer Reports (CR)* magazine study of therapy (which will be discussed later) states the following:

> Alcoholics Anonymous (AA) did especially well, with an average improvement score of 251, significantly bettering mental health professionals.[75]

It is obvious that AA has no psychotherapy professionals that therapize their groups. AA is purposely and conscientiously a laity-led movement. Yet, in the *CR* therapy study, "as a treatment, AA significantly outperformed other mental health professionals."[76]

The following would certainly challenge the notion that professional therapists are superior to nonprofessionals. A series of rigorously controlled double-blind studies, in which the subjects would not know if they are seeing a professional or nonprofessional therapist and which involves an equalizing of "therapists," would really put psychotherapy to the test and we believe it would fail.

A Disagreement

We have presented as legitimate the various positive outcomes from meta-analytic studies, but there are reasons to question them. Even the *Handbook* admits, in its chapter on "Process and Outcome in Psychotherapy—Noch Einmal," the following:

> All the studies reviewed suffer from methodological flaws, some rather more than others; but all studies suffer from some flaws.[77]

In addition, Eysenck, who is a distinguished researcher, has written an article titled "Meta-Analysis Squared—Does It Make Sense?" He says:

> If I am right in my criticism of most meta-analyses, particularly in this field, then piling one inadequate method on top of another is a question of *imponere Pelio Ossam*, as Virgil has it. . . . A method that averages apples, lice, and killer whales (here psychological, educational, and behavioral treatments) can hardly command scientific respect; there is little in common among psychotherapy for [a long list follows]. To combine the outcomes of all these (and many more) meta-analyses seems to me a gigantic absurdity. To pretend that there is anything whatever in common among them seems difficult to justify and to have no ascertainable meaning.[78]

Eysenck maintains:

> Numerous studies since the 1950s have in essence failed to disconfirm the view that various forms of psychotherapy do not show greater effectiveness than spontaneous remission or placebo treatment.[79]

Even the American Psychiatric Association has reached a conclusion regarding the effectiveness of psychotherapy. A book titled *Psychotherapy Research: Methodological and Efficacy Issues*, published by the APA, indicates that a definite answer to the question, "Is psychotherapy effective?" may be unattainable. The book concludes: "Unequivocal conclusions about causal connections between treatment and outcome may never be possible in psychotherapy research."[80] In other words, **they may never know for sure about the effectiveness of psychotherapy**.

In spite of the challenges to the equal outcomes conclusion arrived at by meta-analytic studies, we wanted to present psychotherapy in the best possible light to demonstrate that **even at its best professional psychotherapy is not worth the price**.

Research Conclusion

Dawes is a professor in the Department of Social and Decision Sciences at Carnegie-Mellon University. He is a widely-recognized researcher and offers much academic research support for his thesis that **professional psychotherapy is a "house of cards" and that psychotherapy and its underlying psychologies are built on myths**. In commenting on Dawes's book, Dr. Donald Peterson, a professor at Rutgers University, says:

> What [Dawes] does show, convincingly, is that a large number of studies designed to examine associations between training for psychotherapy and effectiveness of treatment have failed to show any positive relationships. Results as substantial and consistent as these cannot be explained away, and they cannot responsibly be ignored.[81]

In his book bearing the subtitle *Psychology and Psychotherapy Built on Myth*, Dawes says:

> **There is no *positive* evidence supporting the efficacy of professional psychology. There are anecdotes, there is plausibility, there are common beliefs, yes—but there is no good evidence.**[82] (Italics in original; bold added.)

In his introduction, Dawes says:

> Virtually all the research—and this book will reference more than three hundred empirical investigations and summaries of investigations—has found that these professionals' claims to superior intuitive insight, understanding, and skill as therapists are simply invalid.[83]

In reply to his critics, Dawes says:

> Critics of my arguments may well be able to drag out a single study, or even several, that appear to contradict my conclusions. As I pointed out earlier, however, the generality of my conclusions is depen-

dent on multiple studies conducted on multiple problems in multiple contexts.[84]

Dawes says, "Every state requires that practicing professional psychologists be licensed."[85] Throughout his book and particularly in a chapter on licensing, Dawes makes a strong case for abolishing licensing for professional therapists. He says:

> What our society has done, sadly, is to license such people to "do their own thing," while simultaneously justifying that license on the basis of scientific knowledge, which those licensed too often ignore. This would not be too bad if "their own thing" had some validity, but it doesn't.[86]

We agree with Dawes and his interpretation of the research.

Garth Wood ends his book *The Myth of Neurosis* with the following conclusion:

> In other words, all the inferiority complexes, the dream interpretations, the Oedipal factors, the collective unconscious, the free associations, are nothing but red herrings. The vital ingredient is after all merely a caring listener who raises hopes and fights demoralization. . . . But if this is all that is needed, what then of professional training in the intricacies of psychotherapy, what of the huge fees, what of the third-party medical insurance reimbursements, of the pretense and the rhetoric, of all the shams and the charlatans, the sound and the fury signifying nothing? **If this is all the great "science" of psychotherapy is, then let us sweep it away now and bother ourselves with it no more.**[87] (Bold added.)

Consumer Reports: "Invalid Is Invalid"

The *Consumer Reports* (*CR*) magazine published a reader survey regarding personal benefits of receiving psychotherapy.[88] Of the 186,000 *CR* readers surveyed, only 23,400 (13 percent) responded. Of those who responded, only 4,000 (2.2 percent) had sought professional help and 2,900 (1.6 percent) had seen a mental health professional.[89] The 2.2 percent return rate would normally invalidate such a study. However, there has been a drive on the part of mental health professionals to advertise and promote these results. There is also, of course, a financial advantage for them to do so.

The *Consumer Reports* study and Dr. Martin Seligman, consultant to the *CR* study, draw some very positive conclusions about psychotherapy.[90] However, many researchers would challenge, question, and even contradict these positive findings.[91] We will confront one major, fatal flaw on the part of *Consumer Reports* and Seligman.

An efficacy study is the usual "gold standard" in research for measuring the effectiveness of psychotherapy. This involves examining the different variables involved in the actual practice of psychotherapy, some of which we have discussed earlier, such as the client, the therapist, and the therapy used. *CR* and Seligman have now changed this to a new gold standard.[92] Their new so-called gold standard is the use of a consumer satisfaction questionnaire to which a small number of individuals who felt like it responded. If one believes Seligman, this retrospective, self reporting by a small percentage of subscribers to a particular magazine who felt like responding to a questionnaire becomes the new gold standard.

A group from Ohio State University challenged the *CR* study in their article titled "The *Consumer Reports* Study of Psychotherapy: Invalid Is Invalid," published in the *American Psychologist*. They contend that the *CR* findings were "reached after a bravura run across a mine-field of methodological flaws."[93]

Dr. Neil Jacobson, an expert on therapy outcome research, criticizes the *CR* survey for "serious methodological problems."[94] He says of the *CR* survey:

> A long history of research has shown that consumer satisfaction is not correlated with measures of

symptom relief or functioning, and tends to be inflated in results like these.[95]

Dr. Tana Dineen accuses Seligman of confusing what the participants in the *CR* survey "present as subjective opinion for objective reality." She criticizes his new "gold standard" as follows:

> His "gold standard" eliminates the distinction between facts and feelings so that "satisfaction" and "effectiveness" are equated and truth is determined by opinion.[96]

In order to answer the criticism that the *CR* study is merely a study of consumer satisfaction, Seligman compares the *CR* consumer satisfaction study on therapy with a later *CR* consumer satisfaction report on lawyers, in which a similar approach was used.[97] Seligman indicates that the mental health professionals were rated more highly than the lawyers. Now, if *CR* had asked us, we could have saved them a lot of time and money. If *CR* or Seligman do not know that mental health professionals would be better thought of by consumers than lawyers, they are entirely out of touch with reality. Think about all the lawyer jokes told over the years; compare them with the few psychotherapist jokes—enough said? Lawyers are much more often involved in adversarial situations than psychotherapists and spend considerably less time in a nurturant, supportive, intimate relationship with their clients. Also, lawyers are typically not covered by third-party payments as are the mental health professionals. The pay for a lawyer comes out of one's earnings, and lawyers are not usually options but rather requirements. People use lawyers reluctantly out of necessity.

Comments made by Dr. Bernie Zilbergeld would certainly apply to a survey such as the one conducted by *CR*. Zilbergeld says:

> [The reason] clients exaggerate the effectiveness of therapy. . . has to do with the basic nature of

counseling; it is, for most people, a very personal, even intimate, matter. . . . And the therapist is often supportive, understanding, sympathetic. . . . By its very nature, this kind of relationship is hard to criticize. . . . It's hard to say that this kind of relationship or process is useless or harmful.[98]

Dr. Jerome Frank brings another view to this issue when, after commenting about research on brainwashing, he says:

These findings raise some doubts about the claims of certain schools of psychotherapy to produce fundamental personality change. From this perspective, such changes may be analogous to false confessions. That is, the person has not changed fundamentally, but rather has learned to couch his problems and report improvement in the therapist's terms.[99]

If *CR* and Seligman would be willing to risk a study of consumer satisfaction on the part of those who use the professional services of a psychic, an astrologer, or a palm reader, we can easily predict that these groups would definitely beat out lawyers and maybe even mental health professionals as well. Part of the *CR* study obtained data related to the clergy. Those data have not yet been released and, according to a phone call to *CR*, may never be released. However, we predict that the data will reflect a higher rating for clergy than for lawyers. So Seligman's example is a poor one and poorly thought out on his part.

One huge problem with a consumer satisfaction study of an activity like psychotherapy is that the results are dependent upon, to use Dineen's words, "subjective opinion," "feelings," and "satisfaction" of the recipient of that treatment. There are no objective checks, no establishment of facts and no real test of effectiveness. The best person to report on improvement is not always the person being therapized, but rather another person close to the individual. However, rarely is this person asked. There are many therapy consumers who give positive satisfaction reports that would be laughed at by those with whom they interact. We have seen numerous cases of individuals who, as a result of being therapized, have damaged an entire family, including a spouse, children, parents, in-laws, and friends. There are probably millions of nightmares related to those therapy consumers who are expressing their satisfactions in studies like the *CR* one. But, those who best know the satisfied psychotherapy consumers and live with them in real life are not asked. One group of researchers say of the *CR* report:

> This assumes that the *CR* (1994) psychotherapy survey was psychologically akin to all other *CR* surveys, whereas, in fact, it was fundamentally different. While it is nonthreatening to state that a blender is lousy, it is somewhat aversive to indicate that one's current state of mental health is lousy, especially after one has invested considerable time, money, and emotional involvement in therapy. Thus, recipients may have been unwilling to rate their therapy experience negatively, because of its implications for their own self-worth. Client-satisfaction measures can reflect positive outcomes, whereas all objective criteria contradict these rosy reports.[100]

In a previous section in which we compared professionals and nonprofessionals, we gave an equalizing of "therapists" challenge, in which professionals and non-professionals would be made equal with respect to titles, credentials, licensing, etc. Eysenck complains that placebo treatments are not equalized in every way except for the special therapy used and therefore do not really put therapy to the ultimate test. However, if professionals and nonprofessionals were equalized in a way to engender equal trust and confidence and a *CR* questionnaire were then sent to those who were "therapized" it would certainly put psychotherapy to a test it would fail—at least all the evidence points in that direction. But, it is doubtful such a test would be conducted, because resistance would be too great. And, it is our guess that *CR* would run from such a challenge.

Recommendations

Based on the abundance of research already done and for many of the reasons revealed earlier, it is reasonable to recommend that **licensing be abolished for those dispensing psychotherapy**, because there is no benefit to the public for such licensing. The public is in no way protected by those licensing laws. For the same reasons, **insurance companies should cease paying for psychotherapy**.

Of course individuals would be free to pay whomever they wish for advice and comfort. After all, psychic readers bilk people out of all sorts of money and they are not licensed, nor should they be.

Some will ask, what will we do about our problems of living? Zilbergeld, in his book *The Shrinking of America*, discusses much of the research related to psychotherapy.[101] He says:

> If I personally had a relationship problem and I couldn't work it out with my partner, I wouldn't go and see a shrink. I would look around me for the kind of relationship I admire. I wouldn't care if he was a carpenter or a teacher or a journalist . . . or a shrink. That's who I would go to. I want somebody who's showing by [his] life that [he] can do it.[102]

Dawes says:

> If we don't feel so wonderful, there is no shame in seeking a little help from our friends (or a therapist), but there is also no necessity for seeking the services of a high-priced professional who claims to have insights that the research shows are no better than insights inferred from general principles.[103]

In concluding the preface of his book on therapy, Masson says, "What we need are more kindly friends and fewer professionals."[104]

In many research studies the nonprofessionals were given some preliminary, but often minimal training prior to acting as therapists. Many studies refer to these short-term, moderately trained individuals as "paraprofessionals." At this time no one really knows the minimal level of training that might be needed to make an effective therapist. Dawes says:

> More research should be conducted to determine the threshold of intelligence or training that is required for being a therapist who is as effective as most others. Perhaps even a master's degree is unnecessary. Perhaps unemployed college graduates could be as effective as anyone else.[105]

It may be that insurance companies would invest in the research, which would no doubt result in huge financial savings to them. If research led to a cadre of minimally trained and, therefore, less expensive therapists, there should be plenty of them available for those who choose to pay for such services. After all, a professional therapist has been referred to all these years as a "paid friend."

Although Christian psychological counselors claim to have taken only those elements of psychology that fit with Christianity, anything can be forced to fit the Bible, no matter how foolish or ghoulish. Each Christian therapist brings his own individual psychology, borrowed from the world, to the Bible and modifies the Word to make it fit. What they use comes from the bankrupt systems of ungodly and unscientific theories and techniques.

This delicensing would be a real godsend! Then Christians would be left to do what believers did for all the centuries before the rise of psychotherapy. They would function as a priesthood of all believers and depend solely on the Word empowered by the Holy Spirit, ministered one to another.

Szasz is probably one of the best-known psychiatrists in the world. He is Professor of Psychiatry Emeritus, State University of New York and has written numerous books and articles on psychiatry and psychotherapy. He has said about an earlier book of ours:

Although I do not share the Bobgans' particular religious views, I do share their conviction that the human relations we now call "psychotherapy," are, in fact, matters of religion—and that we mislabel them as "therapeutic" at great risk to our spiritual well-being.[106]

Torrey, who is a clinical and research psychiatrist and author of a number of books on psychiatry and psychotherapy, has said about an earlier book of ours:

For people with problems of living who share the Bobgans' spiritual world view, their approach would be the most effective.[107]

After examining the research evidence on psychology, these two secular psychiatrists support the biblical way far better than almost all Bible colleges, seminaries and churches. **If the views of these two secular psychiatrists, as well as the implications drawn from the results of research, were followed, both secular and Christian psychotherapy would almost entirely disappear.** Moreover, Bible colleges, seminaries, and churches could then return to the cure of souls, which was an integral part of the church before the rise of psychotherapy.[108]

Christians and Psychotherapy

In view of all the research evidence, why do people, especially Christians, exhibit such confidence in psychotherapy? Why is it that when Christians experience problems in their lives they turn to this craze? Why do Christian schools and colleges offer these theories as facts? Why do pastors so readily refer their people with problems to licensed professional psychotherapists?

Many Christians were naturally suspicious of psychotherapy in the beginning. However, now that they have uncritically accepted it, they seem reluctant to assume even a reasonably skeptical view. Could it be that, in an attempt to overcome their former image of narrow-mindedness, they have become naive? Or is it because they fear to challenge a system they do not fully understand? Or is it because principles of psychotherapy and psychology have sometimes been so carefully interwoven with biblical principles that the Christian cannot separate the two? Maybe the increasing volume of people with problems has driven the pastors and others to refer problem-laden people away.

However, the main reason why Christians have placed such inordinate confidence in psychotherapy may be that they lack confidence in biblical solutions for problems of living. In a book entitled *The Crisis in Psychiatry and Religion,* 0. Hobart Mowrer asks a penetrating question: "Has evangelical religion sold its birthright for a mess of psychological pottage?"[109] It's time for Christians to look objectively and prayerfully at the birthright and the mess of pottage.

May the Lord have mercy on those who have exchanged their birthright for a mess of psychological pottage. May the Lord have mercy on those who have offered that stew to men, women, and children for whom Christ died. May the Lord have mercy on us all and revive His church with a fresh hunger for His Word, with a renewed confidence in His provisions and promises found in that Word, and with such love for God and one another that oneness in Christ will be our passion and our very life.

5

Rejection of the Living Water

In the past, religion and science were the main ways of achieving our aspirations. More recently, to the consternation of some and the satisfaction of others, the license for ensuring our well-being has apparently been transferred to psychotherapy![1]

Mesmerism

The roots of the religious nature of psychological theories and therapies extend beyond Freud back to Franz Anton Mesmer, an Austrian physician. Mesmer was convinced that he had discovered the great universal cure of physical and emotional problems. In 1779 he boldly declared, "There is only one illness and one healing."[2] He believed that an invisible fluid, which he called "animal magnetism," was distributed throughout the body. He further believed that this invisible fluid influenced illness or health in the mind and emotions as well as in the body. He thought this fluid was an energy existing throughout all of nature and taught that proper health and mental well-being were the result of proper distribution and balance of this animal magnetism throughout the body.

Mesmer's ideas may sound rather foolish today, but they were well received during his era, even though his technique was encumbered by the passing of magnets across a person sitting in a tub of water. His ideas grew even more popular and easier to apply when he dispensed with the magnets. Through a series of progressions, his animal magnetism theory moved away from depending on the effects of physical magnets to stimulating certain psychological affects of mind over matter. As his techniques were modified, they strongly influenced the development of present-day psychotherapy.

Mesmerism became psychological rather than physical with patients entering into trance-like states of hypnosis. Some responders to mesmerism moved into states of consciousness where they spontaneously engaged in what appeared to be telepathy, precognition, and clairvoyance.[3] Mesmerism gradually evolved into a new way of looking at life with its new method of healing by means of conversation undergirded by an intense rapport between practitioner and patient. Medical practitioners also used mesmerism in their search for the possibility of reservoirs within the mind that could potentially heal the body.

Theories and techniques of mesmerism influenced the foundations of psychiatry with such early men as Jean-Martin Charcot, Pierre Janet, and Sigmund Freud. These men used information that had been gleaned from patients while they were in the hypnotic state.[4] Followers of Mesmer promoted ideas about hypnotic suggestion, healing through talking, and mind-over-matter. These three branches of Mesmer's influence became known as hypnosis, psychotherapy, and positive thinking.

In his book *Mesmerism and the American Cure of Souls*, Robert Fuller describes how the thrust of mesmerism changed directions as it came to America.[5] Its promoters garnered great expectations of psychological and spiritual advantage. Non-Christians especially welcomed its promises for self-improvement, spiritual experience, and personal fulfillment. Fuller says that mesmerism offered Americans "an entirely new and eminently attractive arena for self-discovery—their own psychological depths" and that "its theories and methods promised to restore individuals, even unchurched ones, into harmony with the cosmic scheme."[6] The anticipated possibility of discovering and developing human potential, which emerged from mesmerism, stimulated the growth and expansion of psychotherapy, positive thinking, the human potential movement, and mind-science religions. Fuller's description of mesmerism in America accurately portrays twentieth-century psychotherapy.

The American Psychological Association's book on the *History of Psychotherapy: A Century of Change* includes a section titled "Mesmerism: The Beginning of American Psychology," which says:

> Historians have found several aspects of mesmerism and its offshoots that set the stage for 20th-century psychotherapy. It promoted ideas that are quintessentially American and have become permanent theoretical features of our 20th-century psychological landscape.[7]

Among those "theoretical features" developed from mesmerism are the ideas that (1) "individuals suffered from inner emotional or spiritual ills that were caused by personal inadequacies and spiritual deprivation, not by the political and economic conditions of their lives"; (2) "emotional illness was thought to be caused by improper thoughts, usually negative in nature" and positive thinking "could *directly* affect the material world"; (3) through "its healing technology" people could experience "a mystical transformation of identity from an everyday, 'false' self to an extraordinary, 'true' self"; and (4) "personal wealth was limited only by individual psychological development."[8] (Italics in original.)

Mesmer's far reaching influence gave an early impetus to scientific-sounding religious alternatives to Christianity. Moreover, his work established the trend of medicalizing the mind and replacing religion with treatment and therapy. Mesmer gave the world another false religion and another false hope. Professor of psychiatry Thomas Szasz describes Mesmer's influence:

> Insofar as psychotherapy as a modern "medical technique" can be said to have a discoverer, Mesmer was that person. Mesmer stands in the same sort of relation to Freud and Jung as Columbus stands in relation to Thomas Jefferson and John Adams. Columbus stumbled onto a continent that the founding fathers subsequently transformed into the political entity known as the United States of America. Mesmer stumbled onto the literalized use of the leading scientific metaphor of his age for explaining and exorcising all manner of human problems and passions, a rhetorical device that the founders of modern depth psychology subsequently transformed into the pseudomedical entity known as psychotherapy.[9]

The Beginnings of Psychotherapy

Psychotherapy from its very beginning created doubt about Christianity. Each in his own way, two of the most influential inventors of psychotherapy, Sigmund Freud and Carl Jung, eroded confidence in Christianity and established negative ideas concerning Christianity that prevail today. Freud (1856-1939) was a Jew, and Jung (1875-1961) was a Protestant. Both influenced the faith and affected the attitudes of many people concerning Christianity and the role of the church in the healing of troubled souls.

Freud believed that religious doctrines are all illusions and that religion is "the universal obsessional neurosis of humanity."[10] Jung, on the other hand, viewed all religions as collective mythologies, not real in essence, but real in their effect on the human personality. For Freud religion was the source of mental problems, and for Jung religion, though merely a myth, was a solution to mental-emotional problems. Szasz states, "Thus, in Jung's view religions are indispensable spiritual supports, whereas in Freud's they are illusory crutches."[11]

As the views of these two men influenced society, many Christians began to doubt the effectiveness of the Bible and the church in dealing with life's problems. From Freud they heard that if one is religious he must be sick; from Jung they heard that religion is merely a necessary fantasy. While Freud argued that religions are delusionary and therefore evil, Jung contended that all religions are illusionary but good. Both positions are anti-Christian. One denies Christianity and the other mythologizes it.

How did Freud and Jung come to such conclusions about religion? According to Atwood and Tomkins, ". . . all theories of personality will remain colored by subjective and personal influences."[12]

According to Szasz, "The popular image of Freud as an enlightened, emancipated, irreligious person who, with the aid of psychoanalysis, 'discovered' that religion is a mental illness is pure fiction."[13] We mentioned earlier that each psychological theorist's theory arises very subjectively from the theorist's own personal life experiences.

Szasz contends, "One of Freud's most powerful motives in life was the desire to inflict vengeance on Christianity for its traditional anti-Semitism."[14] He also shows how Freud made his hostility towards religion look like an objective conclusion from the realm of science. He says, "There is, in short, nothing scientific about Freud's hostility to established religion, though he tries hard to pretend that there is."[15] Freud was surely not an objective observer of religion. According to Szasz, he was a man who incorporated his personal feelings towards Christians into a supposed scientific theory about all religion. While Freud grew up in a Jewish home, Jung was raised in a Christian home and his father was a minister. Jung wrote of his early experience with the Holy Communion, which seems to be related to his later ideas about religions being only myths. He says:

> Slowly I came to understand that this communion had been a fatal experience for me. It had proved hollow; more than that, it had proved to be a total loss. I knew that I would never again be able to participate in this ceremony. "Why, that is not religion at all," I thought. "It is an absence of God; the church is a place I should not go to. It is not life which is there, but death."[16]

Because of Jung's essential misunderstanding and misconceptions, Christianity, the church, and Holy Communion seemed hollow and dead.

From this one significant incident, Jung could have proceeded to deny all religions as Freud did, but he did not. He evidently saw that religion is very meaningful to many people. Thus, he accepted them all, but only as myths. His choice to consider all religions as myths was further influenced by his view of psychoanalysis. According to Viktor Von Weizsaecker, "C. G. Jung was the first to understand that psychoanalysis belonged in the sphere of religion."[17] Since for Jung psychoanalysis itself was a form of religion, he could hardly reject all religions without rejecting psychoanalysis.

After Jung repudiated Christianity he became involved in idolatry and the occult. He renamed and replaced everything having to do with biblical Christianity with his own mythology of archetypes. As he developed his theories, his archetypes took shape and served him as familiar spirits. One such personal familiar spirit that helped Jung develop his theories was Philemon.[18]

Jung also participated in the occult practice of necromancy. Jung mythologized Scripture and reduced the basic doctrines of the Christian faith into esoteric gnosticism. Freud was also involved in idolatry and the occult. He collected a large number of ancient Greek, Roman, Oriental, and Egyptian artifacts, including rows of statuettes arranged on his desk and around his office. One person who knew the family said that for Freud, "The artifacts weren't only decorative. He used some of them to help him to write."[19] One writer suggests:

> What Freud may have been practicing . . . was an ancient form of magic in which consecrated statues representing spirits or transpersonal powers would engage the magician in imaginal dialogues and supply him with invaluable knowledge. Such magical practices were well known in ancient Egypt, Greece, and Rome, and the very statuettes that Freud owned may have been used for such practices by their contemporaries.[20]

Freud and Jung each turned his own experience into a new belief system called psychoanalysis. Freud denied the spirituality of man by identifying religion as an illusion and calling it a neurosis. Jung attempted to debase spirituality by presenting all religion as mythology and fantasy. Many contemporary psychotherapists have not moved very far from these two positions. They often present religion as an illness at worst and as a myth at best.

Freud and Jung had enthusiastic followers who helped promote their ideas. Furthermore, the media assisted by giving uncritical publicity to the psychoanalytic movement with books, movies, and TV romanticizing this mania. The academic world furthered the cause of psychotherapeutic thinking by failing to identify the shortcomings of the new cult. Even medicine promoted psychiatry by incorporating it as a medical specialty. And worst of all, church leaders helped to propagate the theories of Freud and Jung by embracing the ideas they liked and ignoring the rest, not discerning the anti-Christian cancer that would eat away at the very soul of the church. Abandoning trust in God, Freud, Jung, and other early theorists led their followers in the quest to find answers to life's problems within the limited ideas and standards of men. They developed a philosophy, a psychology, and a psychotherapy of self-deification. In the psychoanalytic, behavioristic, humanistic and existential streams, actions, words, and thoughts are inevitably directed inward. In the psychoanalytic stream, the unconscious and its pathways through free association and dreams constitute the doctrine of this faith. In the behavioristic stream man as animal is emphasized and spirituality is avoided. In the humanistic stream, the self and its pathway of direct experience and feeling are the substance of salvation. In the existential stream, the self is still glorified, but to a higher level of exaltation with so-called higher consciousness as its supreme goal.

Opposing Belief Systems

Because they rest on different foundations, move in contrasting directions, and rely on opposing belief systems, psychotherapy and Christianity are not now, nor were they ever, natural companions in the healing of troubled souls. The "faith which was once delivered unto the saints" (Jude 3) was compromised by a substitute faith, often disguised as medicine or science, but based upon a foundation of humanism, which is in direct contradiction to the Bible. In considering the relationship between psychotherapy and religion, Dr. Jacob Needleman observes:

> Modern psychiatry arose out of the vision that man must change himself and not depend for help upon an imaginary God. . . . mainly through the insights of Freud and through the energies of those he influenced, the human psyche was wrested from the faltering hands of organized religion and was situated

in the world of nature as a subject for scientific study.[21]

From its very beginning, psychotherapy was developed as an alternate means of healing, not as an addition or complement to Christianity or to any other religion. Psychotherapy is not only offered as an alternate or substitute method of healing troubled souls, but also as a surrogate religion.

Dr. Arthur Burton says, "Psychotherapy . . . promises salvation in this life in the same way that theology promises it in the afterlife."[22] In speaking of what psychotherapy has done to religion, Szasz contends:

> . . . contrition, confession, prayer, faith, inner resolution, and countless other elements are expropriated and renamed as psychotherapy; whereas certain observances, rituals, taboos, and other elements of religion are demeaned and destroyed as the symptoms of neurotic or psychotic illnesses.[23]

Referring to the replacement of the biblical with the psychological, Szasz says:

> Educated in the classics, Freud and the early Freudians remolded these images into, and renamed them as, medical diseases and treatments. This metamorphosis has been widely acclaimed in the modern world as an epoch-making scientific discovery. Alas, it is, in fact, only the clever and cynical destruction of the spirituality of man, and its replacement by a positivistic "science of the mind."[24]

It is not only a matter of the "destruction of the spirituality of man," but a destruction of religion itself. Szasz further contends that psychotherapy:

> . . . is not merely indifferent to religion, it is implacably hostile to it. Herein lies one of the supreme ironies of modern psychotherapy: it is not merely a religion that pretends to be a science, it is

actually a fake religion that seeks to destroy true religion.[25]

He warns about the "implacable resolve of psychotherapy to rob religion of as much as it can, and to destroy what it cannot."[26]

Many psychotherapists would agree to the following answer, given by a psychiatrist who was asked whether there is conflict or compatibility between religion and psychotherapy:

> Psychiatry has a quarrel with only those forms of religion which emphasize the doctrine of original sin. Any belief that tends to focus on the idea that man is inherently evil conflicts with the basically humanistic approach to problems that psychiatrists must follow.[27]

God's view of man according to the Bible is not compatible with any psychotherapeutic view of man. Nor is the biblical condition of man accepted or promoted by any of the many brands of psychotherapy.

Psychotherapy has attempted to destroy religion where it can and to compromise where it cannot. A supernatural void has resulted, and the need to believe in something has been filled by making a religion out of the ritual of psychotherapy. Psychotherapy has debased and virtually replaced the church's ministry to troubled individuals. During this time pastors have been devalued and have been intimidated into referring their sheep to professional psychotherapeutic priests. Many people no longer look to pastors and fellow believers for such help; nor do they look to the Bible for spiritual solutions to mental-emotional-behavioral problems.

Szasz tells us that "the psychiatrist displaces the priest as the physician of the soul."[28] The psychotherapists have not only displaced pastors and the priesthood of all believers, but have themselves become god figures. One book refers to "the 'Jehovah effect,' in which the therapist recreates patients into his own image."[29] That book reveals that those patients who become more like their therapists are rated as most improved by their therapists.

Psychotherapists have attained the level of adoration, mystery, and divine regard once accorded to the clergy. They have even become idols, because they supposedly hold the keys to mental health and understand all the mental mysteries of life.

The cycle of deception is complete. The psychotherapist offers humanity a less demanding, less disciplined, more self-centered substitute for religion, for that is what psychotherapy is; a false solution to mental-emotional-behavioral problems, for that is what the psychological way is; and another god figure, for that is what the psychotherapist has become. Now deceived people flock to this surrogate religion with its unproved ideas and solutions. They flock to the counterfeit high priest and worship at strange altars. People have fallen for the false image of the psychotherapist priest and for the theology of therapy.

Different Morality Systems

Psychotherapy is not neutral. It involves values and morals. With respect to treatment, Szasz says that "psychotherapeutic interventions are not medical but moral in character."[30] Robert Watson and Stephen Morse state the obvious, that "values and moral judgments will always play a role in therapy, no matter how much the therapist attempts to push them to the background."[31]

The vast variety of moral standards within the psychotherapeutic framework originate from human conceptions of morality. Psychotherapies have relative, changing, and unreliable morality and value systems and basically disregard God and His Word. Psychotherapists often attempt to free clients from morality systems by changing the standards to fit the person, because they do not recognize the scriptural standards of morality or the biblical means of dealing with guilt. Even if a therapist is a Christian, the psychotherapeutic theories will undermine values and morals that are distinctly biblical.

Psychotherapy is not able to deal adequately with either morality or guilt. Neither is it able to guide a person into a biblically sound, virtuous life.

Cure of Souls or Cure of Minds?

From its inception the Christian church has ministered to those suffering from problems of living. The ministry includes evangelization of the lost, salvation of souls, and sanctification, which involves spiritual growth through life's daily trials. Psychotherapy offers both a substitute salvation and substitute sanctification.

The biblical cure of souls ministers to every believer in every aspect of life and depends upon the Word of God, which describes both the human condition and the process of relief for troubled minds. For centuries there was a prayer and healing ministry that dealt with all nonorganic mental-emotional disturbances. This entire process was known as the "cure of souls." John T. McNeill in A *History of the Cure of* Souls describes this ministry as "the sustaining and curative treatment of persons in those matters that reach beyond the requirements of the animal life."[32]

One aspect in the process of the cure of souls dealt with sin as a basis for mental-emotional-behavioral problems and included forgiveness with healing through repentance and confession. However, the cure of souls includes spiritual activities that encourage spiritual growth, and it thus deals with all nonorganic mental-emotional-behavioral problems. The cure of souls also involves inward change through repentance from sin, which results in a change of mind and heart and of thought and behavior.

The cure of souls, which once was a vital ministry of the church, has been eclipsed by a cure of minds (psychotherapy). The switch from biblical healing to psychological healing was made subtly and quietly. It began in the secular world and then like a little leaven it infiltrated and infected the whole church. The authors of *Cults and Cons* note this shift:

For many, traditional religion no longer offers relevant answers and more and more people are seeking answers in strange, new packages. Thousands, if not millions, are turning to that part of psychology which promises *the answer* and an effortless, painless ride into the Promised Land, perfectly meeting our present and prevailing need for quick solutions to hard problems.[33] (Italics in original).

Martin Gross says:

When educated man lost faith in formal religion, he required a substitute belief that would be as reputable in the last half of the twentieth century as Christianity was in the first. Psychology and psychiatry have now assumed that role.[34]

Carl Rogers admits, "Yes, it is true, psychotherapy is subversive. . . . Therapy, theories and techniques promote a new model of man contrary to that which has been traditionally acceptable."[35]

Bernie Zilbergeld, in his book *The Shrinking of America: Myths of Psychological Change,* says:

Psychology has become something of a substitute for old belief systems. Different schools of therapy offer visions of the good life and how to live it, and those whose ancestors took comfort from the words of God and worshipped at the altars of Christ and Yahweh now take solace from and worship at the altars of Freud, Jung, Carl Rogers, Albert Ellis . . . and a host of similar authorities. While in the past the common reference point was the Bible and its commentaries and commentators, the common reference today is a therapeutic language and the success stories of mostly secular people changers.[36]

Christopher Lasch charges that the "contemporary climate is therapeutic, not religious," and says, "People today hunger not for personal salvation . . . but for the feeling, the momentary illusion of personal well-being, health and psychic security."[37] Lasch also says, "The medicalization of religion facilitated the rapprochement between religion and psychiatry."[38]

Within the church a transition occurred in which people accepted a new message. That new message was a psychological message about the human condition, devoid of the basic biblical principles and, in certain instances, sprinkled with just enough biblical words to make it sound Christian. Many in the church were ignorant of the real meaning of this new message and accepted the new faith in psychotherapy. As a result, a psychology of self became the norm, faith in self became the creed, and the fundamental and eternal truths were laid aside.

With the rise of science and technology, the church has become more materialistic and experience driven than Word directed. As psychotherapy became attached to science and medicine, it became attractive to the church as a seemingly legitimate means of relieving the disturbed soul. Much to their discredit, most church leaders have avoided investigating the essence and value of psychotherapy and have blindly accepted and endorsed its theories and practices. They seem fearful of rejecting the so-called scientific and medical model of the cure of minds. At the same time the church has abandoned one of its most vital responsibilities to its members by giving up the cure of souls ministry as if it were a giant mistake.

Sin or Sickness?

Whereas once the church believed in, spoke of, and practiced the biblical cure of souls, it has shifted its faith to a secular cure of minds. Szasz very ably describes how this change came about: " . . . with the soul securely displaced by the mind and the mind securely subsumed as a function of the brain—people speak of the 'cure of minds.'"[39] The brain is a physical organ; the mind is not. With this subtle semantic twist, the mind (disguised as a bodily organ) was elevated as a scientific and medical concept in contrast to the soul, which is a theological reality. A choice was made between a so-called scientific concept and a theological one.

At the same time that a physical organ (the brain) became confused with a nonphysical human attribute (the mind), another change took place. Whereas the church had believed that there was a relationship of sin and circumstances to the mind, emotions, and behavior, psychotherapists introduced the medical concept of sickness to explain problems of living. Many people easily accepted the word *sickness* to refer to mental-emotional-behavioral problems because that seemed to be the "loving" and "understanding" way to regard such human suffering. Nevertheless, mental-emotional suffering and problematic behavior are not synonymous with sickness, even though such suffering may accompany biological disease.

One of Szasz's main purposes in writing *The Myth of Psychotherapy* was this:

> I shall try to show how, with the decline of religion and the growth of science in the eighteenth century, the cure of (sinful) souls, which had been an integral part of the Christian religions, was recast as the cure of (sick) minds, and became an integral part of medical science.[40]

The words *sinful* and *sick* in parentheses are his. These two words mark the dramatic shift from the cure of souls to the cure of minds.

There is a serious problem when people confuse passion with tissue and sin with sickness. Such confusion of words leads to erroneous thinking, and this very confusion and error were part of what virtually ended the cure of souls ministry in the church. Through a semantic twist, the mind was confused with the brain and the misnomer of sickness replaced the concept of sin. As a result, the entire subjective, theoretical process of psychotherapy hid itself safely in the realm of science and medicine. In reality, psychotherapy is a misfit as medicine and an impostor as science.

The recipe was simple. Replace the cure of souls with the cure of minds by confusing an abstraction (mind) with a biological organ (brain); then convince people that mental healing and medical healing are the same. Stir in a dash of theory disguised as fact. Call it all science and put it into medicine and the rest is history. With the rise in psychotherapy, there was a decline in the cure of souls ministry until it is now almost nonexistent. Secular psychotherapy has taken over to such an extent that Szasz says, "Actually, psychotherapy is a modern, scientific-sounding name for what used to be called the 'cure of souls.'"[41] Thus we have the shell, without the power, without the life, and without the Lord.

Accepting the Living Water

Christianity is more than a belief system or a theological creed. Christianity is not just what happens in church. Christianity is faith in a living Lord and in His indwelling Holy Spirit. Christianity involves the entire life: every day, every action, every decision, every thought, every emotion. One cannot adequately treat a Christian apart from the indwelling Holy Spirit and the Body of Christ. Nor should anyone segment the mind, will, emotions, or behavior from a person's belief system. For too long Christians have looked to the church to answer their theological questions, but looked elsewhere for answers to their life problems. Christians who have God's Holy Spirit living in them are spiritual beings; therefore they need biblical solutions, not merely psychological attempts.

It is understandable that the world would reject the living water in seeking to understand and help individuals suffering from problems of living. However, as the world rejected the biblical answers, the church began to doubt its own doctrine of sin, salvation, and sanctification in the area of mental-emotional suffering and behavioral problems. Many ministers even left their pastorates to become licensed psychotherapists.

During the twentieth century psychotherapy displaced the soul of man with the mind and replaced the cure of souls with the cure of minds. The psychological way has usurped the place of the spiritual, psychological opinions of men have contaminated the Word of God, and even Christians look to psychotherapy rather than to sanctification in dealing with soul problems. It is our position that the Bible provides both a spiritual basis for Christian growth and a spiritual solution for nonorganically caused mental-emotional-behavioral problems.

True mental health involves spiritual and moral health as well as emotional well-being. It is time for Christians to take a fresh look at the Bible and at the provisions which God has available for mental-emotional-behavioral health and healing. The Bible does provide a means of ministry to all who suffer, whether mentally or medically. But, when one suffers problems of living that are not organically related, the cure of souls is truly sufficient for ministering to such a person and psychotherapy has no business there.

Christians are new creatures in Christ, indwelt by the Holy Spirit. They have been born again to new life and are to walk according to the spirit, not according to the flesh (Romans 6:4; Galatians 5:16). From the moment of salvation, Christians are in the process of sanctification, in which they have many opportunities to grow in faith and in the knowledge of the Lord Jesus Christ. Sanctification involves the whole person, through the spirit, which is the deepest and most significant element of one's existence.

The Word of God applies to every aspect of daily life, including mental attitudes and interpersonal relationships. It is alive and powerful to change people from the inside. In addition to the written Word, Christians have the Living Word, Jesus Christ, who will never leave them destitute of daily provisions for wisdom, guidance, and help (Hebrews 13:5). The apostle John describes Jesus as "the light of men," the very source of life and love (John 1:4). God's written Word and Living Word make people whole and holy according to God's way, rather than according to human machinations.

Psychotherapy can cover up a deep spiritual problem, but it cannot transform one spiritually. Psychological theories and therapies attempt to fix up the unregenerate, non-Christian self and/or the Christian who is living by the self-effort of his carnal nature, because they can only manipulate the flesh. Psychotherapy is limited to dealing with what Scripture calls the "old man," the very nature that needs to be replaced with what the Bible refers to as "the new man, which after God is created in righteousness and true holiness" (Ephesians 4:24).

God does not just fix up the "old man." Instead, He counts the old man dead and buried and gives man a new nature which is spiritual and which is centered in Christ.

> Knowing this, that our old man is crucified with him, that the body of sin might be destroyed, that henceforth we should not serve sin. . . .

> Likewise, reckon ye also yourselves to be dead indeed unto sin, but alive unto God through Jesus Christ our Lord. (Romans 6:6,11)

The description of a Christian is thus:

> I am crucified with Christ: nevertheless I live; yet not I, but Christ liveth in me: and the life which I now live in the flesh I live by the faith of the Son of God, who loved me, and gave himself for me. (Galatians 2:20)

What psychotherapy attempts to improve or heal, God has already condemned.

6

Polluted Streams

From Genesis to Revelation, running water symbolizes cleansing, healing, and life. Four pure, life-sustaining rivers flowed forth from the Garden of Eden. The water of life poured forth from the rock to sustain the children of Israel in the wilderness. Jesus offered living water to the Samaritan woman at the well. He further declared to His followers, "He that believeth on me, as the scripture hath said, out of his belly shall flow rivers of living water" (John 7:38). The apostle John recorded his vision in Revelation: "And he shewed me a pure river of water of life, clear as crystal, proceeding out of the throne of God and of the Lamb" (22: 1).

Jesus said, "If any man thirst, let him come unto me, and drink" (John 7:37). Jesus was not speaking of literal thirst, but of spiritual thirst, for He knew that such thirst can only be satisfied with spiritual life. When Jesus gives life, He brings cleansing and healing to the soul, which includes the mind, will, and emotions.

People are at least as thirsty for life and mental-emotional-behavioral health as they have ever been. And yet, in their thirsty quest they have been led to the four polluted streams rather than to the river of living water. These four polluted streams represent the four major models or streams of psychotherapy.

Psychoanalytic Stream

The first polluted stream is the psychoanalytic model, which is based on the work of Sigmund Freud. He believed that those people who were drinking from the river of living water were sick. He decided to devise another stream, emphasizing the mental factors of human behavior and portraying the individual as being dominated by instinctual, biological drives and by unconscious desires and motives. Basic to this view is the belief that our behavior is determined at a very early age. This idea is known as psychic determinism, which is contrary to the biblical concept of personal responsibility and choice.

Behavioristic Stream

The second polluted stream is the behavioristic model, which mostly stresses determinism. This model rejects the introspective study of man and stresses external and observable behavior. Rather than exploring the inner psychic phenomena as explanatory causes, it focuses on the outer behavioristic results. While the psychoanalytic model speaks of psychic determinism, the behavioristic model proposes biological, genetic, and environmental determinism. Two names associated with this model are John Watson and B. F. Skinner.

Humanistic Stream

The third polluted stream of psychology is the humanistic model of man. It emerged as a "third force" in psychology during the 1960s under the leadership of Gordon Allport, Abraham Maslow, and Carl Rogers. Contrary to the first two streams, the humanistic model considers men to be free and self-directed rather than determined. The one unifying theme of this model is the self, which involves self-concept, individuality, search for values, personal fulfillment, and potential for personal growth. On the surface it sounds good, but the focus is on self rather than on God; the source for growth is self rather than the river of living water.

Transpersonal Stream

The fourth polluted stream is the existential or transpersonal model of man. This model, like the humanistic model, considers man to be a free agent who is responsible for his life. It places faith in the inner experience of the individual for dealing with his deepest problems. One important theme of the existential model is that of death. Themes such as what lies beyond death, the meaning of death, and the purpose and value of life are explored in this stream. Although the existential model presents a religious view of man, it encourages the individual to break away from old patterns and to create one's own values, one's own religion, and one's own god. Existential psychotherapists are critical of anyone who is dependent upon a religious creed or authority outside of himself.[1]

It is amazing that it took psychotherapy so long to "discover" the religious nature of man. At its inception, psychotherapy treated religion as a weakness or flaw on the one hand or a myth on the other. However, just because psychotherapy has turned to the religious nature of man does not mean that it is turning people back to God. Psychotherapy does not lead one to worship the God of Abraham, Isaac, and Jacob; nor does it encourage belief in the Bible as the inspired Word of God.

Throughout psychotherapy's history we have seen the rise and wane of one therapy after another, one promise after another, one hope of success after another, and one polluted psychological stream after another. We have swung 180 degrees through four forces of psychotherapy from Freud's rejection of religion as an illusion to new combinations of religion and psychotherapy. Psychotherapy has moved from a dependency upon the natural world as being the sole reality in life to an inclusion of spirituality as a necessity.

This fourth stream of psychotherapy is religion without a creed and faith without a personal God. Although it is an antidote for materialism, it denies biblical absolutes and establishes a divinity of self. It stresses an innate goodness in every person and generally rejects original sin. It is a poor substitute for Christianity but has been accepted by those who have rejected or not known the truth. People have a spiritual vacuum at their very core and it must be filled if they are to be whole. The fourth force in psychotherapy is only a substitute for the reality of God.

Many have run from religion until the emptiness finally caught up with them. Now, instead of returning to the one true God of the universe, they are following the false gods of men's minds. Instead of looking to God, their Creator, many are looking to man as the creator of gods and end up replacing one vacuum with another. Dr. Abraham Maslow is an example of this trend.

Although Maslow is regarded as a key promoter of humanistic psychology, he believed that it was merely a stepping stone to transpersonal or spiritual psychologies. He predicted a move from centering in self to centering in the cosmos, from self-transformation to spiritual transformation. He says:

> I consider Humanistic, Third Force Psychology to be transitional. A preparation for a *still higher* Fourth Psychology, transpersonal, transhuman, centered in

the cosmos rather than in human needs and interests, going beyond humanness, identity, self-actualization and the like.[2] (Italics in original.)

History has proven Maslow correct.

In her article "A New Age Reflection in the Magic Mirror of Science," Dr. Maureen O'Hara says:

It is significant to remember that the present New Age movement has its origins in the counterculture of the sixties and early seventies. Early inspiration came from the writings of Abraham Maslow, Eric Fromm, Rollo May, Carl Rogers, and others.[3]

No one needs the fourth stream, religiously oriented psychotherapists to tell them about the religious nature of man. The church has known about it all along. Moreover transpersonal psychotherapists have a different god and a different gospel. What people do need is to turn to the river of living water given by our Creator and Sustainer.

Mixed Waters

From the four polluted streams flow more than 400 psychotherapeutic approaches. It is from these four streams and many often-conflicting psychotherapeutic approaches that Christian psychologists draw the polluted water of psychological notions and attempt to mix that potion with God's Word.

The apostle Paul warns, "Satan himself is transformed into an angel of light. Therefore, it is no great thing if his ministers also be transformed as the ministers of righteousness: whose end shall be according to their works" (2 Corinthians 11:14,15). An angel of light is one who appears to be righteous but is really not. Jesus used the expression "whited sepulchers" to describe the scribes and Pharisees. They seem beautiful on the outside but are filled with dead men's bones.

Some psychotherapies are like that. They seem to be very Christian in doctrine and principle, but on closer examination they contain only the ideas of sinful humans. Some even contain a "form of godliness," but they lack the power and reality of true godliness. But, because they resemble Christianity on the surface, Christians fall for them in the same way some are led astray by religious cults.

These psychotherapies appeal to Christians because of their emphasis on self-improvement, growth, and change. On the surface they all sound great and often seem like gold, silver, and precious stones. However, all involve self at the center. Self is elevated and a new catechism of cure is preached, based on me, myself, and I. Paul predicted: "This know also, that in the last days perilous times shall come. For men shall be lovers of their own selves, covetous, boasters, proud, blasphemers, disobedient to parents, unthankful, unholy" (2 Timothy 3:1, 2). All of these psychotherapies elevate self and they do it with finesse. They disguise self-love and self-indulgence with such expressions as "I'm OK—You're OK" and "self-actualization." They all deny the authority of the Bible and distort biblical truths. Nevertheless, even though they promise hope for the future, their substance is only wood, hay, and stubble.

Eclecticism

Along with the expanding number of psychotherapies has been an expanding number of therapists using an eclectic approach. The *Handbook* describes eclectic psychotherapy this way:

> The basic assumption of eclectic psychotherapy is that complex patient problems must be addressed using a variety of approaches and techniques. . . . Eclecticism involves "selecting concepts, methods, and strategies from a variety of current theories which work."[4]

Dr. Sol Garfield and Dr. Allen Bergin have said:

> The new view is that the long-term dominance of the major theories is over and that an eclectic position has taken precedence.
>
> The popularity of eclecticism and the trend of psychotherapists to utilize procedures and views from more than one theoretical orientation have been clearly manifested in a number of surveys over the past 15-20 years.[5]

One can see the eclecticism available for Christian therapists. As one integrationist says:

> Man is responsible (Glasser) to believe truth which will result in responsible behavior (Ellis) that will provide him with meaning, hope (Frankl), and love (Fromm) and will serve as a guide (Adler) to effective living with others as a self- and other-accepting person (Harris), who understands himself (Freud), who appropriately expresses himself (Perls), and who knows how to control himself (Skinner).[6] (Parentheses in original.)

While this kind of eclecticism may sound good, one gets a different picture when realizing what these theorists really taught: Glasser's responsibility has nothing to do with God or His measure of right and wrong; Ellis denies the very truth of God; the hope that Frankl gives is not a sure hope because it is man-centered; the love of Fromm is a far cry from the love that Jesus teaches and gives; Adler's guide is self rather than God; Harris's acceptance disregards God's law; Freud hardly understood himself and he repudiated God; Perls' expression focuses on feelings and self; and Skinner's methods of self-control are directed at the human as an animal without a soul.

Psychotherapists are eclectic, but they rarely tell a client which psychotherapeutic approaches they are using. We list and describe a few approaches that have been popular among both secular and Christian psychotherapists. We begin with Sigmund Freud because he started the movement and because his ideas continue to be very prevalent. Following the section on Freud, we briefly describe the theories of Carl Jung, Alfred Adler, Erich Fromm, Abraham Maslow, Carl Rogers, Albert Ellis, William Glasser, Thomas Harris, and Arthur Janov. These are all well-known names and psychotherapeutic approaches. As psychotherapists have become more eclectic the individual names are heard less, but their ideas and methodologies are very active.

7

Sigmund Freud
Psychoanalysis

Probably no single individual has had a more
profound effect on twentieth-century thought than
Sigmund Freud. His works have influenced psychiatry, anthropology, social work, penology, and education and provided a seemingly limitless source of
material for novelists and dramatists. Freud has
created a "whole new climate of opinion"; for better
or worse he has changed the face of society.[1]

Sigmund Freud is the most prominent name in all
psychotherapy. He is considered the father of the
psychotherapy movement and his ideas permeate later
theories and therapies.

Although many of Freud's ideas are under attack by a
number of critics, he still remains one of the most influ-

ential of all psychological theorists. A recent issue of *Scientific American* tells "Why Freud Isn't Dead."[2] The article demonstrates his continuing influence even though some specific Freudian ideas, such as the Oedipus complex, have "fallen out of favor even among psychoanalysts." Morris Eagle, president of the American Psychological Association's psychoanalysis division and professor at Adelphi University says, "There are very few analysts who follow all of Freud's formulations."[3] The *Scientific American* article goes on to state:

> Nevertheless, psychotherapists of all stripes still tend to share two of Freud's core beliefs: One is that our behavior, thoughts and emotions stem from unconscious fears and desires, often rooted in childhood experiences. The other is that with the help of a trained therapist, we can understand the source of our troubles and thereby obtain some relief.[4]

Because of Freud's continuing influence, we give a detailed description of his particular approach called psychoanalysis and pray that it will be helpful to those who want to discern inroads of Freudian thought and practice into the church as well as into Christian counseling.

Freud developed a complex set of theories to describe the human personality and to attempt to understand and treat mental-emotional disorders. Basic to these theories is what Freud described as the unconscious portion of the mind. The unconscious part of the psyche is that which is hidden from us and not open to our direct knowledge. The usual analogy is that of an iceberg, with most of the mind submerged, hidden, and filled with a vast amount of powerful, motivating material.

Freud believed that the unconscious portion of the mind, rather than the conscious, influences all of a person's thoughts and actions. In fact, he believed that the unconscious not only influences, but determines everything an individual does. Such psychic determinism was considered by Freud to be established within the unconscious during the first five years of life. His supposed evidence for the existence of the unconscious is found in dreams, phobias, and "slips of the tongue." A phobia is an irrational fear, while a slip of the tongue is saying something that one does not intend to say.

Since Freud proposed the doctrine of the unconscious and its related theories, his work has been widely accepted and admired and has significantly influenced the writing and thinking of the twentieth century. Yet this constellation of theories about the human psyche is actually only a set of one man's fantasies. These theories have been elevated from fantasy to fact, accepted as gospel truth, and applied to almost every area of human endeavor. Let us remember that we are dealing with unproved opinions, not facts; with ideas, not reality.

Freud invented psychoanalysis as a method for treating mental-emotional disorders and particularly for investigating what he considered to be the unconscious mind. Psychoanalysis has influenced most of contemporary psychotherapy and is one of its most sacred systems. It is only one of the many brand names, but it is considered by some to be the *ne plus ultra* of cures and is known as the fountainhead of Western psychotherapy.

Free Association and Dream Analysis

The psychoanalytic method supposedly exposes the unconscious through the process of free association and dream analysis. In free association, the central activity in psychoanalysis, the patient reveals both his thought life and his dreams. Through this ritual of unrestrained verbalization and dream description, the individual is theoretically unveiling his unconscious to the analyst, who in turn supposedly gains deep understanding into the patient's psyche.

People continually demonstrate both their confidence and ignorance concerning the subjectivity of psychoanalysis and other forms of psychotherapy by asking therapists the meaning of their dreams. The honest answer to any question having to do with what a dream means is that no one really knows. In the Bible, Joseph confessed that he could not interpret dreams, but that only God could explain the meaning of a dream. Just because Freud and numerous others have offered interpretations of dreams, it does not mean that there is any validity to this practice.

At the present time no one really knows what dreams mean. Dream theories range from causation by instinctual drives to mere electrochemical activity.[5] The unfortunate deception is that analysts often give their own subjective dream interpretations as though they are objective truth. And through this process another layer of subjectivity is added to psychotherapy and many people are further duped into believing what is not true.

If one were to ask a Freudian to use one word to describe his theory of dreams it would be *wish-fulfillment*. A symbolic approach to dream content and an emphasis on unconscious conflicts and desires are central to Freud's thinking. As Hilgard et al. say, "Freud felt that dreams were influenced by wishes . . . in the dream, forbidden desires were acted out in disguised form."[6] Freud could imagine all sorts of meanings from dreams because of the highly subjective nature of dream interpretation. He gave himself great latitude by insisting that dreams had both *manifest* and *latent* content. The manifest content consisted of psychoanalytic images, but the latent content was the hidden meaning of those images.[7] Therefore he could create nearly any imaginative meaning, and for Freud the meanings were highly sexual to fit into his Oedipal theory.

In contrast to Freudian beliefs about dreams, Dr. J. Allan Hobson, who is professor of psychiatry at Harvard Medical School, says:

> . . . dreaming is not a response to stress but the subjective awareness of a regular and almost entirely automatic brain process. That is one of many reasons for doubting Freud's theory that dreams are caused by the upsurge of unconscious wishes.[8]

According to Hobson, research suggests that dreams have "causes and functions that are strictly and deeply biological." Hobson asks, "But why are dreams so intensely visual, and why do they produce a sense of constant movement?" He then relates the Freudian explanation:

> Freud thought that the source of these pseudosensory stimuli was a mechanism of disguise and censorship by which "dream work" transformed an unacceptable or latent unconscious wish into images and linked them in a story.[9]

However, Hobson gives a different explanation:

> . . . dream stories and symbols are not a disguise, and the interposition of "defensive modifications" to disguise their origins, as postulated by Freud, is unnecessary. The nonsensical features of dreams are not a psychological defense, any more than the disoriented ramblings of a patient with Alzheimer's disease are.[10]

There is no biblical basis for Freud's theory of the unconscious or for his notion of dreams as wish-fulfillment. Adding nonscience to science does not add up to science, and adding God to this nonscientific conclusion does not add up to biblical truth.

As with nearly all psychotherapeutic concepts, the interpretation of free association is pure unadulterated, unproved opinion. It is actually the loosest kind of theory based upon invented symbols and vague inferences. It is a fuzzy, hazy, soft collection of ideas that have never been proved but are nevertheless propagated as truth. It is a hunting expedition into the unknown. To demonstrate this and to show the pollution in the psychoanalytic stream of thought, let us examine some of Freud's basic theories.

Oedipus Complex

The cornerstone of the psychoanalytic process is an array of theories that revolve around the unconscious.

Contained within the theory of the unconscious is Freud's theory of infantile sexuality and contained within the maze of the infantile sexuality theory is his theory of the Oedipus complex. To understand what psychoanalysis is really all about, one must at least have a glimpse into Freud's theory of infantile sexuality and, in particular, the Oedipus complex. Our purpose in describing these theories is not to surprise or shock, but to reveal the burlesque formulations upon which psychoanalysis proudly stands.

Freud's infantile sexuality theory has captivated the minds of many and easily tantalizes the imagination. The Oedipus complex, the theory within a theory, is a real tour de force of subjective, distorted, and dishonest reasoning presented as truth. It involves feelings of lust, homicide, and incest.

According to Freud's infantile sexuality theory, the first few years of life pretty much determine all that follow. Freud believed that during the first five or six years of life each human being throughout the entire world and since the beginning of mankind is confronted with certain stages of development. Failure to successfully pass through these stages or experiencing a trauma during one of these stages supposedly results in inexplicable damage to one's psyche. Freud identified the four stages as oral, anal, phallic, and genital.

In normal development, these four stages follow one another and occur at certain ages. The oral stage runs from birth to eighteen months; the anal stage from eighteen months to three years; the phallic stage from three to five or six years; and the genital stage runs through puberty. All four stages have to do with sexuality, and Freud has related adult characteristics and mental-emotional disorders to childhood experiences within these various stages. The first three stages will be presented here and particularly the phallic stage with its Oedipus complex.

During the oral stage of development everything centers around the mouth and its activities, which are primarily sucking, biting, chewing, and spitting out. Freud related all of this to sexuality and compared sucking to sexual intercourse. He also considered such infantile activities as thumb or toe sucking to be early forms of childhood masturbation.

During the anal stage, the center of attention shifts to the lower end of the intestinal tract. Here again the main activity, which is defecation, is related to sexuality. Just as there was pleasure associated with sucking and chewing, there is pleasure in the act of expelling waste. According to Freud, this act is also related to sexual pleasure.

The third stage of development is called the phallic stage, and the center of attention is the genital organs. It is in this stage that we see the dark, muddy water of the Freudian psychoanalytic stream. Within this stage of development, Freud identified what he called the Oedipus complex. He considered it to be one of his greatest discoveries because of its supposed universal application. He said, "Every new arrival on this planet is faced by the task of mastering the Oedipus complex; anyone who fails to do so falls a victim to neurosis."[11]

Since the Oedipus complex is Freud's interpretation of the Greek play, *Oedipus Rex*, by Sophocles, let us examine this legend and see what Freud did with it. The play opens with a large crowd of people seeking aid from Oedipus, King of Thebes, because a mysterious pestilence has swept the land. Oedipus informs the crowd that he has sent Creon to seek counsel from the oracle at Delphi. Creon returns with word that the pestilence will abate when the murderer of Laius, the former King of Thebes, has been found and banished.

As the tale unfolds, we learn that many years earlier the oracle of Delphi had prophesied that any son born to King Laius of Thebes would murder him. In response to the prophecy, Laius had taken his infant son, pierced his feet with a nail, and left him on a mountain to die. The child, however, did not die but was found by a shepherd who named him Oedipus. The shepherd then brought

Oedipus to the childless King and Queen of Corinth, who then raised Oedipus as their own son.

When Oedipus became a young man, he happened to seek information from the oracle at Delphi, who predicted that he would kill his own father and marry his mother. Because he loved the only parents he knew, he decided not to return home lest he commit such loathsome acts. Instead, he turned and went the other way. As he traveled along the narrow mountainous roadway, a chariot met him, going the opposite direction. Since the two could not pass one another, the rider in the chariot harshly ordered Oedipus aside. Oedipus stepped aside, but when the chariot's wheels smashed into his foot, he reacted by killing the charioteer and the rider. Although Oedipus did not recognize him, the rider was his own true father, Laius.

Then, after arriving in Thebes, Oedipus solved the riddle of the Sphinx and was rewarded with the hand of the recently widowed Queen Jocasta. Not realizing that she was his mother, Oedipus married her. When the story comes to a close and the truth of the relationship is known, Jocasta hangs herself and Oedipus pierces his own eyes with a pin from her garment and goes blind into banishment.

The story is a classic tragedy in the sense that the main character brings about his own destruction. However, unlike Freud's analysis, Oedipus loved and honored the parents who raised him. Although he did indeed murder his natural father and marry his own mother, he did so without knowing that he was their son. Freud distorted this well-known legend to demonstrate an incredible idea that is more a testimony to his own imagination than a universal truth about mankind. We will now see how Freud transformed *Oedipus Rex* into the Oedipus complex and how he twisted a legend into a supposed reality.

Freud distorted this legend by stating that during the phallic stage of development every boy desires to kill his father and have sexual intercourse with his mother, and every girl has a desire to kill her mother and have sexual intercourse with her father. Freud attributed these desires to all children between the ages of three and six. According to this theory, both the boy and girl love the mother at the beginning and resent the father because he is a rival for the mother's attention. This idea persists in the boy until he finally, unconsciously desires the death or absence of his father, whom he considers his rival, and wants to have sexual intercourse with his mother.

The system is different for girls, however. Freud said that during a girl's early development she discovers that the boy has a protruding sex organ while she has only a cavity. According to Freud's theory, the girl holds her mother responsible for her condition, which causes hostility. She thus transfers her love from her mother to her father because he has the valued organ, which she wants to share with him in sex.

The madness is not yet complete, for Freud describes how this hostility and sensuousness are resolved. In Freud's murky and mad story, filled with fantasy and fabrication, the boy resolves the Oedipus complex through fear of castration. The boy, according to Freud, unconsciously fears that his father will cut off his penis as a punishment for his sexual desire for his mother. This fear successfully brings the boy through this stage of development by causing him to give up or retreat from his unconscious lustful desires.

The girl, on the other hand, fears that her mother will injure her genital organ because of her sexual desire directed at her father. But, within Freud's wild scheme the girl senses that she has already been castrated and thus ends up desiring the male sex organ. The female castration anxiety results in what Freud called "penis envy." According to Freud, every woman is merely a mutilated male who resolves her castration anxiety by wishing for the male sex organ.

To further compound Freud's bizarre beliefs, some analysts apply here a concept called "fellatio" from the oral stage of development. Fellatio, a most hallowed analytic concept, literally means "to suck." According to those analysts, a female may so desperately desire the male sex organ that she wants to take possession of it with her mouth. According to this theory, a woman can, because of her so-called mutilated condition, unconsciously desire to take the valued organ into her mouth to compensate for the penis she wishes she had. There is no complementary statement made about the male in the phallic stage of development. The lopsidedness and extreme chauvinism of Freud's theory is further distorted by those analysts who combine fellatio with penis envy. The concept of fellatio may be the very prism through which a psychiatrist may analyze an unsuspecting female patient.

Do you see how Freud established a system of genital superiority for men and genital inferiority for women? Not only does he designate sexual superiority to the male, but he describes the female as mutilated, with a cavity rather than a powerful protruding organ. Do you see what Freud did with half of mankind? The therapy itself emphasizes a kind of bizarre sexuality that could only have originated in the mind of a male chauvinist. Needless to say, Freud's view of mankind does not fit the Creation during which "God created man in his own image, in the image of God created he him; male and female created he them. . . . And God saw every thing that he had made, and, behold, it was very good" (Genesis 1:27, 31).

Freud went on to postulate that if the Oedipus complex is properly resolved the like-sex parent becomes the child's model. However, he also believed that if it remains unresolved, it can continue to influence subsequent behavior through the unconscious. This myth, raised to the level of reality, is supposed to explain certain mental-emotional-behavioral disorders. Infantile sexuality with its Oedipus complex is the psychoanalyst's divining rod. His hunting expedition into the psychic past is viewed through the lens of infantile sexuality.

Exploring the tabernacle of psychoanalysis, we have come from the outer court of the unconscious to the inner court of infantile sexuality, and finally into the psychoanalytic holy of holies, the Oedipus complex. Unveiling Freud's theories exposes lust, incest, castration anxiety, and, for a woman, penis envy. And Freud was convinced that all of these are psychologically determined by age five or six. Can you think of a more macabre, twisted and even demonic explanation for human sexuality and mental disorders than Freud's central theory of infantile sexuality? Dr. Thomas Szasz says, "By dint of his rhetorical skill and persistence, Freud managed to transform an Athenian myth into an Austrian madness." He calls this "Freud's transformation of the saga of Oedipus from legend to lunacy."[12]

Through the element of Greek drama, Freud has convinced the world that every child is filled with a desire for incest and homicide, every child desires sexual intercourse with the parent of the opposite sex, every child unconsciously wants the like-sex parent to die, and every child is confronted with castration anxiety. Freud so successfully perpetrated his deceit on mankind that otherwise intelligent people not only believe the myth to be reality itself, but actually engage in its madness either as therapists or as patients. People continue to flock to the psychoanalytic couch as lambs to the slaughter, many of them ignorant of what lies in store for them. And we keep on hearing how this country needs more people trained in this mania in order to help us back to mental-emotional-behavioral health.[13]

The elevation of this legend from myth to truth should have been rejected forever at its outset. But instead, Freud's peculiar interpretation and universal application were eagerly received as truth and hailed as the psychological source of salvation for troubled souls. The fallen mind that "strains at a gnat and swallows a camel" opened wide and believed a lie. This mind that could not exercise enough faith to believe in a personal God and a personal Savior took a giant leap of faith and wholeheartedly received the Freudian gospel of salvation. Not able to accept the "faith once delivered unto the saints," the fallen mind canonized Sigmund Freud, believed and proclaimed his impossible dream, and worshiped a goulish nightmare!

When people reject the biblical concept of universal sin, they are open to all sorts of aberrations, one of which is Freud's doctrine of universal childhood fantasies of incest and homicide. Those who denied the very thought of mankind's fallen nature, as described in Scripture, were ready to believe in a powerful unconscious, motivated by infantile sexuality. Many trusted Freudian teachings that the Oedipus complex, castration anxiety, and penis envy (for women) psychically determine the entire life of every individual.

Freud's panorama of ideas is just theory, but not scientific theory. Let us not confuse theory and fact. Let us not confuse reality with one man's perverted explanation of it. Although there is a portion of our minds to which we do not seem to have direct access, it does not follow that Freud's theory about the unconscious is true. And while there is truth in the idea that all infants begin with an intimate relationship with their mothers and that children model themselves after their like-sex parent, it does not follow that Freud's explanations are true.

Because Freud's theory depends upon the unknown, invisible unconscious, there is no way to either prove or disprove the theory. However, there is now more criticism and less confidence in Freud's theories than ever before. Psychiatrist E. Fuller Torrey in his book *The Death of Psychiatry* says, "Psychiatry is dying now because it has finally come to full bloom and, as such, is found not to be viable."[14] Numerous other books, such as *Freudian Fallacy*[15] and *Freudian Fraud: The Malignant Effect of Freud's Theory on American Thought and Culture*,[16] have been written criticizing Freud's ideas.

A number of explanations of how and why Freud came up with such unusual theories as those of infantile sexuality and the Oedipus complex have been suggested. Many believe them to be the result of Freud's own distorted childhood and his own mental-emotional disturbances. In a letter to a friend, dated October 15, 1897, Freud confessed his own emotional involvement with his mother and nursemaid in a series of flowing memories and dreams.[17] Then he announced, "I have found, in my own case too, falling in love with the mother and jealousy of the father, and I now regard it as a universal event of early childhood."[18] Freud referred to his own Oedipus complex as a condition of neurosis, "my own hysteria."[19]

Freud's theory is a projection of his own sexual aberrations upon all mankind. He chose to share his neurosis with the world as a universal psychological absolute. Carl Jung, one of Freud's closest early associates, reported that Freud once said to him, "My dear Jung, promise me never to abandon the sexual theory, that is the most essential thing of all. You see, we must make a dogma of it, an unshakable bulwark."[20] Freud has titillated the minds, tantalized the hearts and foisted a fallacy upon mankind. This is the man who calls those who believe in God "sick" and then offers instead a sick view of mankind, based upon a distorted myth and a theory about a part of the mind that no one has ever seen.

Psychic Determinism

Contained within the theory of the unconscious is not only Freud's infantile sexuality theory, but also his theory of psychic determinism. According to this theory, we are what we are because of the effect of the unconscious upon our entire life. Freud believed that "we are 'lived' by unknown and uncontrollable forces."[21] These forces, according to Freud, are in the unconscious and control us in the sense that they influence all that we do. Thus, we are puppets of the unknown and unseen unconscious, shaped by these forces during our first six years of existence. As we pass from one psychosexual stage of development to another, our psyches are shaped by people in our environment and especially by our parents.

Psychic determinism establishes a process of blame that begins in the unconscious and ends with the parent. Freud removes a person's responsibility for his behavior by teaching that everyone has been predetermined by his unconscious, which has been shaped by the treatment given him by his parents during the first few years of life. The result of this parental treatment, according to Freud, may be abnormal behavior, which he described by such ugly words as *oral fixation, sadistic, obsessive-compulsive,* and *unresolved Oedipus complex.*

The meaning of these psychoterms is not important because they are all theories. They are merely punitive labels that are used to condemn and destroy certain individuals. Moreover, these psychoterms deny personal responsibility and pigeonhole one into an almost no-exit prison for which the psychoanalyst holds the only supposed key. If psychic damage occurs, the only escape is through the ritual of the "wizard of id," the psychoanalyst, who is the great high priest and has access to the mysteries of the psychoanalytic holy of holies, which contains the Oedipus complex. In order to be saved from inner turmoil, desperate souls seek this shaman of symbols, rhetoric, and metaphor.

Each theory within the psychoanalytic framework is based upon merely another theory until one finds himself in a complex labyrinth with the theories of castration anxiety and penis envy within the Oedipus theory within the infantile sexuality theory within the unconscious theory, with the theory of psychic determinism pervading the stagnant water.

The theories within theories related to theories were the threads with which Freud, the master weaver, wove the web of deception so intricately that many souls are trapped within it. Confused by the words and bewildered by the language, most people simply do not know how to either verify or refute such a system of subjectivity that confuses and condemns without proof. It is akin to shoveling smoke.

The whole scheme of the unconscious is a fantasy within a fantasy and a lie within a lie. It is an *Alice in Wonderland* game in which one can give words whatever meanings one chooses.

> "When I use a word," Humpty Dumpty said, in a rather scornful tone, "it means just what I choose it to mean—neither more nor less."
> "The question is," said Alice, "whether you can make words mean so many different things."
> "The question is," said Humpty Dumpty, "which is to be master—that's all."[22]

There is a giant difference between being influenced and being determined. Individuals are not stuck with their early upbringing if it happened to be bad, nor can anyone guarantee that someone with good upbringing will turn out well. However, people have been convinced by the Freudian fallacies that certain kinds of early training fix abnormal behavior in the adult. Thus, if an adult is poorly adjusted, people conclude the person must have had poor early parenting.[23]

Victor and Mildred Goertzel investigated this fallacy. In their book *Cradles of Eminence* they report on the early environments of more than 400 eminent men and women of the twentieth century who had experienced a wide variety of trials and tribulations during their childhood.[24] It is surprising and even shocking to discover the environmental handicaps that have been overcome by individuals who should have been psychically determined failures according to Freudian formulas. Instead of being harmed by unfortunate early circumstances, they became outstanding in many different fields of endeavor and contributed much to mankind. What might have been environmental curses seemed to act, rather, as catalysts to spawn genius and creativity. This study is not an argument for poor upbringing; it is an argument against psychic determinism.

A person need not be trapped in negative patterns of behavior established during the early years of life, for the

Bible offers a new way of life. Put off the old man; put on the new. Jesus said to Nicodemus, "Ye must be born again," and He said elsewhere that new wine could not be put into old wineskins. Jesus offers new life and new beginnings. One who is born again has the spiritual capacity to overcome old ways and develop new ones through the action of the Holy Spirit, the fruit of the Spirit, and the sanctification of the believer. One wonders why so many have given up the hope of Christianity for the hopelessness of psychic determinism.

The psychoanalytic idea of determinism is absolutely contrary to the biblical doctrine of responsibility. From Freudian determinism it follows that people are not responsible for their behavior. After all, if their behavior has already been determined by the age of six by the unseen forces in their unconscious, how can they possibly be responsible for what they do?

The Bible teaches that people do choose and that they are responsible for their actions. Psychic determinism with its accompanying freedom from responsibility is contrary to God's Word. People do make choices and God does hold them responsible for what they do. Psychic determinism has led to moral bankruptcy which in turn has led to or complicated mental failures.

Psychic determinism supports the natural tendency in the human heart to blame circumstances or someone else for one's actions. This pattern emerged in the Garden of Eden when Adam blamed Eve and Eve blamed the serpent. In supporting the natural tendency to place blame elsewhere, psychoanalysis provides extensive explanations and rationale for aberrant behavior. Those who say they are determined by circumstances and other people's actions are lying, fooling themselves, or have truly capitulated to the fallacies of psychoanalysis. In denying responsibility, a person can do what he pleases; that is, he can exercise his own volition under the guise of psychic determinism.

For example, an extensive study of the criminal personality asserts that criminals commit crimes by deliberate choice.[25] This contradicts the idea of psychic determinism and the usual so-called insights of modern psychotherapy that tend to blame the environment and remove responsibility from the individual. Part of the outcry against the criminal personality study occurred because those who conducted and reported the study placed the blame for wrong behavior back on the criminal himself. Responsibility for one's behavior, criminal or otherwise, is not a popular idea in many psychological and sociological circles.

Freudian Theory of Defense Mechanisms

Freud names three parts of the personality as the *id*, *ego*, and *superego*. Dr. Ernest Hilgard et al. say:

> Freud believed that the conflict between id impulses—primarily sexual and aggressive instincts—and the restraining influences of the ego and superego constitutes the motivating source of much behavior.[26]

According to Freud's system, anxiety is the result of restraining the "sexual and aggressive instincts." Freud called the method of reducing the resultant anxiety repression. According to Hilgard et al., "Those methods of anxiety reduction, called defense mechanisms, are means of defending oneself against painful anxiety."[27] They additionally say:

> Freud used the term defense mechanisms to refer to unconscious processes that defend a person against anxiety by distorting reality in some way . . . they all involve an element of self-deception.[28]

Describing repression, Hilgard et al. say:

> In repression, impulses or memories that are too threatening are excluded from action or conscious awareness. Freud believed that repression of certain childhood impulses is universal. For example, he maintained that all young boys have feelings of

sexual attraction toward the mother and feelings of rivalry and hostility toward the father (the Oedipus complex); these impulses are repressed to avoid the painful consequences of acting on them. In later life, feelings and memories that would cause anxiety because they are inconsistent with one's self-concept may be repressed. Feelings of hostility toward a loved one and experiences of failure may be banished from memory.[29]

One last part of the defense mechanisms picture has to do with the individual's desire "to maintain self-esteem." Freud believed that "self-reproaches" diminish self-esteem. He said, "So we find the key to the clinical picture: we perceive that the self-reproaches are reproaches against a loved object which have been shifted away from it on to the patient's own ego."[30] Thus, he believed that people develop defense mechanisms as a means of self-deception "to maintain self-esteem."

Morality

Freud's view of morality is that psychological disorders occur because of society's interference with the instinctual biological needs of the individual. Freud said, ". . . we have found it impossible to give our support to conventional morality [which] demands more sacrifices than it is worth."[31] Freud felt that mental-emotional disorders were caused by the individual being too hard on himself. Freud even encouraged people to free themselves of inhibitions in order to gratify their instincts. Freud's position was that the person's moral standards are too high and that his performance has been too good. Thus, he attempted to compromise the person's conscience.

Freud's moral stance was one of permissiveness with respect to individual action and restraint. In particular, he felt that free fornication would be great preventive medicine and psychoprophylactic for the mind. In fact, he believed in a strong, direct relationship between a person's sex life and mental-emotional disorders. He said,

". . . factors arising in sexual life represent the nearest and practically the most momentous causes of every single case of nervous illness."[32]

However, Freud warned against giving up masturbation for intercourse because of the possibility of contracting syphilis and gonorrhea. But then he suggested, "The only alternative would be free sexual intercourse between young males and respectable girls; but this could only be resorted to if there were innocuous preventative methods," by which he meant birth control.[33] Thus, Freud's only objections to free fornication were the possibilities of venereal disease and pregnancy. Little did he anticipate our present permissive society which has achieved his great therapeutic image of free fornication. Little did he realize the sexual revolution that followed his conjectures. Little did he know that the ensuing sexual permissiveness would not only cause more mental-emotional-behavioral disorders, but rip right into the fabric of society.

The biblical position on fornication is clear: it is forbidden. Biblical restrictions are not a curse, as Freud would want us to believe; they bring health and healing. If such restraints lead to mental disorders, why would the Creator have instituted them? Free fornication, not biblical restraint, leads to human chaos. We see the evidence of this in the high divorce rate and abortions, both of which take a heavy toll in mental-emotional-behavioral pain and stress.

Contrary to what the Freudians would have us believe, it is not freedom in this area that leads to adjustment; it is responsibility and restraint. Acting contrary to God's Word is not only sin; it is poor preventive mental health. Thus, fornication is psychonoxious, not psychoprophylactic. Biblical restraint leads to good mental health, and biblical principles are a balm for anxiety.

The whole failure of the Freudian morality system is permissiveness, and this permissiveness has pervaded not only Freud's thinking, but also the thinking of many who followed. It became part and parcel of public attitudes about social, political, and economic issues as well as about sex. For example, it affected and influenced much of the thinking and teaching about child discipline. One professor who was influenced by Freud used to say, "Never spank a child until he is old enough to understand it and when he is old enough to understand it, never spank a child." Well known pediatrician Benjamin Spock proliferated the no-spank permissiveness in his best seller *Baby and Child Care* [34] and millions of well-meaning parents accepted this Freudian foolishness without question.

There is no doubt that the no-spank position is contrary to Scripture, as we are told in Proverbs 13:24: "He that spareth his rod hateth his son, but he that loveth him chasteneth him early." Discipline is a form of love. Permissiveness, on the other hand, means either indifference or hate. Also, in Proverbs 22:15 we are told, "Foolishness is bound in the heart of a child; but the rod of correction shall drive it far from him."

When Spock realized the kind of damage that his advice in child-rearing had done, he admitted that he and other professionals had actually persuaded the public that they were the only people "who know for sure how children should be managed."[35] He further admitted:

> This is a cruel deprivation that we professionals have imposed on mothers and fathers. Of course, we did it with the best of intentions. . . . We didn't realize, until it was too late, how our know-it-all attitude was undermining the self-assurance of parents.[36]

It is good news that he has recanted his former pro-permissive doctrine. He now says, "Inability to be firm is, to my mind, the commonest problem of parents in America today."[37] He further admits that "parental submissiveness [to children] doesn't avoid unpleasantness; it makes it inevitable."[38]

While both extremes of permissiveness and restrictiveness can be detrimental to a child, the Bible gives us the right balance between the two. Christians don't need Freud or any of his followers to teach them about child discipline.

Current Evidences of Freudian Influence Among Christians

While some Christians still dispense Freud's psychosexual theories, most Christians have dispensed with the Oedipus complex. Nevertheless many continue to promote Freud's fabrication of an unconscious filled with powerful motivating material, accumulated during the early years of life, that determines and directs behavior. They continue to view the unconscious mind as a recorder and receptacle containing everything that ever happened to a person and that these hidden contents exert a powerful force motivating conscious thinking, feeling, and behaving. These people continue to believe Freud's notion that the reason for present behavior is to be found in the past, usually the distant past, especially the first five years of life. Responsibility is shifted to parents and early life circumstances.

Therapy that seeks to find answers for present pain and problems through remembering and reliving the past has its roots in Freudian theory. So-called inner healing is also related to Freudian theory, and all forms of reliving the pain are related to his notion of abreaction, that in reliving the pain one becomes free of its hold. Therapists who believe in a Freudian notion of the unconscious, with its powerful defense mechanisms of repression and denial, have led suffering souls into the morass of false memories, because they believe some hidden trauma is causing the present suffering.

The Freudian Failure

Regarding the results of his own psychoanalysis on his own patients, Freud said:

> Patients are nothing but riff-raff. The only useful purposes they serve are to help us earn a living and

to provide learning material. In any case, we cannot help them.[39]

After examining Freud's theories and the practices and attitudes that followed in his wake, can anyone say Freud has given us a panacea for mental-emotional-behavioral health? Do his theories comprise a solution to human problems? Is infantile sexuality really the magic wand for transforming people? The offerings of Freud and his followers are no more than fallacious substitutes for the spiritual truths which our Creator has given to mankind in His Word and through the life of His Son Jesus.

Freud first mythologized psychotherapy; then he medicalized it, scientized it, and merchandised it. He postulated a supposed universal cure for mankind. But, looking closely, one sees a system that has often been described as merely a white, middle-class, occidental miasma. Its central activity of free association is not so free after all, because the patient tells the therapist what he thinks the therapist wants to hear. Jay Haley contends, ". . . a patient's productions are always being influenced by a therapist, which is why patients in Freudian analysis have dreams with more evident sexual content."[40]

To participate in the psychoanalytic ritual one must "free associate," give up his mental freedom, agree to be determined by his past, blame his parents, become dependent upon the therapist, permit the therapist to take the place of both parents and God, deify sex, denigrate religion, and, above all, pay large sums of money over a long period of time, in spite of the lack of evidence that this Freudian fetish is of any value.

When someone suggests psychoanalysis, beware. And be aware of the intrusion and influence of these ideas into numerous other brands of psychotherapy existent today. Most of them are influenced greatly by Freudian thought. The Freudian fantasies have filtered into nearly all of the psychotherapeutic world. In Dante's *Inferno* there is a sign over the entrance of hell (Hades) which reads,

"Abandon all hope, ye who enter here." We believe that is a safe way for Christians to view psychoanalysis. And, since Freud's theories have seeped into nearly every other form of psychotherapy to one degree or another, we contend that the warning should be written over the door of every provider of psychological counseling.

8

Carl Jung Analytic Psychology

Many Christians have probably never heard of C. G. Jung, but his influence in the church is vast and affects sermons, books, and activities, such as the prolific use of the Myers-Briggs Type Indicator (MBTI). A current, popular example of Jung's legacy can be seen in Robert Hicks's book *The Masculine Journey*, which was given to 50,000 men who attended a Promise Keepers conference. Christians need to learn enough about Jung and his teachings to be warned and wary.

Jung's legacy to Christian psychology is both direct and indirect. Christians, who have been influenced by Jung's teachings, integrate aspects of Jungian theory into their own practice of psychotherapy. They may incorporate his notions regarding personality types, the personal unconscious, dream analysis, and various archetypes in their own attempt to understand and counsel clients. Other Christians have been influenced more indirectly as they have engaged in inner healing, followed 12-step programs, or taken the MBTI, which is based on Jung's personality types and incorporates his theories of introversion and extroversion.

Jung chose psychiatry because it combined his interest in medicine and spirituality. He explained:

> Here alone the two currents of my interest could flow together and in a united stream dig their own bed. Here was the empirical field common to biological and spiritual facts, which I had everywhere sought and nowhere found. Here at last was the place where the collision of nature and spirit became a reality.[1]

Jung was intensely interested in the spiritual realm even though he had rejected Christianity.

As a young child Jung had difficulty distinguishing between Jesus and a monstrous figure encountered in a nightmare, which he later identified as a huge phallus.[2] He wrote:

> At all events, the phallus of this dream seems to be a subterranean God "not to be named," and such it remained throughout my youth, reappearing whenever anyone spoke too emphatically about Lord Jesus. Lord Jesus never became quite real for me, never quite acceptable, never quite lovable, for again and again I would think of his underground counterpart, a frightful revelation which had been accorded me without seeking it. . . . Lord Jesus seemed to me in some ways a god of death, helpful, it is true, in that he scared away the terrors of the night, but himself uncanny, a crucified and bloody corpse.[3]

Jung must have had opportunity to hear the Gospel. Besides Jung's father being a Lutheran minister, all eight of his uncles were pastors as well.[4] He wrote about his continuing distrust of Christ:

> I made every effort to force myself to take the required positive attitude to Christ. But I could never succeed in overcoming my secret distrust.[5]

Between the ages of 17 and 19, Jung engaged in heated theological discussions with his father. He described these encounters as "fruitless discussions" that exasperated both of them. He thus blamed theology for alienating his father and himself. He further concluded the following about his father:

> I saw how hopelessly he was entrapped by the Church and its theological thinking. They had blocked all avenues by which he might have reached God directly, and then faithlessly abandoned him. Now I understood the deepest meaning of my earlier experience: God Himself had disavowed theology and the Church founded upon it.[6]

Even after Jung concluded that all religions are myths that can be helpful to people, he resisted Christianity even as his own personal myth. At a moment of what Jung called "unusual clarity," he thought, "Now you possess a key to mythology and are free to unlock all the gates of the unconscious psyche." Then he recalled how he had "explained the myths of people of the past" and wrote the following:

> But in what myth does man live nowadays? In the Christian myth, the answer might be. "Do you live in it?" I asked myself. To be honest, the answer was no. "For me it is not what I live by."[7]

Jung had more faith in religious myths of ancient cultures than in the God of the Bible. And, he had more faith in his subjective explorations into his own psyche through dreams and fantasies than in the truth of God's Word.

The Collective Unconscious

Jung taught that the psyche consists of various systems including the *personal unconscious* with its complexes and a *collective unconscious* with its archetypes. Jung's theory of a *personal unconscious* is quite similar to Freud's creation of a region containing a person's repressed, forgotten, or ignored experiences. However, Jung considered the personal unconscious to be a "more or less superficial layer of the unconscious." Within the *personal unconscious* are what he called "feeling-toned complexes." He said that "they constitute the personal and private side of psychic life."[8] These are feelings and perceptions organized around significant persons or events in the person's life.

Jung believed that there was a deeper and more significant layer of the unconscious, which he called the *collective unconscious*, with what he identified as *instincts* and *archetypes*, which he believed were innate, unconscious, and generally universal. He believed that these unconscious archetypes are lived out through various behaviors and that they are identifiable through these behaviors as well as through dreams. The archetypes include the *anima* and *animus*, which are the feminine and masculine images which Jung believed play an essential role in every person. Regarding his own experience with the anima, Jung wrote:

> I was greatly intrigued by the fact that a woman should interfere with me from within. My conclusion was that she must be the "soul," in the primitive sense, and I began to speculate on the reasons why the name "anima" was given to the soul. Why was it thought of as feminine? Later I came to see that this inner feminine figure plays a typical, or archetypal, role in the unconscious of a man, and I called her the "anima." The corresponding figure in the unconscious of woman I called the "animus."[9]

Jung went into extraordinary detail in describing the various archetypes, which included the Great Mother, the

Maiden (representing innocence and renewal), the Child, the *Puer Aeternus* (representing eternal youth), the Trickster, the Questing Hero, the Evil Ogre, and the Scapegoat. He believed fairy tale characters often represent these archetypes. He taught that "all archetypes have a positive, favourable, bright side that points upwards," and that they also have "one that points downwards, partly negative and unfavourable."[10] This fits with his concept of the "shadow," which he believed includes negative aspects of both the personal and collective unconscious—sins or faults that have been repressed or ignored because they don't fit with one's self-concept and also those not yet realized.[11]

Jung was intrigued with symbols and thought they represented aspects of the personal unconscious and the collective unconscious and could be accessed through dreams and reflective states of consciousness. He believed that whereas symbols in the personal unconscious originated from the person's own history and functioned to satisfy socially unacceptable instincts and impulses, symbols in the collective unconscious came from collective experiences of the human race and had more to do with total personality and hidden potential. Thus Jungian analysis works to reveal both levels of the unconscious to enable a person to access and know various facets and potential of the inner self.[12]

Jung's *collective unconscious* has been described as a "storehouse of latent memory traces inherited from man's ancestral past, a past that includes not only the racial history of man as a separate species but his pre-human or animal ancestry as well."[13] Jung wrote:

> The ground floor stood for the first level of the unconscious. The deeper I went, the more alien and the darker the scene became. In the cave, I discovered remains of a primitive culture, that is, the world of the primitive man within myself—a world which can scarcely be reached or illuminated by consciousness. The primitive psyche of man borders on the life of the animal soul, just as the cares of

prehistoric times were usually inhabited by animals before men laid claim to them.[14]

Jung's theory incorporates Darwin's theory of evolution as well as ancient mythology. Jung taught that this *collective unconscious* is shared by all people and is therefore universal. However, since it is unconscious, not all people are able to tap into it. Jung saw the *collective unconscious* as the foundational structure of personality on which the *personal unconscious* and the *ego* are built.

Because he believed that the foundations of personality are ancestral and universal, he studied religions, mythology, rituals, symbols, dreams, and visions. He says:

> All esoteric teachings seek to apprehend the unseen happenings in the psyche, and all claim supreme authority for themselves. What is true of primitive lore is true in even higher degree of the ruling world religions. They contain a revealed knowledge that was originally hidden, and they set forth the secrets of the soul in glorious images.[15]

Jung's Psychological Types and the MBTI

Jung developed a psychology of types, which included what he called "attitude types." His two basic types are introversion and extroversion. He extended his typology with what he called "function types."[16] The functions include Thinking, Feeling, Sensation, and Intuition and are further delineated as being rational (judging) or irrational (perceiving).[17]

The Myers-Briggs Type Indicator (MBTI) is a personality inventory based on Carl Jung's theory of psychological types. The MBTI provides the following four bipolar scales:

Introversion—Extroversion
Sensing—Intuition
Thinking—Feeling
Judging—Perceiving

These four scales yield 16 possible types.

After appraising the MBTI, the National Research Council (which is made up of members from the councils of the National Academy of Sciences, National Academy of Engineering, and Institute of Medicine) reported:

> McCaulley (1988) estimates that the MBTI is used as a diagnostic instrument by 1,700,000 people a year in the United States, and Moore and Woods (1987) list the wide variety of organizations in business, industry, education, government, and the military that use it. It is probably fair to say that the MBTI is the most popular "self-insight, insight into others" instrument in use today. Unfortunately, however, the popularity of the instrument is not coincident with supportive research results.[18]

In other words, **research results do not support the popularity**! The Council's particular concern is the **lack of validity** for the MBTI. In concluding the section on validity the Council stated: "The evidence summarized in this section raises questions about the validity of the MBTI."[19]

The Council also criticized the marketing of the MBTI:

> From the perspective of the instrument's developers, the profits from an audience eager for self-improvement encourages them to market the instrument aggressively; aggressive marketing—complete with type coffee mugs, t-shirts, pins, license plates—has apparently increased the number of consumers worldwide.[20]

Prior to their overall "Conclusions" section, the Council said that "the popularity of this instrument in the absence of proven scientific worth is troublesome." In their "Conclusions" section, the Council said very clearly: "At this time, there is not sufficient, well-designed research to justify the use of the MBTI in career counseling programs."[21]

Others have expressed concern about the difficulty of establishing validity for tests that are based upon a theoretical construct. Drs. L. J. Cronbach and P. E. Meehl wrote:

> Unless substantially the same nomological net is accepted by the several users of the construct, public validation is impossible. A consumer of the test who rejects the author's theory cannot accept the author's validation.[22]

In applying this idea to the MBTI, Dr. Jerry Wiggins said:

> The validity of the MBTI can be evaluated independently of the total corpus of Jung's writings but it cannot be fairly appraised outside the more delimited context of Jung's theory of psychological types. As with any construct-oriented test, both the validity of the test and the validity of the theory are at issue.[23]

Please note that the validity of the test and the validity of the theory are inextricably bound.

Theories that underlie personality inventories are not science. They are merely the opinions of men. Jung's fourfold preferences are his opinion about man. The use of them in a personality test such as the MBTI is Jung's theory (which is just his opinion, not science) put in test form.

Just because someone devises a test and uses the four Jungian personality preferences (and 16 types) and uses mathematical means of validating it does not mean that the theory behind it is scientific or factual. At minimum, Jung's theory is merely vain philosophies of men against which we are warned in Scripture. At worst, it originated from Satan through a spirit guide. We would think that no Christian would want Jung's psychological theory or any test that derives from it. Nevertheless numerous Christians use the MBTI to evaluate pastoral and missionary candidates, other job applicants, couples who want to get married, and others for different situations and purposes.

Jung's Spirit Guide

Because Jung turned psychoanalysis into a type of religion, he is also considered to be a transpersonal psychologist as well as an analytical theorist. He delved deeply into the occult, practiced necromancy, and had daily contact with disembodied spirits, which he called archetypes. Jung describes having his whole house "crammed full of spirits" crying out to him. He said that was the beginning of writing "The Seven Sermons to the Dead," which he says flowed out of him.[24] Just prior to that experience he wrote about a fantasy of his soul flying away. He said:

> This was a significant event: the soul, the anima, establishes the relationship to the unconscious. In a certain sense this is also a relationship to the collectivity of the dead; for the unconscious corresponds to the mythic land of the dead, the land of the ancestors. If, therefore, one has a fantasy of the soul vanishing, this means that it has withdrawn into the unconscious or into the land of the dead. There it produces a mysterious animation and gives visible form to the ancestral traces, the collective contents. Like a medium, it gives the dead a chance to manifest themselves.[25]

Because Jung disregarded biblical admonitions against necromancy, he had no problem with contacting the dead and conversing with disembodied spirits. He said:

> These conversations with the dead formed a kind of prelude to what I had to communicate to the world about the unconscious: a kind of pattern of order and interpretation of its general contents.[26]

Therefore, his theories about the unconscious were intrinsically tied to his communication with such entities.

Much of what Jung wrote was inspired by such entities. Jung had his own familiar spirit whom he called Philemon. At first he thought Philemon was part of his own psyche, but later on he found that Philemon was more than an expression of his own inner self. Jung says:

> Philemon and other figures of my fantasies brought home to me the crucial insight that there are things in the psyche which I do not produce, but which produce themselves and have their own life. Philemon represented a force which was not myself. In my fantasies I held conversations with him, and he said things which I had not consciously thought. For I observed clearly that it was he who spoke, not I. . . . Psychologically, Philemon represented superior insight. He was a mysterious figure to me. At times he seemed to me quite real, as if he were a living personality. I went walking up and down the garden with him, and to me he was what the Indians call a guru.[27]

Jung's exploration into what he thought was his unconscious opened him up to demonic influence, which he at first thought emanated from his own unconscious but which existed quite independently from him. He even described himself as having demonic strength and as having a demon in him. He wrote:

> But there was a demonic strength in me, and from the beginning there was no doubt in my mind that I must find the meaning of what I was experiencing in these fantasies. When I endured these assaults of the unconscious I had an unswerving conviction that I was obeying a higher will, and that feeling continued to uphold me until I had mastered the task.[28]

> There was a daimon in me, and in the end its presence proved decisive. It overpowered me, and if I was at times ruthless it was because I was in the grip of the daimon.[29]

Jung was also intrigued with Gnosticism and alchemy. He wrote:

> Grounded in the natural philosophy of the Middle Ages, alchemy formed the bridge on the one hand into the past, to Gnosticism, and on the other into the future, to the modern psychology of the unconscious.[30]

> Only after I had familiarized myself with alchemy did I realize that the unconscious is a process, and that the psyche is transformed or developed by the relationship of the ego to the contents of the unconscious. In individual cases that transformation can be read from dreams and fantasies. In collective life it has left its deposit principally in the various religious systems and their changing symbols. Through the study of these collective transformation processes and through understanding of alchemical symbolism I arrived at the central concept of my psychology: *the process of individuation.*[31] (Italics in original.)

According to Jung, individuation occurs as the psyche develops—as the unconscious becomes conscious.[32]

Symbols of Self-Deification

Another means Jung used to delve into the deeper reaches of his own unconscious was through his numerous renditions of mandalas. A *mandala* is "a circular design containing concentric geometric forms, images of deities, etc. and symbolizing the universe, totality, or wholeness in Hinduism and Buddhism."[33] Jung wrote:

> My mandalas were cryptograms concerning the state of the self which were presented to me anew each day. In them I saw the self—that is, my whole being—actively at work. . . . When I began drawing the mandalas, however, I saw that everything, all the paths I had been following, all the steps I had taken, were leading back to a single point—namely,

to the mid-point. It became increasingly plain to me that the mandala is the center. It is the exponent of all paths. It is the path to the center, to individuation.[34]

Jung did not accept Jesus as God incarnate, but rather believed that God is in every person, at the very center in the collective unconscious and he believed that the mandala signified "the divinity incarnate in man." He wrote:

> The mandala is an archetypal image whose occurrence is attested throughout the ages. It signifies the wholeness of the self. This circular image represents the wholeness of the psychic ground or, to put it in mythic terms, the divinity incarnate in man.[35]

Dr. Richard Noll describes "Jung's solar mandala of his own psyche":

> The inner core of the personality, representing the source of all life, is thus represented in this mandala as a sun. If individuation is adaptation to inner reality, it is a descent into the deepest regions of the psyche to seek closer contact with the source of all life, the inner sun as the god within.[36]

Jung was clearly a neopagan searching for the god within through ancient myths, all the while acting as if he were involved in science. Jung's search was not science, but pagan religion. Noll remarks:

> Jung's familiar psychological theory and method, which are so widely promoted in our culture today, rests on this very early neopagan or völkisch formulation—a fact entirely unknown to the countless thousands of devout Christian or Jewish Jungians today who would, in all likelihood, find this fact repugnant if they fully understood the meaning behind the argument I make here.[37]

In other words, Jung searched for ancient mysteries in myths and pagan religious sources to connect with the god within, to discover that his true self was, after all, god. Noll demonstrates that Jung's life work was driven by "his fascination with the self-deification experiences of the ancient mysteries, and his own secret experience of being deified."[38] No wonder new agers are interested in Jung!

Jung's AA Influence

Jung also played a role in the development of Alcoholics Anonymous. Cofounder Bill Wilson wrote the following in a letter to Jung in 1961:

> This letter of great appreciation has been very long overdue. . . . Though you have surely heard of us [AA], I doubt if you are aware that a certain conversation you once had with one of your patients, a Mr. Roland H., back in the early 1930's did play a critical role in the founding of our fellowship.[39]

Wilson continued the letter by reminding Jung of what he had "frankly told [Roland H.] of his hopelessness," that he was beyond medical or psychiatric help. Wilson wrote: "This candid and humble statement of yours was beyond doubt the first foundation stone upon which our society has since been built."

When Roland H. had asked Jung if there was any hope for him Jung "told him that there might be, provided he could become the subject of a spiritual or religious experience—in short, a genuine conversion." Wilson continued in his letter: "You recommended that he place himself in a religious atmosphere and hope for the best."[40] As far as Jung was concerned, there was no need for doctrine or creed, only an experience.

It is important to remember that Jung could not have meant conversion to Christianity, since as far as Jung was concerned all religion is simply myth—a symbolic way of interpreting the life of the psyche. To Jung, conversion simply meant a totally dramatic experience that would profoundly alter a person's outlook on life.

Jung himself had blatantly rejected Christianity and replaced God with a myriad of mythological archetypes. Jung's response to Wilson's letter included the following statement about Roland H.:

> His craving for alcohol was the equivalent, on a low level, of the spiritual thirst of our being for wholeness; expressed in medieval language: the union with God.[41]

In his letter Jung mentioned that in Latin the same word is used for alcohol as for "the highest religious experience." Even in English, alcohol is referred to as *spirits*. But, knowing Jung's theology and privy counsel with a familiar spirit, one must conclude that the spirit he is referring to is not the Holy Spirit, and the god he is talking about is not the God of the Bible, but rather a counterfeit spirit posing as an angel of light and leading many to destruction.

Jung's Blasphemy

Jung's neopaganism and his desire to replace Christianity with his own concept of psychoanalysis can be seen in a letter he wrote to Freud:

> I imagine a far finer and more comprehensive task for [psychoanalysis] than alliance with an ethical fraternity. I think we must give it time to infiltrate into people from many centers, to revivify among intellectuals a feeling for symbol and myth, ever so gently to transform Christ back into the soothsaying god of the vine, which he was, and in this way absorb those ecstatic instinctual forces of Christianity for the one purpose of making the cult and the sacred myth what they once were—a drunken feast of joy where man regained the ethos and holiness of an animal.[42]

Thus Jung's goal for psychoanalysis was to be an all-encompassing religion superior to Christianity, reducing its truth to myth and transmogrifying Christ into a "soothsaying god of the vine." For many people, Jung seemed to reach this goal as they turned to what Noll titles his book, *The Jung Cult*. Noll says:

> For literally tens of thousands, if not hundreds of thousands, of individuals in our culture, Jung and his ideas are the basis of a personal religion that either supplants their participation in traditional organized Judeo-Christian religion or accompanies it. For this latter group especially, the Jungian experience, as it is promoted by its specialized caste of analysts, holds out the promise of mystery and the direct experience of the transcendent that they do not experience in any church or synagogue.

Regarding the individual followers of Jung's personal religion, Noll says:

> Although all are united by a common belief in individuation and a transcendent, transpersonal collective unconscious that is said to manifest itself through the individual psyche, the emphasis remains on the personal experience of the universal in the particular. . . . The entire pantheon of all the world's mythologies, torn out of any semblance of its original cultural contexts, is utilized as an "objective" reference point for the interpretation of personal experience.[43]

Erica Goode comments on Jung's popularity:

> Thirty-one years after the Swiss psychiatrist's death, Jung's theories are surging in popularity, becoming a cultural touchstone, a lens for processing experience, in some cases almost a religion. In churches, quotes from Jung's work spill from the pulpit.[44]

Goode quotes from Kendra Smith's paper, "With Jungian Psychology, Do We Need Religion?" in which she reports on a woman who "claims Jungian psychology as her spiritual path and dream analysis as her spiritual discipline."[45]

Christians dabble in Jung's religion when they incorporate his notions about man and deity through imbibing in his theories, therapies, and notions that have filtered down through other psychotherapies, through 12-step programs, inner healing, dream analysis, and personality types and tests.

9

Alfred Adler Individual Psychology

Alfred Adler was an associate of Freud, but broke away from him as he developed his own theory of Individual Psychology. While Adler's theory contained many of Freud's ideas, such as a modified psychic determinism, unconscious motivation, and the importance of a client gaining insight into his unconscious motives and assumptions, he did not believe that people were motivated by sexual impulses.[1] Instead, he initially contrasted Freud's theory of sexual instincts with his own theory of aggressive instincts motivating individuals. Next, he "scientized" Friedrich Nietzsche's "will to power" theory, but later substituted it with his own "striving for superiority" theory.[2]

Adler had a penchant for assuming that his psychological ideas applied to everyone. He frequently used such words as *all, always,* and *every.* Thus he decided that "striving for superiority" was the universal motivation of mankind. Adler also believed that all humans are motivated by a need to overcome feelings of inferiority. He further taught that, in addition to everyone having the same goal of superiority, early in life each person develops his own "style of life" for pursuing his goal.[3]

Adler believed that his theory of Individual Psychology incorporated the whole person and that all behavior is motivated by a self-created, goal-oriented life plan, which he later called "life style." Adler wrote:

> For general guidance I would like to propound the following rule: *as soon as the goal of a psychic movement or its life-plan has been recognized, then we are to assume that all the movements of its constituent parts will coincide with both the goal and the life-plan.*[4] (Italics in original.)

He believed that the person's life style is based on his perceived meaning of life formed within the first five years. Adler thus said that the psychologist must "look below the surface" of any activity and expression of the client's goal. He said: "We must still look for the underlying coherence, for the unity of the personality. This unity is fixed in all its expressions."[5]

Although Adler stressed the unity of the whole person, he ignored the most important aspect of humanity: that God created man in His own image. This gross omission not only left a huge gap in his understanding of individuals; it also distorted the rest of his theory. The few references to religion reveal his evident disregard of God and the Bible. At one point in his career he betrayed his Jewish heritage and was baptized as a Christian, although, according to Walter Kaufmann, Adler "did not believe in Christianity."[6] His personal religion was neither Judaism nor Christianity. His faith rested on his own theory of Individual Psychology, which he believed was superior to the efforts of religion.[7]

Motivational Goals

Alder saw every attitude and activity in terms of the individual striving towards a goal. He proposed "the following law holding in the development of all psychic happenings: we cannot think, feel, will, or act without the perception of some goal."[8] He declared, "All psychic activities are given a direction by means of a previously determined goal."[9] He said:

> The conclusion thus to be drawn from the unbiased study of any personality viewed from the standpoint of individual-psychology leads us to the following important proposition: *every psychic phenomenon, if it is to give us any understanding of a person, can only be grasped and understood if regarded as a preparation for some goal.*[10] (Italics in original.)

Adler believed that everyone is motivated by a common goal that shapes all behavior. He identified the common goal as one of superiority, power, security, and significance, but also stressed the need for social responsibility. Adler taught that "two great tendencies dominate all psychological activities." He wrote:

> These two tendencies, social feeling and the individual striving for power and domination, influence every human activity and colour the attitude of every individual both in his striving for security and in his fulfillment of the three great challenges of life: love, work, and relationships.[11]

According to Adler, if the goal of superiority is not accompanied by social feelings and a desire to cooperate with others, life will not work for the person.

Adler taught that while the goal of superiority is universal, the goal is nevertheless unique to each individual, depending on the meaning he gives to life and on the life style he has developed to reach the goal.[12] Thus he declared: "Nobody knows his own goal of superiority so that he can describe it in full."[13]

Adler saw nothing wrong with the superiority goal itself, only how effectively a person was able to move towards his goal. Nor did he see any advantage in changing the goal itself. Christians should clearly see that such a goal belongs in the kingdom of darkness and reflects Satan's proud desires. Christians have other goals, to love and glorify God and to become like Jesus. Of course, Adler even distorts the goal of becoming like Jesus as being one of superiority, becoming like God.[14] Thus, attempts to incorporate Adler's teachings into Christian ministry can be disastrous.

Adler believed that the constant striving for superiority is what motivates mankind to be socially responsive and personally responsible. He explained:

> It is the striving for superiority which is behind every human creation and it is the source of all contributions which are made to our culture. The whole of human life proceeds along this great line of action—from below above, from minus to plus, from defeat to victory. The only individuals who can really meet and master the problems of life, however, are those who show in their striving a tendency to enrich all others, who go ahead in such a way that others benefit also.[15]

Adler believed that a person's entire style of life works to fulfill this goal of superiority but that, unless social feeling and cooperation have been developed, the goal of superiority can become the driving force for neuroticism and criminal behavior.[16]

Adler also attributed great motivating force to inferiority feelings. These would naturally work together with the goal of superiority, the desire to be superior rather than inferior. He said:

> This feeling of inferiority is the driving force, the starting point from which every childish striving originates. It determines how this individual child acquires peace and security in life, it determines the

very goal of his existence, and prepares the path along which this goal may be reached.[17]

Everyone, according to Adler, experiences inferiority feelings and works to rid himself of these feelings. However, he explained that, if a person cannot imagine improving the situation, he will try other methods of getting rid of the inferiority feelings, such as trying "to hypnotize himself, or auto-intoxicate himself, into feeling superior," his inferiority feelings "accumulate, because the situation which produces them remains unaltered."[18] Adler further taught that continued self-deception and useless attempts to feel superior lead to what he called the "inferiority complex," in which the person appears to "be more occupied in avoiding defeat than in pressing forward to success."[19]

Adler is well known for his concept of the inferiority complex, although the term was also used by Freud and Jung.[20] He said, "Every neurotic has an inferiority complex,"[21] and, "Every neurosis can be understood as an attempt to free oneself from a feeling of inferiority in order to gain a feeling of superiority."[22] Adler further contended: "Behind every one who behaves as if he were superior to others, we can suspect a feeling of inferiority which calls for very special efforts of concealment."[23]

Along with the common goal of superiority and common inferiority feelings, Adler taught, "All our strivings are directed towards a feeling of security."[24] He believed in a common striving for significance. He wrote:

> Every human being strives for significance, but people always make mistakes if they do not recognize that their own significance lies in their contribution to the lives of others.[25]

Adler's books are filled with case studies of people who have made numerous mistakes in attributing meaning to situations, in attempting to reach their goals, and in their strivings for security and significance. He contends that all of these mistakes are due to the development of the creative self during the first five years of life.

Adler's case studies serve to promote his theory and perspective, because he describes people in such a way as to fit his theory. This can be very deceptive because when people read the case studies they begin to see people through Adler's eyes rather than from a biblical perspective. If the same individual in the same situation were used as a case study by each of the more than 400 different systems of therapy, the person would be described according to the controlling theory.

The Creative Self, Style of Life, and Determinism

His concept of the "creative self" is considered to be "Adler's crowning achievement as a personality theorist." His theory of the creative self purports that each person creates his own personality through a combination of "stimuli acting upon the person and the responses he makes to these stimuli."[26] Adler's ideas about the creative self grew out of his "style of life" theory, which is considered "the most distinctive feature of his psychology."[27] These two notions are so closely interwoven that it is difficult to separate them. According to Adler, each person develops his own unique way of reaching his goals during the first four or five years of life. Once the person's style of life is formed, his own unique style (including attitudes and feelings) remains relatively fixed throughout his entire lifetime. Through one's own unique style of life, a person's creative self interacts with the environment and interprets reality in such a way as to create and reach the characteristic goal.[28] For instance, he said:

> Once a child has learned that he can tyrannize his environment by fury, or sadness, or weeping, arising out of a feeling of neglect, he will test this method of obtaining domination over his environment again and again. In this way he falls easily into a behavior pattern which allows him to react to insignificant stimuli with his typical emotional response.[29]

Adler believed that if such a pattern is repeated often enough it becomes part of the person's life style. Adler declared: "Emotions are as fixed as one's life style."[30] He wrote:

> In every individual we see that feelings have grown and developed in a direction and to a level that were essential to the attainment of her personal goal. . . . A person who accomplishes her goal of superiority through sadness cannot be cheerful and satisfied with her accomplishments. She can only be happy when she is miserable![31]

Adler did not agree with Freud's determinism, but actually created another form of psychic determinism as powerful as Freud's. Freud's determinism depends on what happens to a person during the first five years of life. Adler's depends on what the child makes of his circumstances during the first five years of life. Adler taught that "the foundations of the human psyche are laid in the earliest days of childhood."[32] He believed that a person is determined during the first five years of life, not by circumstances themselves, but rather by how the child interprets the circumstances and thus forms an attitude towards life. He wrote:

> This is where Individual Psychology diverges from the theory of determinism: no experience is in itself a cause of success or failure. We do not suffer from the shock of our experiences—the so-called trauma— but instead make out of them whatever suits our purposes. We are not determined by our experiences but are self-determined by the meaning we give to them; and when we take particular experiences as the basis for our future life we are almost certain to be misguided to some degree. Meanings are not determined by situations. We determine ourselves by the meanings we ascribe to situations.[33]

Adler taught that "the particular pressure [a child] has felt in the days of earliest infancy will colour his attitude towards life and determine in a rudimentary way his view of the world, his cosmic philosophy."[34] He further declared: "Every marked attitude of a man can be traced back to an origin in childhood. In the nursery are formed and prepared all of man's future attitudes."[35]

Although the child's response is involved, it nevertheless ends up being determinism in that the child creates his own life style during these early years and, once created, the life style determines how the person will pursue his goals throughout life. Adler said:

> By the end of the fifth year of life, a child has adopted a unified and crystallized pattern of behaviour, with his own distinct style of approaching problems and tasks which we would call his 'life style'. **He has already fixed his deepest and most lasting conception of what to expect from the world and from himself. From now on, the world is seen through an established scheme of apperception.** Experiences are interpreted before they are accepted, and the interpretation is always in accordance with the original meaning that the child has ascribed to life.[36] (Bold added.)

Adler confidently declared a theory of determinism when he wrote:

> By the end of the fifth year her personality has formed. The meaning she ascribes to life, the goal she pursues, her style of approach and her emotional disposition have all been determined.[37]

According to Adler this determinism is both universal and complete. No one escapes it and everything everyone does is determined by the life style created during the first five years of life. He wrote:

> Every crisis of adult life is met in accordance with our previous training: our response always conforms with out life style.[38]

Thus, according to Adler, the style of life, created during one's first five years of life, determines how one will attempt to reach one's goals.

The Unconscious

Adler also believed in a powerful unconscious filled with motivating material driving behavior. He contended that for many people, especially those who experience problems of living, the determining factors regarding goals and life style lie hidden in the unconscious. He believed that people are often unaware of how their early life perceptions are now determining their behavior. He wrote, "We may seek and find the behavior pattern of a man in the unconscious. In his conscious life we have but a reflection, a negative, to deal with."[39]

What a hopeless theory! Adler's theory is devoid of new life. It leaves people in the hopeless darkness of infantile perception. Nevertheless, Christians have taken Adler's ideas of the creative self, life style, and goal of superiority and added them to the Bible, supposing that Scripture alone cannot deal with the human condition.

Changing the Self Through Insight

Along with every secular theory of why people are the way they are, why they do what they do, and how they change is a methodology. Adler thought that through his psychological methods, people could gain insight into their unconscious and thereby overcome mistakes that were made in the early development of their life style. In fact, Adler believed that only his method could accomplish this task, for he said:

> It is **only** the individual-psychological method that can then throw light upon these phenomena of the unconscious and that can attempt to correct a false development.[40] (Bold added.)

Adler believed that the key to understanding a person was to be found in the meaning the person ascribed to life.[41] He said, "We experience reality only through the meaning we ascribe to it: not as a thing in itself, but as something interpreted."[42] Adler taught that, while all have a common goal of superiority and strivings for security and significance, "There are as many meanings ascribed to life as there are human beings and perhaps, as we have suggested, each meaning is mistaken to some extent."[43] Thus he taught that the task of the psychologist was to "find and understand the meaning a person ascribes to life" and to help the individual to gain a better understanding of his meaning in life and his goals and to find new meanings and thereby new means to the goals.[44]

But, how might one person know and understand the inner life of another person? Adler thought it was possible for specially trained people who were able to read people as one might read and interpret a poem. He wrote:

> Understanding a style of life is similar to understanding the work of a poet. . . . The greatest part of his meaning must be guessed at: we must read between the lines. So, too, with that profoundest and most intricate creation, an individual style of life. The psychologist must learn to read between the lines; he must learn the art of appreciating life-meanings.[45]

Adler's method of reading between the lines includes assembling and arranging the many puzzle pieces of memories and dreams. Thus, the Adlerian analyst is limited to his own subjective perception about the client's perceptions. To arrange all the components according to Adler's theoretical structure, one must "become an expert guesser."[46] All in all Adler's method was highly speculative even though he contended that what he did was science.[47] Adler admitted his true method: guessing and reading between the lines. Does that sound even remotely scientific? Is that a method Christians should use to understand each other's style of life and so-called unconscious motivation?

Memories and Dreams

Adler searched for an individual's meaning of life through memories and dreams. He said:

The greatest help of all, however, in unlocking the meaning an individual ascribes to himself and to life is his store of memories.[48]

He believed that the earliest memories were the most significant in discovering an individual's life style. He said, "The first memory will show the individual's fundamental view of life, her first satisfactory expression of her attitude." He declared, "I would never investigate a personality without asking for the first memory."[49] Adler firmly believed that talking about early childhood events could reveal a person's style of life and that if a person could understand his style and how it was not working he could change. He said, "Early memories are especially significant. To begin with, they show the life style in its origins and in its simplest expressions."[50]

While Adler primarily depended on an individual's memories to find out about the person's meaning in life and life style, it did not matter to him if the memories were even true. He said:

It is of no importance for the purposes of psychology whether the memory an individual considers the earliest is really the first event that he can remember—or even whether it is a memory of a real event. Memories are important only for what they represent, for their interpretation of life and their bearing on the present and future.[51]

He also said:

It is comparatively unimportant whether the memories are accurate or not; what is most valuable about them is the fact that they represent the individual's judgment.[52]

One has to wonder if truth meant anything to Adler. His teachings about the unimportance of whether or not memories are true have influenced countless therapists who do not care whether or not their clients' memories are true. This attitude on the part of therapists has unwittingly led many clients in the direction of false memories. Christians, on the other hand, should believe that the truth is extremely important. Jesus said, "If ye continue in my word, then are ye my disciples indeed; And ye shall know the truth, and the truth shall make you free" (John 8:31,32).

Besides working with memories, without caring whether they were true or not, Adler worked with dreams. He said: "Dreams offer us important insights into the problems of someone's emotional life."[53] What he looked for in dreams was not so much the content as the feeling tone. He wrote: "The aim of the dream is the feelings it leaves behind. The feelings an individual creates must always be consistent with his life style."[54] He explored clients' dreams to gain insight into the life style, because he believed that dreams serve to support that life style. He wrote:

> The purpose of the dream will be to support and reinforce the dreamer's life style, to arouse the feelings best suited to it. But why does the life style need support? What can possibly threaten it? It is vulnerable to attack from reality and common sense. The purpose of dreams, therefore, is to defend the life style against the demands of common sense.[55]

It is interesting to note that therapists will generally find what they are looking for in dream analysis, especially when the client wants to cooperate. Once clients understand what the therapists are looking for, they will dream accordingly. If the therapists are looking for childhood sexual abuse, the clients will have those kinds of dreams. If the therapists are looking for Jungian archetypes and symbols, the clients will have those kinds of dreams. However, this has more to do with suggestion and cooperation than with the validity of dream analysis.

The Adlerian Therapeutic Process

In Adlerian psychology, the first phase of therapy consists of the therapist establishing rapport with the patient. The second phase is devoted to learning "to understand the patient's life style and goal."[56] This consists of gaining insight into the client's motivations, his inner intentions, through guessing and reading between the lines. Adlerian therapy is generally long-term. After extensive analysis (speculation and guessing) to determine the life style, the therapist has to convince the client of his findings and then help him change through small increments of so-called insight over the months and even years of therapy. Adlerian case histories include such phrases as "A year went by," "almost two years into therapy," and "during the two and a half years of treatment."[57]

The Adlerian analyst does not work on behavior directly, but rather on meaning and on interpretation. Since Adler did not believe that what happens to a person determines behavior, but rather the person's interpretation is the determining factor, he contended that people will "never change their actions unless they change their interpretations."[58] He said:

> We must never treat one symptom or one single aspect of someone's personality. We must discover the wrong assumption the person has made in choosing her life style, the way her mind has interpreted her experiences, the meaning she has ascribed to life, and the actions with which she has responded to the impressions received from her body and from her environment.[59]

Looking for a person's style of life is a hunting expedition. This can be seen in case studies written by Adlerian therapists. Consistent in all of them is that the style of life is what the person does to reach his goal. The hunting expedition into an individual's past is fraught with subjective interpretation, imagination, speculation, and preconceived notions.

Both the therapist's imagination and the client's introspection are required in Adlerian psychology. Adler said: "Fundamental changes are produced only by means of an exceedingly high degree of introspection or among neurotics by means of the physician's individual psychological analysis."[60] He also said:

> Generally, the most effective way to revise an individual's life style is with the assistance of someone trained in psychology, in the understanding of these meanings, who can help him to discover the original error and suggest a more appropriate meaning.[61]

Thus the Adlerian-trained therapist must glean from bits and pieces of memories and dreams, come to a subjective understanding of what these might reveal about the client, and then convince the client to believe the interpretation and cooperate by making the appropriate changes in meaning. All this must be done in a way that fits Adler's theoretical framework.

While people may indeed change aspects of their lives through this kind of psychological therapy, they are limited to superficial change, not the deep inner change imagined by Adler. There is only one way to truly transform a person and that is God's way. Every other effort pales in comparison. Nevertheless Christians have turned to Adler's wisdom and watered down the power that they have in Christ for changing lives.

Adler's theories are human attempts to interpret what people do. They are at the same level of scientific validity as the collected, often contradictory notions of the now over 400 different psychological counseling approaches. It is possible to use any of those theoretical frameworks to view humanity, but they are merely the lenses of human interpretation, mainly based on the various theorists' own personal experiences. What Adler and others contributed are not simply objective observations about what people do. Instead, they sought through their own fallenness to see into the inner man.

Humanistic Goals

Although his Individual Psychology employs much introspection and concentrates a great deal of time on an individual's goals and life style, Adler also included social concern. In fact, as mentioned earlier, he believed that "true meaning of life depends on contribution and co-operation."[62] He said: "Only the individual who understands that life means contribution will be able to meet his difficulties with courage and with a good chance of success."[63] However, regarding those who approach problems in this seemingly giving manner, Adler says:

> They will say, "We must make our own lives. It is our own task and we are capable of performing it. We are masters of our own actions. If something new must be done or something old replaced, no one can do it but ourselves." If life is approached in this way, as a co-operation of independent human beings, there are no limits to the progress of our human civilization.[64]

The best Adler has to offer is godless humanism, a system to help people do a better job of creating their own life styles, a means of becoming one's own god.

Adler believed that where religion fails, his humanistic system will succeed. In reference to his statement about the true meaning of life depending upon contribution and cooperation, he wrote the following:

> There have always been people who understood this fact, who know that the meaning of life was to be interested in the whole of mankind, and who tried to develop social interest and love. In all religions, we find this concern for the salvation of mankind.[65]

Then he arrogantly declared:

> Individual Psychology arrives at the same conclusion in a scientific way and proposes a scientific method to achieve it. This, I believe, is a step forward.[66]

No wonder the apostle Paul warned believers about "science falsely so-called." But many have failed to heed Paul's warnings and have incorporated Adler's theories and methods into their own ministry. Adler's psychology is not a step forward, but a step backward right into the Garden of Eden, for he was echoing the serpent saying to Eve, "ye shall be as gods, knowing good and evil" (Genesis 3:5).

Adler's humanistic personality theory imputes to every person righteousness, humanitarianism, uniqueness, dignity, worth, and power to direct and change his own life.[67] Such a theory naturally arises out of an evolutionary viewpoint, in which the human is the most highly evolved being in the known universe.

As with the other self theorists, Adler left out God. He was a humanistic psychologist who placed man at the center and designed a doctrine of the creative self whereby man supposedly creates his own personality, gives meaning to life, and creates his own goals and means of reaching them.[68]

10

Erich Fromm Unconditional Love

Erich Fromm was trained in both sociology and psychoanalysis. As with Adler, Fromm's work was grounded in Freudian psychoanalytic theory but evolved into humanistic psychology. As both a sociologist and a psychologist he opposed all forms of authoritarian government, including God's. In fact, he portrayed the God of the Old Testament as a self-seeking authoritarian.

Fromm did not seek to understand the human condition from a position of faith in God or from a desire to understand and exegete God's Word. Instead, he was an atheist who argued against the fundamentals of the Christian faith. He was the psychoanalyst who taught the old Greek philosophy of Protagoras, that man is "the measure of all things."[1]

Fromm did not oppose religion as long as a person's god is merely a symbol for his own subjective idea of "the highest value, the most desirable good." Since Fromm did not believe that there is any Being who transcends the human, he said that "the specific meaning of God depends on what is the most desirable good for a person."[2] Not only did Fromm deny God's existence; he fought vehemently against the idea of God's sovereignty. Furthermore, he equated faith in God the Father with infantile behavior. He says:

> Quite obviously, the majority of people have, in their personal development, not overcome this infantile stage, and hence the belief in God to most people is the belief of a helping father—a childish illusion.[3]

Fromm taught that one must love himself, accept himself, and esteem himself to reach his highest potential. That is because he did not believe in God as a helping Father who loves His children and recreates them into the image of Christ. For him, such faith in God the Father was the "childish illusion" of those who had not overcome their infantile stage of development. Nevertheless many Christians knowingly or naively support Fromm's teachings on self-love.

Fromm's religion was secular humanism. While he recognized man's sense of separation, he rejected God's plan for reconciliation. He declares:

> Man—of all ages and cultures—is confronted with the solution of one and the same question: the question of how to overcome separateness, how to achieve union, how to transcend one's own individual life and find at-onement.[4]

Fromm substituted biblical atonement through Christ's death with the myth of a self-produced "at-onement." Instead of reconciliation with God, Fromm insisted that man's solution "to overcome separateness" is to be found within himself, through unconditional self-love, which he believed would enable individuals to love the whole world.

Fromm was an early proponent of unconditional love, which he equated with a mother's love, in contrast to conditional love, which he equated with a father's love. While he wrote about conditional/unconditional love in his earlier books, his clearest statements about this contrast are in his book *To Have or To Be*:

> The motherly principle is that of *unconditional love*; the mother loves her children not because they please her, but because they are her (or another woman's) children. For this reason the mother's love cannot be acquired by good behavior, nor can it be lost by sinning.[5]

> Fatherly love, on the contrary, is *conditional*; it depends on the achievements and good behavior of the child; father loves that child most who is most like him, i.e., whom he wishes to inherit his property. Father's love can be lost, but it can also be regained by repentance and renewed submission.[6] (Italics in original.)

Unconditional love and acceptance are now dominant teachings in the church. However, unconditional love is a myth. That is because the human is naturally self-biased and the human heart is so deceitful that one can fool himself into thinking that he is loving unconditionally, when in fact he has all kinds of conditions. For instance, what kind of unconditional love is at work when the client can no longer pay for services and therapy is discontinued?

In humanistic psychology, parents and society are always the culprits. Since they believe that every person is born with intrinsic worth and innate goodness, psychologists contend that one main reason people experience emotional and behavioral problems is because they have not received unconditional love from their parents. Following that thesis, Christians have come to believe that the best kind of love is unconditional love. It is the highest love secular humanists know. It is touted as a love that makes no demands for performance, good behavior, or the like. It has also been associated with a kind of permissiveness, even though the promoters of the unconditional love jargon would say that unconditional love does not have to dispense with discipline.

Because the concept of unconditional love permeates society and because it is often thought of as the highest form of human love, it is natural for a Christian to use this term to describe God. After all, His love is far greater than any human love imaginable. God's love is so great that "He gave His only begotten Son that whosoever believeth in Him should not perish, but have everlasting life" (John 3:16). Oh, the magnitude of the cost! We cannot even fathom His love even though our very breath depends upon it! His love indeed reaches to the heights and depths. Nevertheless, *unconditional* is a misleading term when used to describe God's love. The word is loaded with too many secular, humanistic, psychological connotations. God's love is so great that He gave His only begotten Son to pay the price and thereby to meet all the conditions.

Fromm also taught that the source of love is within the self. Rather than faith in God and in His love, Fromm insists, "What matters in relation to love is the faith in one's own love; in its ability to produce love in others, and in its reliability."[7] He says:

> Infantile love follows the principle: "*I love because I am loved.*" Mature love follows the principle: "*I am loved because I love.*"[8] (Italics his.)

He would identify all Christians as having infantile love, since the Christian's love is in response to God's love, as stated in 1 John 4:7 and 14:

> Beloved, let us love one another: for love is of God; and every one that loveth is born of God, and knoweth God. . . . We love Him, because He first loved us.

While the Bible declares that God, not self, is the source of love, Fromm called that kind of love "infantile." When he equated mature love with "I am loved because I love," he set up self as the source and self-love as the necessary beginning of love for others.

In spite of the fact that Fromm adamantly opposed the God of the Bible, he did not hesitate to use the Bible for his own cause. And yet, to do so, he misinterpreted it to fit his own scheme. Here is his twisted, secular humanistic interpretation of Matthew 22:39:

> If it is a virtue to love my neighbor as a human being, it must be a virtue—and not a vice—to love myself, since I am a human being too. There is no concept of man in which I myself am not included. A doctrine which proclaims such an exclusion proves itself to be intrinsically contradictory. The idea expressed in the Biblical "Love thy neighbor as thyself!" implies that respect for one's own integrity and uniqueness, love for and understanding of one's own self, can not be separated from respect for and love and understanding of another individual. The love for my own self is inseparably connected with the love for any other self.[9]

Fromm's seductive reasoning has been so successful that many people bend Scripture in the same way in order to justify self-love. However, a careful look at Matthew 22:37-40 does not support current self-love and self-esteem teachings.

> Jesus said unto him, Thou shalt love the Lord thy God with all thy heart, and with all thy soul, and with all thy mind. This is the first and great commandment. And the second is like unto it, Thou shalt love thy neighbour as thyself. On these two commandments hang all the law and the prophets.

Notice that Jesus gave only two commandments: to love God and others as much as one **already does** love himself. Then He said, "On these two commandments hang all the law and the prophets." On the other hand, those who attempt to use those verses to promote self-love and self-esteem have added a third commandment to Scripture. And such a commandment to love and esteem self is in direct contradiction to the entire thrust of Scripture.

While many Christians do not see the contradiction between the biblically-based theology and self-love/self-esteem psychology, Fromm certainly did! He quoted the following from Calvin's *Institutes* to illustrate the opposite of what he himself believed and taught.

> We are not our own; therefore let us not propose it as our end to seek what may be expedient for us according to the flesh. We are not our own; therefore, let us, as far as possible, forget ourselves and all things that are ours. On the contrary, we are God's; for Him therefore, let us live and die.[10]

Fromm contended that Calvin's doctrine was rooted in self-contempt and self-hatred. He used the same fallacy as many Christians do today in thinking that the only alternative to self-love is self-hatred. The biblical alternative to self-love is love in relationship with God and others. Self is already loved. Therefore the Bible emphasizes love for God and others. Teachings of self-love, self-acceptance, and self-esteem focus on the self.

The current teachings on self-love and self-esteem both inside and outside the church come from the broken cistern of self, not from God's Word. In contrast to Christianity, Fromm defines the "truly religious person" as one who "does not pray for anything, does not expect anything from God." He says that a "truly religious person . . . does not love God as a child loves his father or his mother." He then equates humility with unbelief, for he says that the "truly religious person" has "acquired the humility of sensing his limitations, to the degree of knowing that he knows nothing about God."[11] Thus faith in God is replaced by faith in self, and love for God is replaced by love for self. And in many ways, the self-love and self-esteem teachings in the church move in the same direction.

Fromm obviously did not understand the Bible. He did not even have the slightest understanding of the love of God or the truth of the Gospel of Jesus Christ. He saw the God of the Bible as a cruel dictator who drove Cain to murder Abel. Here is Fromm's interpretation of Genesis:

> The Biblical report of Cain's crime and punishment offers a classic illustration of the fact that what man is most afraid of is not punishment but rejection. God accepted Abel's offerings but did not accept Cain's. Without giving any reason, God did to Cain the worst thing that can be done to a man who can not live without being acceptable to an authority. He refused his offering and thus rejected him. The rejection was unbearable for Cain, so Cain killed the rival who had deprived him of the indispensable. What was Cain's punishment? He was not killed or even harmed; as a matter of fact, God forbade anyone to kill him (the mark of Cain was meant to protect him from being killed). His punishment was to be made *an outcast;* after God had rejected him, he was then separated from his fellow men. This punishment was indeed one of which Cain had to say: "My punishment is greater than I can bear."[12] (Italics in original.)

Fromm saw God as evil and Cain as a helpless victim. But the Lord says: "Yet the children of thy people say, The way of the Lord is not equal: but as for them, their way is not equal" (Ezekiel 33:17).

Fromm's notions about God represent the kind of theology that is at the root of the self-love, self-acceptance and self-esteem teachings that have been brought into the church. One cannot separate the teachings of self-love, self-acceptance and self-esteem from their rotten source. While current self-teachings may appear wonderfully loving, they are as deceptive as the serpent in the Garden. They come from the same source and ultimately deny Christ. As much as psychology lovers say that their self-love and self-esteem teachings do not contradict Scripture, the entire thrust of Scripture is toward loving God and others. Self does not need any encouragement to be concerned about and to pay attention to itself.

11

Abraham Maslow Need Psychology

Along with Carl Rogers, Abraham Maslow is considered by many to be one of the founders of humanistic psychology.[1] Maslow began his work in behavioral psychology, in which he studied reactions of laboratory animals. He regarded himself as both a psychoanalyst and behaviorist,[2] and one can see the influence of both in his writings even as he moved into the humanistic stream under the influence of Erich Fromm.[3] While Maslow carried vestiges of psychoanalytic and behavioristic theory into his work and even though his later interest was in transpersonal psychology, he is best known for his humanistic psychology and especially for his "hierarchy of needs" model.

Maslow believed that contemporary religions of his day, including Judaism and Christianity, had "proven to be failures . . . nothing worth dying for."[4] Yet he was convinced that a "human being needs a framework of values, a philosophy of life, a religion or religion surrogate to live by and understand by."[5] Thus he presented his own philosophy of life, framework of values, and humanistic religion.

As with other secular humanists, Maslow believed in an innate goodness of man at his very core. In contrast to the Scriptures, which say that foolishness is bound up in the heart of a child, Maslow contended that when a child develops normally "he will choose what is good for his growth."[6] Maslow taught that a child "knows better than anyone else what is good for him" and that adults should "not interfere too much . . . but rather *let* them grow and help them grow in a Taoistic rather than an authoritarian way."[7] (Italics in original.)

Maslow wanted to study healthy people. He said, "Freud supplied to us the sick half of psychology and we must now fill it out with the healthy half."[8] Just as with many humanistic psychologists, Maslow did not entirely abandon Freudian theory. He firmly believed in a powerful Freudian-like unconscious that motivates behavior outside a person's awareness. He said:

> It is not necessary at this point to overhaul the tremendous mass of evidence that indicates the crucial importance of unconscious motivation. . . . What we have called the basic needs are often largely unconscious although they may, with suitable techniques, and with sophisticated people, become conscious.[9]

He also believed, along with Freud, in a powerful, motivating unconscious filled with everything that ever happened to a person.

> The serious thing for each person to recognize vividly and poignantly, each for himself, is that every falling away from species-virtue, every crime against one's own nature, every evil act, *every one without exception records itself* in our unconscious

and makes us despise ourselves.[10] (Italics in original.)

This model of the mind as recorder and receptacle of everything has since been discredited in the research.

Maslow's Hierarchy of Needs

Maslow taught that people are motivated by their needs in an hierarchical order, beginning with physiological (bodily) needs, such as the need for food. According to his system, the levels proceed up the scale from bodily needs to safety needs (protection, security), to love needs (affection, friendship, belonging), to esteem needs (respect, approval), and finally to the need to self-actualize (to develop to one's highest potential). As each level is satisfied to a certain degree, a person will supposedly be motivated by the so-called needs of the next level. For instance, according to Maslow's system, if a person's bodily and safety needs are fairly well met, he will be motivated by the so-called needs of the next level, the need for love. Then when that need is met to a certain degree he will be motivated by his so-called need for approval, and so forth.

Maslow's terminology reveals the influences of behaviorism and evolutionism as he discussed physiological needs and said:

> If all the needs are unsatisfied, and the **organism** is then dominated by the physiological needs, all other needs may become simply nonexistent or be pushed into the background . . . . But what happens to man's desires when there is plenty of bread and when his belly is chronically filled?
>
> *At once other (and higher) needs emerge* and these, rather than physiological hungers, dominate the **organism**. And when these in turn are satisfied, again new (and still higher) needs emerge, and so on. This is what we mean by saying that the basic

human needs are organized into a hierarchy of relative prepotency.[11] (Italics in original, bold added.)

Notice that Maslow referred to the human being as an organism. Yet, according to Maslow, as the person proceeds through the hierarchy, the organism becomes almost godlike as he reaches self-actualization and finally transcendence, which he refers to as "divine or godlike."[12] By divine or godlike he does not imply a supernatural being, but rather something that is "part of human nature . . . a potentiality of human nature."[13] In Maslow's hierarchy, needs motivate people to evolve from organisms teeming with potential to godlike creatures as various needs are met at various levels.

While Maslow taught that people are motivated by the basic needs of his hierarchy, he was not totally rigid about one right after the other up the scale. He said that "most behavior is multimotivated" and that:

> Within the sphere of motivational determinants any behavior tends to be determined by several or *all* of the basic needs simultaneously rather than by only one of them.[14] (Emphasis in original.)

Nevertheless, he was certain about the importance of each level of need.

Referring to love needs, Maslow declared, "In our society the thwarting of these needs is the most commonly found core in cases of maladjustment and more severe psychopathology."[15] He wrote:

> Love hunger is a deficiency disease. . . . The healthy person, not having this deficiency, does not need to receive love except in steady, small, maintenance doses and he may even do without these for periods of time.[16]

Maslow also contended that self-esteem is a universal need. He stated:

> All people in our society (with a few pathological exceptions) have a need or desire for a stable, firmly

based, usually high evaluation of themselves, for self-respect, or self-esteem, and for the esteem of others. These needs may therefore be classified into two subsidiary sets. These are, first, the desire for strength, for achievement, for adequacy, for mastery and competence, for confidence in the face of the world, and for independence and freedom. Second, we have what we may call the desire for reputation or prestige (defining it as respect or esteem from other people), status, dominance, recognition, attention, importance, or appreciation.[17]

He further taught:

Satisfaction of the self-esteem need leads to feelings of self-confidence, worth, strength, capability, and adequacy, of being useful and necessary in the world. But thwarting of these needs produces feelings of inferiority, of weakness, and of helplessness. These feelings in turn give rise to either basic discouragement or else compensatory or neurotic trends.[18]

Maslow emphasized self-esteem in spite of negative results. He contrasted two types:

Person A, who has both personal strength and love for his fellow man, will naturally use his strength in a fostering, kindly, or protecting fashion. But B, who has equal strength but has with it hate, contempt, or fear for his fellow man, will more likely use his strength to hurt, to dominate, or to assuage his insecurity. His strength must then be a threat to his fellows. Thus we may speak of an insecure quality of high self-esteem, and we may contrast it with a secure quality of high self-esteem.[19]

Maslow thought the reason for the difference was in the person's security level.

In addition to the bodily, safety, love, and esteem needs, Maslow saw yet another need that must be fulfilled and that was the need for what he called "self-actualization," which he defined as "man's desire for self-fulfillment, namely, to the tendency for him to become actualized in what he is potentially," that is, to reach his highest potential.[20] He said:

> So far as motivational status is concerned, healthy people have sufficiently gratified their basic needs for safety, belongingness, love, respect and self-esteem so that they are motivated primarily by trends to self-actualization (defined as ongoing actualization of potentials, capacities and talents, as fulfillment of mission (or call, fate, destiny, or vocation), as a fuller knowledge of, and acceptance of, the person's own intrinsic nature, as an unceasing trend toward unity, integration or synergy within the person).[21]

Maslow believed that when a person is motivated at the higher levels of need gratification, society would benefit. He said:

> *The pursuit and the gratification of the higher needs have desirable civic and social consequences. . . .* People who have enough basic satisfaction to look for love and respect (rather than just food and safety) tend to develop such qualities as loyalty, friendliness, and civic consciousness, and to become better parents, husbands, teachers, public servants, etc.[22] (Italics in original.)

Therefore, according to Maslow, doing unto others is motivated by gratification of one's own so-called needs at whatever level they seem to appear.

Maslow saw everything in human terms, as if humans in and of themselves possess all that is necessary for growth and change. He wrote:

> To make growth and self-actualization possible, it is necessary to understand that capacities, organs and organ systems press to function and express themselves and to be used and exercised, and that such use is satisfying, and disuse irritating . . . .

Capacities clamor to be used and cease their clamor only when they *are* well used. That is, capacities are also needs.[23] (Italics in original.)

Because Maslow refused to recognize the Creator, he believed that all resources for need gratification and self-actualization resided within the human.

Utopia Beyond the Reaches of Human Nature

Maslow looked forward to a type of Utopia of self-actualized persons. In *New Pathways in Psychology* Colin Wilson says Maslow "felt that a sane, healthy society should not be a utopian dream—that the *nature of things as they are* means that it is perfectly possible under present circumstances."[24] (Italics in original.) When he wrote *Motivation and Personality* (1954), Maslow was highly optimistic about his system. He envisioned how wonderful the world would be when more and more needs would be gratified in more and more people. His illustration reveals his optimism about our society:

> . . . most members of our society who are normal are partially satisfied in all their basic needs and partially unsatisfied in all their basic needs at the same time. A more realistic description of the hierarchy would be in terms of decreasing percentages of satisfaction as we go up the hierarchy of prepotency. For instance, if I may assign arbitrary figures for the sake of illustration, it is as if the average citizen is satisfied perhaps 85 percent in his physiological needs, 70 percent in his safety needs, 50 percent in his love needs, 40 percent in his self-esteem needs, and 10 percent in his self-actualization needs.[25]

However, by the time he wrote *Toward a Psychology of Being* he was beginning to see that in spite of all the psychology and the apparent amount of need gratification, his theory of self-actualization was not working as expected. He wrote:

> Though, in principle, self-actualization is easy, in
> practice it rarely happens (by my criteria, certainly
> in less than 1% of the adult population).[26]

But, Maslow did not blame the failure on his own godless
system. Instead, he placed the blame on the Bible and
biology when he wrote:

> We have already mentioned one main cultural
> reason, i.e., the conviction that man's intrinsic
> nature is evil or dangerous, and one biological deter-
> minant for the difficulty of achieving a mature self,
> namely that humans no longer have strong instincts
> which tell them unequivocally what to do, when,
> where and how.[27]

It is interesting that he not only blames Christian
teachings about the Fall in the Garden of Eden; he also
rejects the God of the Bible who has given His Word to do
what instinct does not do—that is, to authoritatively
guide and direct the individual as to "what to do, when,
where and how." In spite of all of his talk about personal
freedom and autonomy, it appears Maslow would have
preferred instinct-driven robots to Spirit-directed Christians.

Even though he had to make some adjustments to his
earlier theories, Maslow continued his optimism for
discovering a psychology of health. He wrote in his introduction to the second edition of *Toward A Psychology of
Being*:

> There is now emerging over the horizon a new con-
> ception of human sickness and of human health, a
> psychology that I find so thrilling and so full of
> wonderful possibilities that I yield to the temptation
> to present it publicly even before it is checked out
> and confirmed, and before it can be called reliable
> scientific knowledge.[28]

Following that he listed "basic assumptions of this point
of view." These include his belief that each person has "an
essential biologically based inner nature," which can be

studied "scientifically," and which is intrinsically "good or neutral rather than bad."[29] He said:

> Perhaps we shall soon be able to use as our guide and model the fully growing and self-fulfilling human being, the one in whom all his potentialities are coming to full development, the one whose inner nature expresses itself freely, rather than being warped, suppressed, or denied.[30]

Because Maslow did not believe in the biblical doctrine of original sin, he had to find an explanation for evil. He thought he found the answer to evil in what he referred to as the "huge, rich, and illuminating literature of dynamic psychology and psychopathology, a great store of information on man's weaknesses, and fears." He declared:

> We know much about *why* men do wrong things, *why* they bring about their own unhappiness and their self-destruction, *why* they are perverted and sick. And out of this has come the insight that human evil is largely (though not altogether) human weakness or ignorance, forgivable, understandable, and also curable.[31] (Italics in original.)

According to Maslow, evil is the result of ignorance and weakness. His solution to conquering evil was giving knowledge to help people gain ego-strength. He wrote, "Self-knowledge seems to be the major path of self-improvement," and although "self-knowledge and self-improvement are very difficult for most people . . . the help of a skilled professional therapist makes this process much easier."[32] In other words, knowledge makes all the difference, but since people protect themselves from any self-knowledge that might lower their self-esteem, they may need a therapist to help them face truths about themselves.[33]

Nevertheless Maslow admitted a shortcoming of therapy when he wrote:

The higher the need level the easier and more effective psychotherapy can be: at the lowest need levels it is of hardly any avail.[34] (Italics in original.)

Here again is an admission that talk therapy works best for those who need it least. In contrast, God is involved at every level of need and in every aspect of a person's growth.

Self-Actualization Actualized

Maslow's dream for a Utopia inhabited with self-actualized persons of high self-esteem was realized in the Haight-Ashbury district of San Francisco, as the flower children of the sixties took his theories to heart and lived a life of free love and self-gratification. Maslow did not teach self-indulgence, but that can be the result of any system which emphasizes the self, presupposes the goodness of the human, and claims that people will develop their highest potential if so-called needs are met.

Adrianne Aron describes this problem in "Maslow's Other Child." She says:

> To examine some of the more menacing aspects of a pursuit of self-actualization that disregards political and ethical matters, I shall discuss here the dominant social pattern of the hippie movement in its early days. In the hippie pattern Maslow's dream of a compassionate, reciprocal, empathic, high-synergy scheme of interpersonal relations gets lost behind a reality of human exploitation. Where the theorist prescribed self-actualization the hippies produced mainly self-indulgence. Yet, I shall argue, the hippie result is not alien to the Maslovian theory, for when the relationship between self and society is left undefined and unattended by a theory of self-development, one social pattern is as likely to emerge as another.[35]

Because of the heavy focus on self and its so-called needs and because external standards are looked down on in humanistic psychology, a dangerous type of tolerance follows. Aron says:

> In the hippie view, true toleration demands a respect for the inviolability of each idiosyncratic way of coping with the world. . . . One of the ways the hippies hoped to eliminate intolerance was by making no judgments. . . . Hence people worked at developing flexibility and broadmindedness, unaware that suspension of judgment would inevitably lead to exploitation, either of their own trusting selves or of other seemingly free spirits. Without judgment, there was nowhere to place blame, and without blame, there was no way to assign responsibility or to differentiate between good and bad behavior.[36]

Humanistic teachings of unconditional acceptance were also shown for what they really are. Aron says:

> The tendency to accept oneself and others unconditionally, as they are, laying no stress and placing no contingency on what they might become, is to take away from the individual incentives for struggle and personal growth. In various forms hippie interviews echo Maslow's prescription, "Do you want to find out what you ought to be? Then find out who you are!"[37]

In their well-reasoned book *Psychology's Sanction for Selfishness*, Dr. Michael and Lise Wallach say:

> Maslow and Rogers certainly want people to be caring and helpful to one another, to pursue common goals, to try to deal with the problems of their communities and broader groups. But what they advocate seems designed rather to prevent this than to bring it about. . . . If we are always to be determined by what is within rather than outside ourselves, if we are always first and foremost to seek our own growth and actualization, this inevitably seems to push toward concern for the self at the expense of others.[38]

Dr. William R. Coulson, a former colleague of Carl Rogers and Abraham Maslow, says that in his later years Maslow did not agree with much of what he had theorized in his earlier years. Unfortunately Maslow did not make corrections loud enough for people to hear. His hierarchy of needs and related theories were already accepted as a system and people were enamored with it. And, one of the most dangerous places it was being used was on children. Yet Coulson says:

> In truth, he [Maslow] finally believed children *mustn't* be brought under the self-actualization umbrella. Their purchasing power was something new in history; couple it with parents who were falling for the new permissiveness and it made for great danger. Humanistic psychology was actually helping to make children vulnerable to exploitation. Giving direction was being left to family outsiders.[39] (Italics his.)

Coulson also demonstrates how Maslow tried to curb the enthusiasm over developing high self-esteem. Coulson refers to the second edition of *Motivation and Personality* where Maslow reported:

> The high scorers in my test of dominance-feeling or self-esteem were more apt to come late to appointments with the experimenter, to be less respectful, more casual, more forward, more condescending, less tense, anxious, and worried, more apt to accept an offered cigarette, much more apt to make themselves comfortable without bidding or invitation.
>
> In still another research, their sexual reactions were found to be even more sharply different. The stronger [high self-esteem] woman is much more apt to be pagan, permissive, and accepting in all sexual realms. She is less apt to be a virgin, more apt to have masturbated, more apt to have had sexual relations with more than one man, much more apt to have tried such experiments as homosexuality,

cunnilingus, fellatio, and anal sexuality. In other words, here too she is apt to be more forward, less inhibited, tougher, harder, stronger.[40]

In other words, Maslow discovered that satisfying the so-called self-esteem needs did **not** produce the desired results. And that is the problem with so many of the self theories. They begin with fallen flesh and simply end up with another face of fallen flesh. Christians who use Maslow's teachings seem to ignore these results.

The Religion of Psychology

When he did not find his utopian dream fulfilled in humanistic psychology, Maslow moved into transpersonal psychology, which is a godless spiritual psychology. All the while rejecting God, Maslow wrote:

> These psychologies give promise of developing into the life-philosophy, the religion-surrogate, the value-system, the life-program that these people have been missing. Without the transcendent and the transpersonal, we get sick, violent, and nihilistic, or else hopeless and apathetic. We need something "bigger than we are" to be awed by and to commit ourselves to in a new, naturalistic, empirical, non-churchly sense, perhaps as Thoreau and Whitman, William James and John Dewey did.[41]

While recognizing that people need something bigger than themselves, Maslow held that "truth in unrighteousness" (Romans 1:18) and "changed the truth of God into a lie, and worshipped and served the creature more than the Creator" (Romans 1:25). Maslow rejected the God of the Bible and foolishly hoped to find this "something bigger" through transpersonal psychology.

Besides replacing the biblical doctrine of man, Maslow offered a new religion with values and peak experiences. Through his influence, even Christians have embraced humanistic values, which appeal to human pride. Maslow believed that one could form a "descriptive, naturalistic science of human values" and thereby discover "which values men trend toward, yearn for, struggle for, as they improve themselves, and which values they lose as they get sick." He contended that these values "are intrinsic in the structure of human nature itself, that they are biologically and [genetically] based, as well as culturally developed."[42] He believed in "the existence of the highest values within human nature" and boldly declared:

> This is in sharp contradiction to the older and more customary beliefs that the highest values can come only from a supernatural God, or from some other source outside human nature itself.[43]

Along with humanistic values and notions about how people can live productive, satisfying lives, Maslow offered a substitute religious experience he variously called the "core-religious experience," "transcendent experience," and "peak-experience."[44]

Maslow reduced Christian conversion experiences to peak-experiences common to all religions and also available without faith in God or in any religion. He hypothesized: "to the extent that all mystical or peak-experiences are the same in their essence and have always been the same, all religions are the same in their essence and always have been the same."[45] Maslow not only believed that such experiences were very important in human development; he also believed they could be investigated scientifically:

> In the last few years it has become quite clear that certain drugs called "psychedelic," especially LSD and psilocybin, give us some possibility of control in this realm of peak-experiences. . . . Perhaps we can actually produce a private personal peak-experience under observation and whenever we wish under religious or non-religious circumstances. We may then be able to study in its moment of birth the experience of illumination or revelation.[46]

Besides proposing to induce peak-experiences for observation purposes, Maslow suggested the possibility of using LSD to produce peak-experiences in people who might appear to benefit. He wrote:

> Even more important, it may be that these drugs, and perhaps also hypnosis, could be used to produce a peak-experience, with core-religious revelation, in non-peakers, thus bridging the chasm between these two separated halves of mankind.[47]

His book *The Farther Reaches of Human Nature*, which was published after his death, illustrates how humanistic psychology moves into the transpersonal realm. In that book he wrote about peak experiences, mysticism, Taoistic receptivity, unitive consciousness, transcending time and space, and Eastern religious influences. But what is seen as sacred and divine is not the God of the Bible, but rather the human and his potential. He declared:

> . . . any full perception of any woman or man includes their God and Goddess, priest and priestess possibilities, and mysteries embodied in and shining through the actual and limited human individuals before one's eyes: what they stand for, what they could be, what they remind us of, what we can be poetic about.[48]

Maslow's thinking moved right into the new age movement. In an article from *The 1988 Guide to New Age Living*, Jonathan Adolph wrote:

> Perhaps the most influential ideas to shape contemporary new age thinking were those that grew out of humanistic psychology and the human potential movement of the 60's and 70's. The fundamental optimism of new age thinking, for example, can be traced to psychologists such as Carl Rogers and Abraham Maslow.[49]

Maslow placed his hope in man instead of God. His theories of self followed the deterioration described in Romans 1:

> Because that, when they knew God, they glorified him not as God, neither were thankful; but became vain in their imaginations, and their foolish heart was darkened. Professing themselves to be wise, they became fools, And changed the glory of the uncorruptible God into an image made like to corruptible man . . . and worshipped and served the creature more than the Creator . . . (Romans 1:21-23, 26).

12

Carl Rogers Client-Centered Therapy

One of the best-known and most admired humanistic psychologists of the twentieth century is Dr. Carl Rogers. Rogers spent a lifetime studying human behavior and developed a technique of treatment called "nondirective" or "client-centered" therapy. It is nondirective in that the therapist does not lead the client's attention to any topic or material. The client chooses. It is client-centered in that it proposes to allow the client to have his own insights and to make his own interpretations rather than looking to the therapist to provide the insights and interpretations.

Carl Rogers, in his nondirective therapy, claims that he does not influence the client in any way. Because the person expresses himself any way he chooses, many believe nondirective therapy is value-free. However, Jay Haley says:

> Actually nondirective therapy is a misnomer. To state that any communication between two people can be nondirective is to state an impossibility.[1]

Without intending to do so, a counselor will communicate some response and thus influence the client's thoughts, words, and actions.[2] Two independent studies, conducted ten years apart, showed that Rogers himself was, in fact, a directive counselor.[3] His response to his clients rewarded and punished and therefore reinforced or extinguished certain expressions of the clients. If Rogers cannot be nondirective, it is certainly unlikely that any other psychotherapist or counselor can refrain from being directive in one way or another. The therapist's values will seep through any system and influence clients.

Rogers developed a theory of personality called the "self theory," which assumes that everyone has the ability to change and that everyone has a measure of freedom for self-direction and growth. He placed great importance on the uniqueness of the individual. His view of human nature is positive, which was a welcome contrast to the negative and deterministic view of man presented by both the psychoanalytic and behavioristic models.

The self theory with its positive possibilities came during a time of material affluence but spiritual emptiness. Rogers' theory seemed to fill the emptiness and provide new hope to match the new affluence. It emphasized the kind of personal values and self-determination that permitted one to enjoy the material prosperity more fully.

Besides emphasizing the innate goodness of man, Rogers saw self as central, in that each person lives in his own special world of experience, in which he is the center and forms his own judgments and values. Although Rogers placed strong emphasis upon values for guiding behavior and for living a meaningful life, he taught that these values should be based upon internal, individual decisions rather than blind acceptance of values in one's environment. In self theory, all experiences are evaluated in relation to the individual's self-concept.

Rogers believed that a person's inner tendencies are toward what he called "self-actualization," which he identified as the basic force motivating the person. Through self-actualization, the person tries to maintain his personhood and strives to grow towards a greater sense of fulfillment in relation to his self-concept and in relation to how other people relate to him. Rogers believed that the natural man's basic inner direction is towards health and wholeness.

Rogers and Christianity

Important to Rogers' self theory is his view of Christianity. Christianity was not foreign to Rogers. He described himself as "the middle child in a large, close-knit family, where hard work and a highly conservative Protestant Christianity were about equally revered."[4] At one time he attended Union Theological Seminary and he confessed that during a seminar he, as well as others, "thought themselves right out of religious work."[5] He felt that on the one hand he would probably always be interested in the "questions as to the meaning of life,"[6] but on the other hand he said, "I could not work in a field where I would be required to believe in some specified religious doctrine."[7] Obviously he saw Christianity as having requirements rather than privileges.

Rogers explained, "I wanted to find a field in which I could be sure my freedom of thought would not be limited."[8] He did not want to be what he calls "limited" by biblical dogma, but by his very act he set up another kind of dogma. Instead of an external dogma (Bible), he set up an internal dogma (self). He restricted himself by refusing Christianity. His refusal of Christian doctrine placed restrictions upon his own thought and influenced his entire work. Rogers eventually became involved in spiritism, consulted the Ouija board, and even became involved in necromancy.[9]

We will first examine how his rejection of Christianity colors his theories; then we will consider three important ideas which he discovered during his career and compare them with biblical principles. Basically, some of Rogers' theory and therapy sounds biblical, without giving credit to the Bible, but other parts are absolutely contrary to Scripture.

Rogers received enough Christianity to deny determinism but not enough to escape self-exaltation. He rejected the external authority of Scripture and established an internal authority of self. This rejection changed the course of his career from theology to psychology and from worshiping God to worshiping self. His psychological theories exalt self rather than God. The apostle Paul describes this move from serving God to serving self in the first chapter of Romans. Paul says that men "changed the truth of God into a lie, and worshipped and served the creature more than the Creator" (Romans 1:25).

Rogers is to be commended for his break with psychoanalytic and behavioristic determinism, but not for his self theory. Steeped in the philosophy of humanism, Rogers believed in the basic goodness of man, and his system establishes the self as the final authority rather than God. His avoidance of religious dogma was a rejection of external authority and placed self at the center of all experience. Rogers stressed freedom of choice based on each person's internal value system, rather than on the external authority of Scripture. The value system focuses upon the earthly and immediate rather than on the heavenly and eternal. It is based upon the natural without regard to the supernatural and divine.

For the Christian, the Word of God is supreme; for the self theorist, the word of self is supreme. When the self is thus exalted, the biblical concept of sin goes out the window and is replaced by another concept of sin, which is based on standards established by self. Although

Rogers can be commended for recognizing the uniqueness of man, he rejected the universality of sin.

The concept of self-actualization sounds quite lofty and wonderful, but it is merely a disguise for self-indulgence. Self theory has self at the center of all things, and this position of self has been and always will be contrary to Scripture. We live in a God-centered (theocentric) universe with theocratic rule, not in a self-centered (egocentric) universe with egocratic rule.

Rogers' Three "Discoveries"

Rogers claimed to have discovered three important principles during his lifetime of studying human behavior and practicing his therapy.[10] The first principle is that of listening. He pointed out that people have a real need to be heard and that seemingly unbearable problems become bearable when someone listens. He further believed that a sense of utter loneliness occurs when no one listens.

There is no question that listening is a vital response. However, this "fact of psychotherapy," newly "discovered" by Rogers, was long known and used by the church. James wrote to the early church, ". . . let every man be swift to hear, slow to speak, slow to wrath" (1:19). This is a necessary function of every man, not a special gift given only to a chosen few.

Rogers did seemingly discover something of value, but it was a simulation of Scripture rather than the truth of God. One need not follow Rogers into the web of self theory just because of one truth which sounds biblical. Rogers completely omitted the crucial concept of listening to God and of His response of listening to our words, our thoughts, and our unspoken yearnings.

Rogers' second important principle is "to be real." By this he meant being oneself and not playing a role or being phony. Being honest with oneself and others is a principle found throughout Scripture. For instance, the writer of Hebrews says, "Pray for us: for we trust we have a good conscience, in all things willing to live honestly"

(13:18). Paul exhorted believers to "walk honestly" (I Thessalonians 4:12). He encouraged servants to serve "not with eyeservice, as menpleasers; but as the servants of Christ, doing the will of God from the heart" (Ephesians 6:6). The Bible teaches that God looks upon the heart, the real inner person, and that people are to be honest and true. Being unreal is a form of deception and false witness; being unreal is labeled sin in the Bible.

Although both Rogers and the Bible encourage a person to be real, do Rogers' concepts harmonize with the Bible on this basic principle? If by "being real" Rogers meant following whatever internal value system one has developed, good or bad, his form of being real is not biblical truth; it is just another form of self-deception which could lead to disaster.

Attached to Rogers' principle "to be real" is his concept of "unconditional self-regard," which is merely a euphemism for self-love. Rogers said that unconditional self-regard occurs when the person "perceives himself in such a way that no self experience can be discriminated as more or less worthy of positive regard than any other."[11] According to Rogers, the individual becomes the "locus of evaluation," the final authority and evaluator of all experience.

After much research in the area of human judgment, Hillel Einhorn and Robin Hogarth point out the paradox of a person's high confidence in his own judgment in spite of its unreliability. They bemoan the fact that, because of a person's tendency to rely on his own fallible judgment, theories such as Rogers,' which totally depend upon a person's subjective perception and evaluation, will continue to be popular.[12]

Rogers' system puts self in the position to say such things as "I am the one that evaluates all experiences and I am the one who sets up my own value system. Nothing is in and of itself more valuable than anything else unless I say so." This is surely contrary to Scripture, because it eliminates the Bible and sets up self as the center of authority and the creator of values. Rogers rejected the biblical doctrine of being real and substituted a false doctrine, which eliminates the Bible as the source of truth and denies the biblical concept of sin.

Rogers' third important principle, which he considered to be his crowning discovery, is that of "love between persons." When Jesus was asked, "Which is the great commandment in the law?" He answered:

> Thou shalt love the Lord thy God with all thy heart, and with all thy soul, and with all thy mind. This is the first and great commandment. And the second is like unto it, Thou shalt love thy neighbour as thyself (Matthew 22:37-39).

Jesus further said to His disciples, "Love one another, as I have loved you" (John 15:12). In addition, 1 Corinthians 13 ends: "And now abideth faith, hope, charity [love], these three; but the greatest of these is charity [love]." Love is one of the most obvious and repeated principles in all Scripture.

Before we criticize or compliment Rogers, we need to understand what he meant by "love between persons." Rogers was only speaking about human love. While human love is an admirable virtue, it does not compare with divine love. Human love without the divine is merely another form of self-love. Divine love, on the other hand, encompasses all the qualities listed in 1 Corinthians 13. Rogers was only speaking of love between humans. He ignored the great commandment to "love the Lord thy God." Moreover, he never mentioned God's love, which is demonstrated throughout the Bible.

Rogers' crowning discovery is a limited human love between persons, which excludes the love of God and love for God. In excluding God, Rogers set up me, myself, and I as the evaluator and prioritizer of all experiences. The self, rather than God, becomes the center of the universe, and love apart from God becomes only a self-rewarding activity. In leaving out God, Rogers ended up with a love between persons, which is hardly more than a feeble extension of self-love.

Here is an example of the kind of love which Rogers advocated:

> The man of the future . . . will be living his transient life mostly in temporary relationships . . . he must be able to establish closeness quickly. He must be able to leave these close relationships behind without excessive conflict or mourning.[13]

Obviously love between persons is not intended to be for the sake of Christ or for the sake of the other person, but rather for the sake of self. When one leaves out the God of love and the love for God, he is left with love as a self-centered activity.

Any important ideas about the human condition did not originate with Rogers. They have always existed. Rogers merely found three principles that are superficial substitutes for the deep divine principles of Scripture.

In both theory and therapy, Rogers managed to elevate self to the position of being a god. With self at the center of the universe and God completely ignored, self theory exists as a counterfeit religion. Self theory is an influential system that wears an effective disguise. As any convincing counterfeit, it may look like the real thing, but in reality it is essentially contrary to Scripture.

Rogers' Broad Influence

Rogers has profoundly influenced society through his personality theories and "client-centered therapy." His ideas and methods became extremely popular, not only in the therapeutic world, but also in the church. E. Brooks Holifield describes Rogers' influence on pastoral counseling in his book *A History of Pastoral Care in America: From Salvation to Self-Realization*. He says:

> Rogers offered a method of counseling that could be taught—or at least introduced—in the brief period available in the seminary curriculum. . . . But Rogers was popular with the religious liberals because they liked his optimistic image of the self as

capable of growth and change, because their distaste for moralistic legalism corresponded to his notion that conventional social expectations inhibited the true self.[14]

Rogers' influence has not been limited to the liberal end of the religious continuum. His ideas have also filtered into the most conservative, evangelical seminaries and churches through the broad acceptance of psychological presuppositions, such as self-love, self-esteem, and self-acceptance (unconditional positive regard).

Rogers did not limit his concern to psychological counseling, but believed that all people could benefit from therapy. Therefore, he and his protégé William Coulson introduced group therapy into children's classrooms. After founding the Center for Studies of the Person in La Jolla, California, they organized encounter groups and developed a therapy-type of school program. Like many self-esteem movements, their goal was to counteract drugs.

Since Rogers believed that to be real, the self must operate according to its own internal value system, he and Coulson worked to help children replace external values (from parents, etc.) with internal values (indirectly influenced by the teachers/leaders). Since that time Coulson has seen the horrendous error of the work. Rather than helping children develop strong moral fiber to resist drugs, just the reverse happened. Not only did the groups destroy learning, in that they spent more time in "group" than in the three R's, but they also destroyed the moral fiber of both the children and the teachers/leaders.[15]

Similar values clarification programs continue to exist and undermine values already established by parents. It is interesting to note that values clarification programs also focus on building self-image, self-esteem, self-love, and self-acceptance. The 1989 California State Conference on Self-Esteem included the Center for Self-Esteem and the Values Clarification Institute. There is a close connection between self-esteem and being one's own standard for right and wrong. When there is no external code of ethics higher than the child's internal feelings, permissiveness reigns.

Instead of using the Bible as the standard of evaluation, the subjective self is the standard. That is mankind's natural condition; that is mankind's fallen condition. The entire self-esteem movement is an activity of fallen humanity. When parents are encouraged to build self-esteem in their children they are abetting the ways of fallen humanity, ways to be one's own king and judge, and ways to be one's own little god.

Even people who may have nothing to do with Rogers' "client-centered therapy" may be living according to some of Rogers' "discoveries." In doing so they are practicing another religion, because the self-love/self-esteem movement is religious. While it may not include the entire religion of secular humanism, it is nevertheless the essence of that religion. People believe in self-esteem. They hold the doctrines of self as tenaciously as any religious fanatic.

13

Albert Ellis Rational Emotive Behavior Therapy

Cognitive-behavioral therapies attempt to help people change their feelings and behavior through changing how they think and what they believe. One of the most popular cognitive-behavioral therapies is Albert Ellis's Rational Emotive Behavior Therapy (REBT), formerly called Rational-Emotive Therapy (RET). Ellis contends that people's "psychological problems arise from their misperceptions and mistaken cognitions about what they perceive" and from the emotional responses to those misperceptions and mistaken cognitions and the resulting "habitually dysfunctional behavior patterns." Therefore the therapy emphasizes "deep philosophical change."[1]

Because Ellis's therapy emphasizes "deep philosophical change" and involves disputing the "irrational beliefs" of the client, one needs to consider what kinds of beliefs are foundational to Ellis's theory. Atheism is the controlling philosophy behind Ellis's theory. Atheism is not simply Ellis's personal preference. It is basic to the "deep philosophical change" emphasized by the theory.

The ABC's of REBT

The ABC's of REBT are appealing both in their simple explanation for complex behavior and in the truth they seem to reflect. Ellis's REBT explanation for human behavior is (1) that emotional problems come from the person making himself disturbed through irrational beliefs and (2) that the person can make himself undisturbed through the ABC's of REBT, that is, through admitting his feelings and then exploring what irrational beliefs are causing them and then by changing his beliefs. The following is a brief outline of Ellis's ABC's:

A. "Activating Experience." Other expressions used by Ellis for this category are: "Activity," "Action" or "Agent," also referred to as "Adversities."
B. "The Individual's Belief System," which includes "irrational Beliefs" and "rational Beliefs."
C. "Emotional Consequences," either "rational Consequences" or "irrational Consequences."
D. "Dispute the irrational Beliefs." The therapist disputes the client's "irrational Beliefs" and guides the client to dispute his own "irrational Beliefs" for himself.
E. "Effects, also called "functioning Effects," which are the "cognitive Effect" and "behavioral Effect."

Ellis contends that circumstances themselves (A) do not cause "dysfunctional Consequences" (C), but that the person himself causes his own painful emotions through his "irrational Beliefs" (B). Thus he needs to have his thinking straightened out through "disputing" (D) his "irrational Beliefs" (B) and replacing them with "rational Beliefs" (B). This process is to bring about both "cognitive Effects" and "behavioral Effects" (E).

At first glance one might see a clear parallel to Christianity in the emphasis on beliefs and how they can affect behavior. That what we believe influences our feelings and actions predates REBT by centuries. This similarity is probably what attracts Christians to this system. Examining the system more closely, however, one will see that although REBT and the Bible seem parallel at this point, they are heading in opposite directions. Just because there are similarities between a psychological counseling system and the Bible does not mean that they are compatible.

Turning God into an "Irrational Belief"

REBT leads away from God to a man-centered universe. Ellis says:

> Unlike the orthodox psychoanalytic and the classical behavioristic psychologies, rational-emotive therapy squarely places man in the center of the universe and of his own emotional fate and gives him almost full responsibility for choosing to make or not make himself seriously disturbed. . . . Moreover, when he unwittingly and foolishly *makes* himself disturbed by devoutly believing in irrational and unvalidatable assumptions about himself and others, he can almost always *make himself* undisturbed again, and can do so often—if he utilizes rational-emotive procedures.[2] (Italics in original.)

Ellis is an avowed atheist who repeatedly through his writings insists that faith in God is an "irrational Belief." Ellis declares, "The very essence of most organized religions is the performance of masochistic, guilt-soothing rituals, by which the religious individual gives himself permission to enjoy life." He continues, "Religiosity, to a large degree, essentially is masochism; and both are forms of mental sickness."[3] Ellis declares:

> If one of the requisites for emotional health is acceptance of uncertainty, then religion is obviously the

unhealthiest state imaginable: since its prime
reason for being is to enable the religionist to
believe in a mystical certainty."[4]

Ellis believes that faith in God is not based on reality,
but on fantasy. He says about the human condition:

One of his highly human, and utterly fallible, traits
is that he has the ability to fantasize about, and to
strongly believe in, all kinds of nonhuman entities
and powers such as devils, demons, and hells, on the
one hand, and angels, gods, and heavens, on the
other hand.[5]

He responds to reports about people benefiting from
religion by saying:

REBT acknowledges that a belief in religion, God,
mysticism, Pollyannaism, and irrationality may at
times help people. But it also points out that such
beliefs often do much more harm than good and
block a more fully functioning life.[6]

His antagonism toward people believing in God is not
always that mild. Elsewhere he disputes against faith by
saying:

Relying on God, or supernatural spirits or forces, or
on fanatical cults, may well become an obsessive-
compulsive disturbance in its own right and lead to
immense harm to other people and to oneself.[7]

Remember that in REBT the therapist disputes
against so-called "irrational Beliefs." Thus, the disputing
would be similar to the above quote. What a person
believes is central to REBT. Ellis says:

[REBT] employs a large variety of evocative-emotive
and behavioral-motorial methods of helping troubled individuals change their basic irrational values
and philosophies and acquire more sensible, joy-pro-
ducing and pain-minimizing ideas. . . . it is excep-
tionally hard-headed, persuasive, educational, and

active-directive and because it straightforwardly attacks many of the sacred myths, superstitions, and religiosities that are so prevalent among human beings.[8]

While he does not specify Christianity here, it is definitely included in his designation "sacred myths, superstitions, and religiosities." He is especially concerned about religions with "*shoulds, oughts,* and *musts*" and asserts that "*all* human disturbance is the result of magical thinking (of believing in *shoulds, oughts,* and *musts*) and can therefore be directly and forthrightly eliminated by the individual's sticking rigorously to empirical reality."[9] (Italics in original.)

Unconditional Self-Acceptance

Ellis opposes faith in God in his category of "irrational Belief." He does not accept God in any way whatsoever. On the other hand, he encourages unconditional self-acceptance as the primary "rational Belief" that one must (though he hates the word *must*) believe. Ellis is opposed to all musts, shoulds, and absolutes. Yet he teaches the absolute of self-acceptance. Although he hates religious dogmatism, he declares his own:

> Dogmatically tell yourself, "I am alive, and I am good because I am alive." This simple formula, if you really believe it, will work, and will be virtually unassailable. For, believing it, you will never feel terribly anxious or self-deprecating as long as you are alive. And when you are dead, you still won't have much to worry about![10]

Indeed, Ellis's system is a faith system with no final judgment. It is a religion of secular humanism, pragmatism, and hedonism with its own dogma, doctrines, and tenets. The primary doctrine of REBT is that the individual is worthwhile simply because he exists. Ellis says:

> Quite didactically, moreover, I present to the client what is usually, for him, a quite new, existentialist-

oriented philosophy of life. I teach him that it is possible for him to accept himself as being valuable to himself just *because he exists,* because he is alive, and because as a living person he has some possibility of enjoying himself and some likelihood of combating his own unhappiness. I vigorously attack the notion that his intrinsic value to himself depends on the usual socially promulgated criteria of success, achievement, popularity, service to others, devotion to God, and the like. Instead, I show him that he had better, if he is really to get over his deep-seated emotional disturbances, come to accept himself *whether or not* he is competent or achieving and *whether or not* he has a high value to others.[11] (Italics in original.)

The doctrine also opposes people comparing themselves to any external standard or evaluating themselves according to what they do. He says:

A basic tenet for rational living is that people not rate themselves in terms of any of their performances, but instead fully accept themselves in terms of their being, their existence. Otherwise, they tend to be severely self-deprecating and insecure, and as a consequence they function ineffectively.[12]

This tenet is essential for the goal of hedonism. Ellis sees nothing wrong with hedonism as long as a person seeks it effectively, that is with a minimum of anxiety or hostility.

The goal of REBT therapy is to reduce anxiety and hostility through convincing the client that he is not worthless. Self-acceptance is presented as a definitional concept rather than a rating concept. Therefore, everyone can have self-acceptance merely through the definitions he chooses.[13] As negative circumstances happen to him, he learns to identify "irrational Beliefs" that supposedly cause such feelings as anxiety, worthlessness, or depression, rather than what might be normal "feelings of disappointment, sorrow, regret, frustration, and annoyance."[14]

Ellis presents the following as a successful outcome:

> On one occasion I very firmly gave a thirty-year-old male, who had never really dated any girls, an assignment to the effect that he make at least two dates a week, whether he wished to do so or not, and come back and report to me on what happened. He immediately started dating, within two weeks had lost his virginity, and quickly began to overcome some of his most deep-seated feelings of inadequacy. With classical psychoanalytic and psychoanalytically oriented psychotherapy, it would have taken many months, and perhaps years, to help this man to the degree that he was helped by a few weeks of highly active-directive rational therapy.[15]

The goal of feeling good about oneself without being disturbed about breaking God's commandments can certainly be met through REBT.

Man-Centered Values

Ellis's belief system dispenses with God, places man at the center, and declares him worthwhile and good. Ellis insists that his method is scientific,[16] rather than religious, but it is really a value system. He says:

> The cognitive therapies make maximum use of a humanistic, scientific methodology that is based on relevance and pleasure seeking but that also is closely tied to scientific empiricism, objectivity, and controlled experimentation. RET starts frankly with a human value system—namely, the assumption that pleasure, joy, creativity, and freedom are good or efficient for human living, and that pain, joylessness, uncreativeness, and bondage are bad or inefficient. It also assumes that what we call emotional, disturbance is largely self-created and can therefore be self-dispelled.[17]

Ellis does not notice the inherent contradiction in his attempt to make his system both scientific and value-laden. He contends that it is a "scientific methodology that is based on relevance and pleasure seeking," but these are simply human values based on what appears to work for the individual. Relevance? Yes, because Ellis will tolerate no external standard. Pleasure seeking? Yes! Empiricism? Only from a highly subjective perspective. Science? No!

Ellis says, "All psychotherapy is, at bottom, a value system"[18] But, values are nonmeasurable and beyond science. Values are in the realm of religion. Ellis's therapy system is a religious system based on the religion of secular humanism and hedonism. Ellis boasts:

> RET, being philosophic and nonextremist, emphasizes both the releasing pleasures of the here-and-now and the longer-range goals of future gain through present-day discipline. It holds that humans have the capacity to be contemporary *and* future-oriented hedonists.[19] (Italics in original.)

REBT is not a neutral system with neutral techniques. It has its own form of morality and right-and-wrong. Ellis says:

> Psychotherapy had better be largely concerned with clients' sense of morality and wrongdoing. An effective therapist will help clients see that they are acting immorally (destructively) to themselves and to others, that they can correct their unethical behavior in most instances, and that when they cannot or do not correct it they are still not bad or immoral *persons*.[20] (Italics in original.)

Notice that in Ellis's system of morality, people are separated from what they do. No matter what they do, "they are still not bad or immoral *persons*." The Bible does not make this distinction between the person and what the person does, but many Christians do because of their exposure to humanistic psychology. Christ died on the cross to save sinners. The magnitude of God's grace is minimized through humanistic psychological systems that refuse to call people *sinners* with the full impact of the word.

Along this same line of separating the doer from the deed, is Ellis's statement, "Accept the 'sinner,' but not necessarily the 'sin.' But preferably don't label a person as a 'sinner.'"[21] Why is Ellis opposed to calling a person a "sinner"? His reason is that by believing you are a sinner, you might "actually *make yourself* continue to act immorally and mistakenly in the future."[22] (Italics in original.) Unfortunately there are Christians who reason in the same manner. When they do so, their source is not Scripture, but rather humanistic psychology, the religion of humanism. Referring to oneself as a sinner saved by grace does not cause a Christian to "continue to act immorally and mistakenly in the future." Paul declared: "This is a faithful saying, and worthy of all acceptation, that Christ Jesus came into the world to save sinners; of whom I am chief."

To be expected, the values of religious humanism vary according to the person and group. Ellis says:

> Although humans are never likely to determine any absolute, final, or God-given standard of morals or ethics, they can fairly easily agree, in any given community, on what is "right" and what is "wrong" and can therefore rate or measure their thoughts, feelings, and acts as "good" or "bad."[23]

Ellis opposes belief in any "God-given standard of morals or ethics." For that reason, he does not even like using the words *sin* and *sinner*.

> You preferably should not use words like "sin" and "sinner," because they imply absolute, God-given (or devil-given) standards that help to condemn your self, your entire being, for some of your mistaken acts.[24]

Christians should be wary of incorporating anything from other value systems. It is tantamount to incorporating parts of other religions. Use the Bible. It is the only inerrant and authoritative document for a Christian.

Ellis elevates human reason above God's Word. He uses his fallible reason to judge God out of existence and to call faith in Him "irrational Belief." Nevertheless Christians have attempted to Christianize his system. How does one integrate a psychological theory that denigrates God and faith in His Word and somehow come up with anything remotely biblical? Combining heresy and blasphemy with certain ideas from Scripture is indeed psychoheresy!

Enticing Christians into an Atheistic System

Atheism is so strong within the framework of REBT that it affects every part. One cannot take part of REBT and truly divorce it from this atheistic system, because it still ends up being man-centered rather than God-centered. Man is at the center of the universe as far as Ellis is concerned and everything he has written clearly demonstrates a theology of no-god-exists except in the irrational beliefs of fallible people.

The cognition (thinking) that Ellis teaches people to use regarding God and self forms the context in which a person is to dispute irrational beliefs. If a person repeatedly argues against so-called irrational beliefs with the doctrines of "I am good and valuable and God does not really exist," he merely moves further into the kingdom of darkness and further away from the only truth that can set him free.

If one attempts to Christianize the system by leaving out Ellis's doctrine of God-does-not-really-exist, he is still stuck with Ellis's doctrines of man, which are heretical, without recognition of either the Creation or the Fall. Ellis's rationality is irrational because of the noetic effects of the Fall. What he says about man as an autonomous being is anti-rational at the root, because it depends on his say-so and circular reasoning. He recognizes only human desire and comfort, and his hatred for God is so intense that he tries to obliterate His very being. He is like a child who covers his eyes to make people disappear. With his mind closed to God and His Word, Ellis vainly tries to help people move from irrational beliefs to rational beliefs. Truly he is an example of the blind leading the blind.

What Ellis's theory boils down to is this: The human is worthy because he exists. God does not exist. Therefore the human's worth exceeds God's worth. This anti-God doctrine controls and colors every part of his theory. Nevertheless, after the development of so-called Christian psychology, Ellis saw a whole new group to proselytize and even wrote an article titled "Can Rational Counseling Be Christian?" His article was published in a series titled "Can Counseling Be Christian?" in the integrationist publication *Christian Counseling Today*.[25]

Ellis's response to the question, "Can Rational Counseling Be Christian?" reveals that he is ignorant about true Christianity. He says:

> Much counseling, by both religionists and nonreligionists, is irrational; some of it is actually harmful. As the founder of Rational Emotive Behavior Therapy (REBT), I naturally think that this particular form of counseling helps more people more thoroughly than other methods. I also believe that some kinds of Christian counselors are quite rational and can and do use REBT successfully.[26]

The ones who are rational according to Ellis cannot include the full character of God. Thus the only Christian counselors who can use REBT successfully are those who are willing to present a distorted view of God and who are willing to ignore such verses as Romans 12:19, which refers to God's vengeance: "Dearly beloved, avenge not yourselves, but rather give place unto wrath: for it is written, Vengeance is mine; I will repay, saith the Lord."

Throughout most of his writings, Ellis has made it clear that belief in any deity is irrational and harmful. In fact, Ellis has declared that his system of therapy is "one of the few systems of psychotherapy that will truly **have no truck whatever** with any kind of miraculous cause or cure, **any kind of god** or devil, or **any kind of sacredness**."[27] (Bold added.)

Now that Christian psychology is big business and loaded with people who might want to attend the Albert Ellis Institute for Rational Emotive Behavior Therapy, Ellis is making some special allowances, but only if the counselor is willing to create a god who is limited to being "a warm fuzzy." Ellis's system could not accommodate the Sovereign God who created the universe and who holds man accountable, who both rewards and punishes, and whose Word is both authoritative and absolute. Neither can Ellis fathom a future judgment of mankind.

Ellis is familiar with Christian psychologists who have willingly subsumed Scripture to REBT, at least as far as the character of God and the absolutes of Scripture. Ellis tells about two clinicians who, at an annual conference of the American Psychological Association, "showed how REBT can be effectively integrated with a Christian outlook."[28] What kind of Christian outlook might accommodate a psychological theory that denies the existence of God, but is willing for people to have an irrational belief in a god that does not disturb their thinking with absolutes or with such concepts as original sin and hell?

If Ellis can contribute to the watering down of Christianity by condescending to have his REBT "integrated with a Christian outlook," he may war more effectively against God than he has done through his earlier, dedicated atheism. His article shows that every religious system integrating with REBT must conform itself to REBT. Ellis explains how that works: "Because some of the main 'rational' philosophies that it promotes are also part of the Christian tradition and are specifically advocated in the New Testament and in various other Christian writings."[29] He obviously thinks more highly than he ought about his own system and does not admit that seeming similarities are superficial. Ellis's view of faith, hope, love, truth, and compassion are humanistic rather than godly or biblical. Furthermore, he would continue to call much of what the Bible teaches irrational, and whatever part he might condescend to call rational must be transmogrified to fit his system.

Whereas in Ellis's REBT the person himself affirms his own unconditional acceptance to himself. In the so-called Christian version the person has God doing it for him. Although the Bible does not teach unconditional love, the so-called Christian version has Jesus and God loving the client unconditionally so that the person does "not need the love and approval of other people." The person simply uses God to reinforce the REBT philosophy. God is relegated to the role of psychological assistant in REBT therapy.[30]

During the same time that he wrote the article "Can Rational Counseling Be Christian?" and answered that question in the affirmative, Ellis also affirmed his negative stance regarding Christianity in a *Free Inquiry* interview titled "Why I Am a Secular Humanist." The following is one of the items:

> *FI*: "You have said before that you thought most religion most of the time does harm. What exactly is the harm?
>
> Ellis: Religion usually entails belief in a god who sets up certain rules that are to be obeyed. If not, terrible things will happen—you will roast in hell for eternity or will be ostracized.[31]

Ellis then refers to the Ten Commandments and says, "Such absolutist rules are unworkable and unrealistic." He says:

> Most people wrongly think that religions create moral rules. Actually religions just take moral rules from different cultures and dogmatize them. The Ten Commandments are a very good example of this. Obviously, Moses didn't go up the mountain and speak to God. How did he create the Command-

ments? He took the mores of his time and rewrote them. He took some of the laws and the customs that he thought were the best and put them in the Ten Commandments.[32]

Thus Ellis, with his "rational" thinking has dismissed God's Word and prophets.

Ellis also believes that "religion is much like bad therapy."[33] He says:

Religion helps you feel better because, presumably, Jesus, God, or Allah or some other deity loves you. Therefore, you feel (a) there is a God—which almost certainly there isn't—and that (b) God is on your side, will take care of you, love you, give you the right rules to live by, etc.[34]

Then he goes on to say why this is bad:

Religion prevents you from getting the ultimate solution, which is that, despite the fact that the universe has no supernatural meaning whatsoever—there's no God, no devil, no fairies, no nymphs—*you can still take care of yourself.*[35] (Italics in original.)

Therefore, it is obvious that from Ellis's perspective the business of having God accept one unconditionally, as in his "Can Rational Counseling Be Christian?" article, will prevent one from "getting the ultimate solution," being *"you can still take care of yourself."* Perhaps he's hoping that people will cross the REBT bridge built by Christian psychologists and at last find their ultimate solution in self rather than in an imaginary god.

Christians need to reject REBT and other forms of cognitive-behavior therapies that deal with one's belief system. Christians must study their Bibles to deal with their beliefs in reference to problems of living, rather than systems controlled by humanistic psychology.

14

William Glasser
Reality
Therapy

Reality Therapy is a radically non-Freudian type of therapy developed by psychiatrist William Glasser and described in his book *Reality Therapy*. The reality therapist is not interested in becoming involved in the two Freudian demons: the past history of the client and the unconscious determinants of behavior.

Concerning the client's past, Glasser says that "we can neither change what happened to him nor accept the fact that he is limited by his past."[1] If a client does mention the past, it is always to be related to the present and the future. Although Glasser believes in unconscious motivation for behavior, he says:

> . . . knowledge of cause has nothing to do with therapy. Patients have been treated with conventional

psychiatry until they know the unconscious reason for every move they make, but they still do not change because knowing the reason does not lead to fulfilling needs.[2]

He argues that unconscious motivations are often just used as excuses for continuing undesirable behavior.

Reality Therapy's core is the three R's: *reality, responsibility,* and *right-and-wrong.* These not only read like motherhood and apple pie, but they have a distinctly Christian ring. Therefore it is necessary to examine these three concepts and the process of therapy to see whether Glasser's system is truly biblical.

Reality

Glasser stresses the importance of helping a person see and deal with life as it really is. A distorted view of other people's actions, events affecting the person's life, and one's own actions can lead to emotional problems and hinder that person from behaving in appropriate ways. Glasser believes that "all patients have a common characteristic: *they* all deny *the reality of the world around them.*"[3] (Italics in original.) Thus, one main responsibility of the therapist is to bring the person in touch with the reality of his environment and of himself.

Glasser encourages his clients to develop behavior that is realistic in terms of both the present and the future. In doing this, he differentiates between immediate and long-range consequences of behavior. He points out that realistic behavior is that which results from a consideration of both long-range and short-range consequences, since some behavior, though immediately satisfying, may be unsatisfactory in the long run.

Responsibility

Glasser says "It is not enough to help a patient face reality; he must also learn to fulfill his needs."[4] Responsibility, according to Glasser is "the ability to fulfill one's needs, and to do so *in a way that does not deprive others*

of the ability to fulfill their needs."⁵ (Italics in original.)
Such behavior is the primary goal of Reality Therapy.

Glasser has an interesting notion about the relationship of behavior to human thought and emotions. He believes that people do not act responsibly just because they are happy, but rather that people who act responsibly are more likely to be happy. Happiness or the lack of it is thus dependent upon responsible behavior, rather than the circumstances. Therefore, the therapist's job is to help clients become responsible.

Although Glasser uses reason and logic in counseling, he does not concentrate heavily on either thoughts or emotions. Most psychotherapists try to change thoughts and emotions; Glasser works directly with outward behavior. He contends that responsible behavior shapes positive thoughts and emotions, just as irresponsible behavior causes unhealthy attitudes and emotions.

There is an old saying that if you knew better you would do better. However, experience in life tends to disprove this, since people often do not perform according to what they know. Glasser's theory stresses doing better rather than just knowing better, because he believes a change in behavior will lead to a change in thinking. Thus, he concentrates on teaching his clients responsible ways to respond.

Glasser not only holds the client accountable for his own behavior, but refuses to take the responsibility away from him. Clients very often attempt to make others responsible for their behavior, but Reality Therapy denies them this privilege. The client is encouraged to perform responsibly and to be responsible for his performance. Glasser does not waste time asking why a person acted irresponsibly; instead, he assumes that the client can act responsibly and proceeds to help him do so.

Right-and-Wrong

Responsibility suggests morality of some kind, and, indeed, Reality Therapy includes a concept of right and wrong. Glasser says:

. . . to be worthwhile we must maintain a *satisfactory standard of behavior.* To do so we must learn to correct ourselves when we do wrong and to credit ourselves when we do right. . . . Morals, standards, values, or right and wrong behavior are all intimately related to the fulfillment of our need for self worth.[6] (Italics in original.)

Glasser's position is a refreshing contrast to most psychotherapies, which either stress the adverse effects of the moral standards of society on the individual or refuse to impose these, or any other standards, on the client. In the Freudian system, a conscience which makes too many demands on the individual must be reformed to lower the moral expectations so that the person can feel good about himself.

Numerous psychotherapeutic systems encourage the individual to satisfy the instincts and impulses by reducing the demands of the conscience. These therapies are based on the theory that lowering the standards of conventional morality is beneficial and necessary for improved mental-emotional-behavioral health. They focus on internal desires rather than external behavior. Glasser, on the other hand, does not believe in decreasing standards but, rather, in increasing performance. Reality Therapy devaluates the biological desires and elevates the social needs of the individual.

Process of Therapy

Reality Therapy treatment is usually about six months and rarely longer than a year. Of crucial importance in the process is the relationship between the therapist and the client. Glasser believes that the therapist, as a person, provides the missing link to positive change. He says:

We know, therefore, that *at the time any person comes for psychiatric help he is lacking the most critical factor for fulfilling his needs, a person whom he genuinely cares about* and *who he feels genuinely cares about him.*[7] (Italics in original.)

In Reality Therapy the therapist must become this special person to whom the client can respond.

Glasser believes that without involvement, there can be no therapy. The therapist must be both a friend to the client and a model of responsibility for the client to follow. As a friend he is to exhibit compassion and a caring attitude, but he is not to respond to unnecessary demands for sympathy nor react to criticism from the client. Ideally the relationship becomes the motivation for responsible behavior.

Throughout therapy the major goal is to teach the client to become responsible. As such, the therapist becomes a teacher as well as a friend. The therapist rejects irresponsible, unrealistic, and wrong behavior, but at the same time maintains an attitude of accepting the client as a person. In fact, the therapist makes it clear that he will never reject the client, no matter what. Rather, it is the behavior the therapist rejects and that only for the ultimate good of the client.

Through acceptance of the person and rejection of negative behavior, the therapist tries to help the client evaluate his own behavior. The therapist also attempts to help his client to make plans for change and gives suggestions for carrying out the plans. Glasser claims that through this process, the client develops more realistic and responsible behavior and thus finds self-fulfillment and happiness.

Criticisms of Reality Therapy

Well, what can be wrong with Reality Therapy? It sounds wholesome, good, and even biblical with such concepts as reality, responsibility, and right-and-wrong. Let's examine this seemingly virtuous system in the light of the Bible.

According to Glasser the individual has two basic psychological needs. He says they are *"the need to love and be loved and the need to feel that we are worthwhile to our-selves and to others."*[8] (Italics in original.) While the Bible teaches the importance of love, Glasser's concept is lacking in that it only emphasizes human relationships and totally ignores a loving relationship with God.

The Bible says, "We love him, because he first loved us" (I John 4:19). God's love for us is so great that He gave His Son that we might have eternal life, and therefore we love Him. Jesus taught that the greatest commandment is, "And thou shalt love the Lord thy God with all thy heart, and with all thy soul, and with all thy mind, and with all thy strength" (Mark 12:30). The love relationship between God and man is one of the greatest doctrines of the entire Bible. It is of supreme importance to man and a powerful force in an individual's life. It has immeasurable "therapeutic" value and is of far greater value than love between persons. Moreover, human love relationships are far better and more complete when supernatural love is a reality.

Glasser, like Rogers, deals only with a natural love relationship and not the divine love relationship. Just as Rogers, Glasser emphasizes the need for caring and involvement between persons, but ignores a person's greatest need for a love relationship with God.

Along with the need for love, Glasser noted that people need to feel worthwhile to themselves and to others. He says that although this need is separate from the first need, the person who satisfies the need to love and be loved will usually feel worthwhile. This sounds like a beautiful generalization, but here again it is incomplete and ignores the Bible. The important word in this second need is *feel*. A man can feel worthwhile under a variety of circumstances. Feeling worthwhile is merely an internal evaluation, which might not be at all realistic or accurate. A person may feel he is worthwhile and establish his own system for saving the world and end up like Hitler. *Feeling* has to do with self and subjectivity, while Scripture deals with truth.

The Bible does not stress self-worth or feeling worthwhile. Instead it encourages believers to esteem others more than themselves and to attribute all worthiness and glory to God Himself. Christianity is not about feeling or being worthwhile but rather entering into a relationship with the Creator of the universe, to whom all glory is to be given. When people truly know God they need not concern themselves with independent worthwhileness.

The apostle Paul confessed he had previously considered himself a very worthwhile individual. Not only did he have the perfect heritage, but he had followed the Jewish law and customs with great zeal and righteousness. However, when he came face to face with the resurrected Christ, he discovered that all he had considered worthy in himself was empty, because he had not been in the proper relationship with God. And from that point, he desired to "be found in him, not having mine own righteousness, which is of the law, but that which is through the faith of Christ, the righteousness which is of God by faith" (Philippians 3:9).

Glasser defines moral behavior as, *"When a man acts in such a way that he gives and receives love, and feels worthwhile to himself and others, his behavior is right or moral."*9 (Italics in original.) In other words, if a person gives and receives love according to his own definition and feels good about himself, "his behavior is right and moral" according to Glasser. But, not according to God. Scripture clearly reveals both the sinfulness of every person and the inherent self-deception of a deceitful heart (Jeremiah 17:9). Because Glasser's theory is devoid of God, he places undue confidence in man.

Glasser exhibits confidence in man because of his humanistic ideology, which says people are basically good in themselves and which denies the fundamental nature of sinful, fallen man. We can expect both moral and immoral behavior from persons because of their fallen nature. Glasser would call immoral behavior "irresponsible," but it would be more appropriate to call it "sinful." Glasser cares more about the so-called rights and liberties of persons than about godly righteousness, biblical beliefs, or the true freedom which can only be found in Jesus.

Glasser's therapy system centers directly on behavior, but he completely ignores the Bible, which is filled with exhortations to behave wisely and responsibly, and substitutes it with society's current moral code. For example, if two people are in love and wish to live together without the commitment of marriage, they would certainly be conforming to Glasser's definition of responsible behavior, since it fulfills their needs, does not deprive or restrict others from fulfilling their needs, and fits into current moral practices. But the Bible is opposed to such relationships, and responsible Christian behavior conforms to God's Word.

Societal standards, the laws of men, and the prevailing moral code change, but God's Word is eternal. What is the sense of responsible behavior limited to outward conformity to a current moral code if it is divorced from an internal change caused by the supernatural presence of God? Glasser is more concerned with outward behavior than with inner attitudes, but God looks on the heart rather than the external appearance. For Glasser it doesn't matter what you believe as long as you act according to current mores. The Bible deals with the whole man, with his inner and outer behavior.

Although people can change their behavior to a certain extent, they are nevertheless restricted by the inherent tendency to sin because of the fallen nature. Only God's grace enables a person to act fully responsible, and even then there are slips and sins. Paul expressed this quandary in Romans 7 when he said that with the mind he wanted to do the right thing, but he did just the opposite anyway because of the sin principle within him. He found that the power to act responsibly, both inwardly and outwardly, was only through the grace of God in his life and through the power of the indwelling Holy Spirit. Throughout the entire Old Testament, the Israelites were unable to follow the law of God. However, when Jesus came and gave His life for those who believe, He enabled them to receive His own perfect life. He transforms their hearts and lives so that they can be new creatures in both inner and outer behavior.

Upon examination, Glasser's view of reality, responsibility, and right-and-wrong communicates a worldly system which sounds somewhat biblical, but is not. Besides failing to conform to the Bible, Reality Therapy proposes to heal mental-emotional-behavioral problems through self-effort. As in other psychotherapies, self, not God, is at the center of Reality Therapy. The system uses biblical sounding concepts like love, but in a shallow, self-centered, human sense. Ingredients necessary to dissolve mental-emotional-behavioral problems are biblical truth, biblical love, and biblical behavior, not the three R's of Glasser.

Christians have been deceived by a system that relies upon worldly standards of reality, responsibility, and right-and-wrong. The Bible describes reality and teaches responsibility and right and wrong behavior. Although Glasser's counterfeit system may look biblical, he has struck out on all three since his concepts are nonbiblical, worldly, and self-oriented.

According to Reality Therapy, the therapist is the client's model for attaining the goal of responsible behavior. On the other hand, the Bible teaches that Christ is the model and our goal is to be like Him. The Bible presents Christ, not the therapist; Christ, not fallen nature; Christ, not self. One who provides help based on the Bible will constantly refer to and exhibit scriptural love, mercy, and grace, as well as scriptural reality, responsibility, and right-and-wrong. The Bible teacher will use Christ as the model and Christ's overcoming victory as the example, rather than himself and his own ability. These are the only truly valid and reliable mental-emotional-behavioral health principles because they have been given by the Creator. Christians would do well to stay away from biblical sounding therapies and return to

the Word, which is the Christian's source of all mental-
emotional-behavioral healing and health.

15

Thomas Harris Transactional Analysis

Transactional Analysis, a therapeutic system that examines interactions between people, was very popular among Christians for a number of years. Although its popularity has waned, some of its central ideas continue to thrive in the current eclectic environment. To understand the weaknesses of Transactional Analysis (TA), we examine some of its concepts, its four life positions, and its unproved theories.

Dr. Thomas Harris, in his book *I'm OK—You're OK: A Practical Guide to Transactional Analysis,* quotes the work of neurosurgeon Wilder Penfield and offers it as a basis for his own theory. Under Penfield's influence, Harris believes that both past events and feelings accompanying those events are recorded in the brain in such a way that each event is forever united with the emotion.

According to Harris, events and emotions remain linked together in the brain throughout life. Harris refers to the brain as a high fidelity tape recorder and uses this metaphor to describe his system. He constantly refers to events being recorded or played back.

Harris says that during his early years a child is recording volumes of negative feelings, which greatly influence his entire life. These negative recordings come from certain demands imposed on him and accompanied by parental approval or disapproval. Toilet training is one example. During this training time, the child's natural inclinations are curbed, and the child must form new habits according to parental demands. There is often a conflict between what the child is doing naturally and what the parent wants him to do.

Harris says that negative feelings from the civilizing process bring a child to the conclusion that he is not OK. Harris is not necessarily blaming the parents, for he says, "It is the *situation of childhood* and *not* the intention of the parents which produces the problem."[1] (Italics in original.) Even the child of loving parents comes to the same conclusion according to Harris.

Four Life Positions

Harris does indicate that the child receives OK recordings as well as not OK ones, but he believes that the not OK feelings predominate.[2] His belief in the universal not OK experience of mankind is the key to TA and to his four life positions, which are:

> I'm not OK—You're OK
> I'm not OK—You're not OK
> I'm OK—You're not OK
> I'm OK—You're OK

The first position, I'm not OK—You're OK, is established by a decision every young child makes. The child concludes that he is not OK because the not OK feelings ultimately outweigh the OK feelings. The child concludes that the parent is OK because the parent provides what

Harris labels "stroking," which is "repetitious bodily contact."[3] The child evaluates a parent's goodness through the amount of stroking he receives. Since the parents, particularly the mother, provide stroking, the child concludes You're OK. Harris says the conclusion I'm not OK—You're OK is the "universal position of early childhood" and is "the most deterministic decision of his life."[4]

If there is an absence of necessary stroking, the child moves from position one to life position two: I'm not OK—You're not OK. This is a position of abandonment and despair and the beginning of deep mental-emotional problems. There is no hope because no one is OK. Harris believes that many in this position give up and may eventually end up in mental institutions.

If, on the other hand, the absence of stroking is combined with verbal abuse and/or physical brutalization, the child may move on into the next life position: I'm OK—You're not OK. This move comes from self-stroking. As the child is recovering from being beaten he learns to comfort (stroke) himself and concludes I'm OK by myself. A person who remains in this life position is not objective about his actions. He continually excuses himself and blames others. He says, "It is never my fault, always their fault." This position is occupied by incorrigible criminals.

The fourth and best life position, according to Harris, is I'm OK—You're OK. While the presence or absence of stroking determines the first three positions, the faculties of reason and choice determine the fourth position.[5] Harris compares choosing this new position to a conversion experience. The stated aim of Harris's book is "to establish that the only way people get well or become OK is to expose the childhood predicament underlying the first three positions and prove how current behavior perpetuates the positions."[6]

Harris and Freud

Harris uses the Freudian ploy of relating psychotherapy to medicine in order to give it credibility and make it acceptable. This might explain why he begins his book by first referring to Freud and then to neurosurgeon Penfield. Referring to Penfield's work, Harris says, "The evidence **seems** to indicate that everything which has been in our conscious awareness is recorded in detail and stored in the brain and is **capable** of being 'played back' in the present."[7] (Bold added.) The word *seems* means "appears like" or "may possibly be" and the word *capable* means "can." However, Harris has concluded from Penfield's work that all this material is stored in the brain and **does determine** one's present behavior. He maintains that *"our earliest experiences, though ineffable, are recorded and do replay in the present."*[8] (Italics in original.) In addition, he contends that "the past invariably insinuates itself into our present life."[9] Harris calls this "the hook of the past."[10]

How Accurate Are Our Memories?

Many people believe that memory is like a tape recorder that records every event accurately and keeps it intact. But, research on memory has debunked that myth and raised many questions about common misconceptions about remembering and forgetting.

In his book *Remembering and Forgetting: Inquiries into the Nature of Memory*, Edmund Bolles says, "The human brain is the most complicated structure in the known universe."[11] In introducing his book he says,

> For several thousand years people have believed that remembering retrieves information stored somewhere in the mind. The metaphors of memory have always been metaphors of storage: We preserve images on wax; we carve them in stone; we write memories as with a pencil on paper; we file memories away; we have photographic memories; we retain facts so firmly they seem held in a steel

trap. Each of these images proposes a memory ware-
house where the past lies preserved like childhood
souvenirs in an attic. This book reports a revolution
that has overturned that vision of memory. Remembering is a creative, constructive process.[12]

How accurate are childhood memories? Does the
vividness of the recall increase the validity of a memory?
Swiss psychologist Jean Piaget described a clear memory
from his own early childhood:

> I can still see, most clearly, the following scene, in
> which I believed until I was about fifteen. I was sit-
> ting in my pram, which my nurse was pushing in
> the Champs Elysées, when a man tried to kidnap
> me. I was held in by the strap fastened round me
> while my nurse bravely tried to stand between me
> and the thief. She received various scratches, and I
> can still see vaguely those on her face. Then a crowd
> gathered, a policeman with a short cloak and a
> white baton came up, and the man took to his heels.
> I can still see the whole scene, and can even place it
> near the tube station.[13]

Notice the details of this memory. Nevertheless,
Piaget then revealed that his vivid memory was of an
event that never happened. Piaget said that, when he
was about fifteen years old, his nurse had confessed that:

> She had made up the whole story, faking the
> scratches. I, therefore, must have heard, as a child,
> the account of this story, which my parents believed,
> and projected into the past in the form of a visual
> memory.[14]

Memories are created out of images, overheard
conversations, dreams, suggestions, and imagination as
well as out of actual events. And they change over time.
Even as we remember we tend to fill in the gaps. Therefore, each time a memory is recalled it is also recreated
with the emotions accompanying the recall and with the
imagination which fills in the gaps.

Remembering is not running an invisible tape recorder back to an event. It is pulling together bits and pieces of information that logically fit together. Nor can we depend on accuracy. Even immediate recall may be inaccurate simply because of an initial failure to perceive accurately. That is why those who testify about a particular event may have completely different stories.

Memories are also very malleable. They change even as we recall past events. Dr. Elizabeth Loftus, a well-known memory researcher, says:

> With the passage of time, with proper motivation, with the introduction of special kinds of interfering facts, the memory traces seem sometimes to change or become transformed. These distortions can be quite frightening, for they can cause us to have memories of things that never happened.[15]

Even under the best circumstances, memory is incomplete. People creatively fill in details with probabilities. Because of this natural inclination and because of the possibility of creating new memories through hypnosis and other forms of suggestion, Christians should be cautious about any counseling that looks for the keys of today's behavior in so-called repressed memories in some controlling unconscious.

Even if it had been or could be proven that all of the experiences in our awareness are recorded in detail and remain in the brain, it is only a giant leap of faith that would cause us to conclude that they universally determine our behavior. It is not past experiences but present decisions that govern behavior. Because of Harris's psychiatric training, he is no doubt fixated on the past as a powerful determinant of present decisions and behavior and has merely redressed the Freudian fiction.

On the other hand, Harris does seem to hold an anti-Freudian position on personal volition, because he believes a person can choose the fourth position, I'm OK—You're OK. He seems, on the surface at least, to have escaped Freud's unconscious determinants of behavior and preoccupation with the past. Nevertheless, Harris has not really escaped them; he has only limited their influence. According to Harris individuals are unconsciously determined by their early experiences to end up in the position of I'm not OK. But he claims that this position is not permanent if one decides to change.

Harris contends that people can choose to be different, but that until they consciously decide to change they are conditioned and determined by their unconscious and past history. In other words, people are not only determined to end up in one of the first three life positions, but the position established during childhood determines present behavior unless they decide to move into the fourth position. Excluding this decision to change, Harris ends up with the same old Freudian determinism.

Harris has committed the further Freudian error of making I'm not OK—You're OK the universal neurosis of man. To support his position he quotes L. S. Kubie and adds his own italics:

> The clinical fact which is already evident is that once a central emotional position is established early in life, it becomes the affective position *to which that individual will tend to return automatically for the rest of his days* .[16]

Harris and Christianity

Harris stresses volition, responsibility, and even morality. In fact, his book contains an entire chapter on his personal view of morality, in which he also presents his own personal view of Christianity. Because his view of Christianity sounds somewhat biblical, many Christians have erroneously accepted "the gospel according to Harris." Remembering that "all scripture is given by inspiration of God, and is profitable for doctrine, for reproof, for correction, for instruction in righteousness" (2 Timothy 3:16), does what Harris says about Christianity stand the test of Scripture?

Sin

Harris claims that the universal human condition is I'm not OK—You're OK. How the child arrives at this position underlies Harris's personal theology. Harris does not believe that a child is born into the condition of sin but rather that the child chooses this position.[17] For Harris sin is a decision a child makes about himself, rather than a condition in which a child finds himself. There is a subtle, but gigantic theological difference here. One idea is biblical; the other is not. The biblical position is that all are born sinners. The fallen nature is inherited from Adam and is not an individual human decision. People do not decide I'm not OK; they already have a sinful nature. "Wherefore, as by one man sin entered into the world . . ." (Romans 5:12). "For as by one man's disobedience many were made sinners . . ." (Romans 5:19).

According to the Bible, man does not arrive at the position I'm not OK; he is born into a biblically defined condition of sin. People sin because that is their natural condition, not because of unconscious determinism or past circumstances. Not OK is just a humanistic substitute for the biblical truth about the sinful condition of man as a result of the Fall; this is a condition for which there is only one cure and that is a right relationship with the Creator, not a theory and system of TA.

Born Again

With a massive misconception of sin, Harris's resulting understanding of the born-again experience is also unbiblical. Harris quotes Jesus' words, "Except a man be born again, he cannot see the kingdom of God" (John 3:5) and then distorts the meaning. According to Harris, it is the civilizing process that forces a person into the position of sin, and one is born again by using his reason to understand his condition and to decide to change that position from one of I'm not OK to I'm OK.[18] Here again there is a subtle, but powerful, difference between deciding to make a change by virtue of the nature of human reason and believing what the Bible declares to be the source of new life. According to Harris, one merely decides to be OK and he is. It is a natural, humanistic, internal act. According to the Bible, one is born again by God's grace through faith. Being born again by the Spirit of God is a supernatural, external provision received by faith.

According to Harris, human action makes a person OK, but according to Scripture, it is divine action. Harris's theory of OKness relies solely on human works; biblical truth is that salvation is God's work. According to the Bible, being born again relies upon the provision of salvation and sanctification by the Creator, rather than on a process of self-transformation. The sin condition is not erased or removed or changed by self; it is removed by God as one trusts in the sacrifice Jesus provided for new life and as one receives the power of the indwelling Holy Spirit to live the new life.

The peak experience of Transactional Analysis is I'm OK—You're OK, and the method of arrival is faith in self and in the TA system. However, the biblical truth is that God sent His supernatural Son into this natural world to redeem a people for Himself. No amount of theory or brilliance in writing will ever replace or erase the essence of biblical salvation and sanctification.

Transactional Analysis is a simple, easy-to-learn theory—high in simplicity but low in truth about the human condition and the means of change. Harris evidently doesn't know the truth about why man is not OK nor how he can become OK. The idea that I decide to be OK and then I am OK, without repentance and forgiveness, is an heretical theology and a disguise for self-indulgence and self-centered love. It puts mere humanity at the center of both deciding to change and providing the means of change. It is, to use Harris's words, a system of "self-stroking" par excellence.

Harris's theology tranquilizes people to the truth about the human condition and the Gospel. Harris has replaced the biblical concept of mankind's fallen condition and Christ's provision for change with his own personal theology of unconscious determinism and self at the center of all things. Harris's theology is: I decide, I do, and I arrive.

One Way

The Bible declares very plainly that there is only one way of salvation: "Neither is there salvation in any other; for there is none other name under heaven given among men, whereby we must be saved" (Acts 4:12). According to the Bible there is only one way to God, and, as much as some may not like it, Christianity is in this sense an exclusivistic religion.

This exclusivism is a doctrinal absolute, but Harris declares, "There are no doctrinal absolutes."[19] He contends:

> The truth is not something which has been brought to finality at an ecclesiastical summit meeting or bound in a black book. *The truth is a growing body of data of what we observe to be true.*[20] (Italics in original.)

This is Harris's subtle way of saying that the basis for truth is not what is in the Bible, but rather what is in man. Truth, according to Harris, depends on self and what self observes to be true.

Harris bases his ideas on the unproved theory of evolution and denies the claims of Christianity by saying that a small percentage of the world's population could not possibly have exclusive truth. He quotes statistics on world population and the distribution of money, material possessions, food, life span, and religion. He concludes by saying:

> We are deluded if we continue to make sweeping statements about God and about man without continually keeping before us the facts of life: the long history of the development of man, and the present day diversity of human thought.[21]

What Harris is really saying is that, considering mankind's late arrival in so-called evolution and considering how any society compares with the rest of the world materially, religiously, and numerically, no one has a claim to exclusive truth. What Harris may not realize is that God's Word is exclusive truth revealed by God, and that no matter what Harris may say, God's Word is eternal and exclusive.

Opinions about evolution and the ideologies of the majority of the world have nothing to do with whether or not one has exclusive truth. Christians do not evaluate their view of God and the universe merely by present-day circumstances, the theory of evolution, or any other unproved theory.

> For what if some did not believe? Shall their unbelief make the faith of God without effect? God forbid: yea, let God be true, but every man a liar (Romans 3:3-4).

Grace

Besides rejecting the exclusiveness of Christianity and distorting the biblical concept of sin, Harris has also mutilated the biblical concept of grace. He has misshapen it to fit his own gospel of self-forgiveness and salvation through self. He says:

> The concept of grace . . . is a theological way of saying I'M OK—YOU'RE OK. It is not YOU CAN BE OK, IF or YOU WILL BE ACCEPTED, IF, but rather YOU ARE ACCEPTED, unconditionally.[22]

He quotes Paul Tillich's explanation of the incident in which a prostitute came to Jesus. Tillich says, "Jesus does not forgive the woman, but he declares that she *is* forgiven. . . . The woman came to Jesus because she was forgiven," and then Harris adds "not to be forgiven."[23] (Italics in original.) Forgiveness, according to Harris, is an unconditional given, like unconditional acceptance, for all people, no matter what.

At the end of this incident Jesus says, "Thy faith hath saved thee; go in peace" (Luke 7:50). According to the Bible, she received forgiveness and salvation through exercising faith. Acceptance comes with salvation. Those who have been saved are "accepted **in** Christ Jesus." God loves and is merciful to the just and unjust. However, He does not accept sinful people in the manner promoted by Harris. Instead, God has provided the means of forgiveness and salvation by faith, wherein believers are given new life, not an old one fixed up by a secular salvation from not OK to OK unconditionally.

Faith is necessary for receiving forgiveness and salvation. "For by grace are ye saved through faith" (Ephesians 2:8). This faith means faith in God, not faith in self or a TA system. Harris is biblically wrong again. One does not become OK unconditionally. God set the conditions; Christ paid the price. Believers respond by grace through faith.

After Jesus says, "Thy sins are forgiven," the Bible says, "And they that sat at meat with him began to say within themselves, 'Who is this that forgiveth sins also?'" (Luke 7:48, 49). Regardless of whether she was forgiven before or after she arrived, the important point is that forgiveness is necessary and that Jesus is the one who forgives, because of who He is.

Harris further confuses the concept of grace by returning to his theme of the positions of persons. He argues that a person's main problem is the not OK position of sin, not *acts* of sin, and that a person need only acknowledge or confess that he is in the wrong position to become OK. Such transition from not OK to OK is grace according to Harris. He foolishly argues that confessing sinful *acts* is ineffective for change and that such confession cheapens the concept of grace and strengthens a not OK position.[24]

According to the Bible, our primary problem is both a position and an act. All were born in sin (position) and everyone does sin (act). 1 John 1:8 declares, "If we say that we have no sin, we deceive ourselves, and the truth is not in us." The Bible enjoins those who have been born again to "confess your faults one to another . . ." (James 5:16), and, "If we confess our sins, he is faithful and just to forgive us our sins, and to cleanse us from all unrighteousness" (1 John 1:9). According to the Bible it is necessary to recognize and confess both the condition and act of sin and to receive God's forgiveness.

A New Gospel?

In the midst of writing his unbiblical gospel, Harris declares:

> If Transactional Analysis is a part of the truth which helps to liberate people, the churches should make it available. Many ministers who have been trained in Transactional Analysis agree and are conducting courses in Transactional Analysis for members of their churches as well as using it in pastoral counseling.[25]

For many years TA was much loved in Christian circles, much taught in Christian colleges, and much practiced by Christian psychotherapists. Residues of the theory continue to contaminate Christian counseling.

TA is accepted by many as truth because it sounds so close to the truth. Harris speaks of morality, sin, born again, and grace. However, Harris's concept of morality is not biblical; nor are his concepts of sin, born again, and grace. Harris preaches a false gospel of universalism and a false path of salvation through mere self-forgiveness. About all Harris has done is to attempt to replace the fundamental truths of Scripture with a self-help game called Transactional Analysis. Upon close scrutiny and careful observation, one sees Harris with his TA game as just another deception.

16

Arthur Janov
Primal Therapy

Within the muddy waters of the psychoanalytic stream are numerous tributaries of Freudian theory, and among them flows the questionable Primal Scream therapy, created by Dr. Arthur Janov. Janov superimposed his theories upon the unconscious determinants of behavior, the vast influence of the early formative years on present behavior, and the need to return to the past to uncover early traumas which are buried in the unconscious.

There is a little psychoanalytic leaven in too many a psychotherapeutic loaf, but Primal Therapy has a particularly strong Freudian flavor. Janov invented a novel twist to the Freudian framework. He took the basics and added some excitement, drama, and stimulus for violent expression. He has popularized the psychic trip into the past and claims a 95 percent cure rate for customers.[1]

Soon after Janov completed his doctorate in psychology from Claremont Graduate School in 1960, he opened his private practice. Primal Therapy began during a session with a college student whom he calls Danny Wilson. In this session Wilson told Janov about a comedian whose act consisted of wandering around the stage dressed in diapers, drinking out of a baby bottle, and calling out, "Mommy! Daddy! Mommy! Daddy!" The comedian ended his act by passing out plastic bags, vomiting into a bag, and inviting the audience to do likewise. Because of Wilson's obvious fascination with the act, Janov suggested that he might want to cry out "Mommy" and "Daddy" just as the comedian had done. Although Wilson first refused, he finally gave in and began calling out, "Mommy! Daddy! Mommy! Daddy!" The next few minutes provided the basis for Janov's new therapeutic system.

Janov noticed that Wilson became very upset and began turning and twisting in agony, with his breathing becoming rapid and sporadic. Then Wilson screeched, "Mommy! Daddy!" His movements became more convulsive and finally he let out a piercing, deathlike scream. With this scream, Janov launched Primal Therapy. Janov began trying it out on other clients and developed his theory accordingly. Then, he published a description of his methodology in his best-selling book *Primal Scream*, which has been translated into every major language.[2] At the time Janov had to build special, soundproof facilities to protect the community from the ear-piercing screams and violent verbalizations expressed during the sessions.

The sacred words of Primal Therapy are *Primal Pain*, which Janov capitalized for emphasis. These words form the core around which the central Primal Therapy doctrines revolve. According to Janov, as the child grows he has a dilemma between being himself and conforming to his parents' expectations. During this developmental period, the child accumulates pain from the injuries of unmet needs, such as not being fed when hungry, not being changed when wet, or being ignored when needing attention. Primal pain occurs as the result of the conflicts between self-need and parental expectation. Through the process of growth as conflicts continue to occur, the accumulation of primal pain results in what Janov calls the "Primal Pool of Pain."

When the pool gets deep enough, just one more incident supposedly pushes the child into neurosis. This single significant incident is labeled the "major Primal Scene." Janov contends:

> The major Primal Scene is the single most shattering event in the child's life. It is that moment of icy, cosmic loneliness, the bitterest of all epiphanies. It is the time when he begins to discover that he is not loved for what he is and will not be.[3]

It is at this point that the child finally gives up the idea of being himself in order to gain his parents' love. In the process of gaining parental approval, the child supposedly seals off his real feelings and becomes an unreal self. Janov calls this disassociation from one's feelings "neurosis."

Janov teaches that the primal scene occurs between the ages of five and seven and is buried in the unconscious. According to Janov, the individual builds a network of defenses against even the awareness that the pain is there and he develops a life style that hides the origin of the pain and merely releases the tension caused by the pain, but he is not able to eliminate it.

Notice here, as with the Freudian process of blame and the voyage into the past, Janov's culprits are the parents and the solution is to be found in the past. In both theories only a return to the early years can bring healing for present anxieties. Janov specifies a single cause of neurosis: blocked pain; and he offers a single cure as the one and only cure in all the world for neurosis: Primal Therapy.

Janov theorizes that to be cured, the neurotic must return to his major primal scene where he decided to give up his real self and his real feelings in exchange for the possibility of parental love. He must experience the emotions, the events, and the expectations of others as well as the accompanying pain in order to be cured. The experience of returning to the primal scene and suffering the primal pain is called a "Primal." Primals are a necessary part of the healing process as far as Janov is concerned.

Reading Janov's book one sees an absence of joy in the Primals. They seem to be universally filled with such negative human emotions as anger, fear, loneliness, and rejection. Although Primal Therapy involves both a talking out and a feeling out, feeling is supreme. The way into and out of neurosis, according to Janov, is through feeling. He says, "Neurosis is a disease of feeling."[4]

Primal Therapy promises a quickie cure. It involves three weeks of intensive individual therapy, followed by six months of weekly group sessions, and culminating in one week of intensive private therapy. After this, the patient is free to have Primals on his own. During the first three weeks of individual therapy, the patient usually has his first Primal. After that, he continues to have more Primals during post-period group sessions. The therapist does everything he can to encourage the patient to get in touch with his internal Pain. A number of props, such as baby bottles, cribs, cuddly toys, life-sized photographs of parents, and even a birth simulator made out of inner tubes, had originally been used during these sessions.

In group sessions there is little interchange among those present. The Primal is king and the individual experience is supreme. As you can imagine, it would seem like utter chaos and outright bedlam to stumble upon such a group at the time. One might find some adults sucking baby bottles, others cuddling stuffed toys, still others in adult-sized cribs, one man standing with his genitals exposed, and a woman with her breasts uncovered. Then there was the birth simulator for those who wanted to experience the Primals that go all the way back to the womb and the birth process. Additionally, picture thirty or forty adults on the floor, gagging, thrashing, writhing, gurgling, choking, and wailing. Listen to the sobbing and screeching, "Daddy, be nice!" "Mommy, help!" "I hate you! I hate you!" "Daddy, don't hurt me anymore!" "Mommy, I'm afraid!" And all of this is punctuated by deep rattling and high-piercing screams. Today the atmosphere is less chaotic—gone are many of the props originally used. However, the theory is still the same.

Does Primal Therapy really bring emotional stability into a person's life? Janov enthusiastically claims a 95 percent cure rate. But, it depends on whom you ask. Just as with many forms of therapy, there are many testimonials, but little verifiable research. Janov's critics have accused the patients of either consciously or unconsciously faking the Primals. No doubt there is some self-hypnosis and gullibility involved. Others have warned that this type of treatment could cause psychological deterioration or permanent psychosis. Some former patients have even called it emotional brainwashing.

If one listens to testimonials of satisfied customers, one might well be impressed with the glowing claims of emotional healing and the elimination of migraine headaches, ulcers, arthritis, menstrual cramps, and asthma. Janov states that many dramatic physical changes result from his therapy. "For example," he says, "about one-third of the moderately flat-chested women independently reported that their breasts grew."[5] Janov claims that Primal Therapy is a cure-all when he declares, "But Primal Therapy *should* be able to do away with all symptoms or the premise—that symptoms are the result of Primal Pains—is not valid."[6] (Italics in original.)

Such testimonials are not backed with any kind of unbiased research. Since outside research teams were not allowed to conduct studies, the success or failure of Primal Therapy cannot be determined apart from the subjectivity of testimonials which range all the way from praising to damning. Without outside validation from objective research groups, no one can know the extent of help or damage that occurs.

This sick psychotherapy is only one of a host of similar therapies that are attracting a large number of adults seeking to find solace for the troubled soul. It is impossible to tell how many are in Primal Therapy or any one of its "friends and relations." However, one can see the influence of Primal Therapy in inner healing and in expressive therapy, where people are encouraged to re-experience the pain of the past.

Dr. Leonard Berkowitz, who has extensively studied violence and aggression, disagrees with the idea that it is desirable to let out one's aggressive feelings. Those therapists that encourage such active expressions of negative emotions are called "ventilationists." Their therapies, according to Berkowitz, stimulate and reward aggression and "heighten the likelihood of subsequent violence."[7] He declares, "The evidence dictates now that it is unintelligent to encourage persons to be aggressive, even if, with the best of intentions, we want to limit such behavior to the confines of psychotherapy."[8]

Berkowitz criticizes the rejection of the intellect in these expressive therapies, as well as the popular view held by ventilationists and others that it is unhealthy to suppress one's feelings. He believes that "in the long run, our social and human problems can be solved only with intelligence."[9]

Desperate and naive Christians are just as likely to undergo ventilationist therapies as any other, and there are Christian psychotherapists using such regressive and expressive therapies. Janov and others have not only capitalized on Freud's fantasies, but also on the public's gullibility. People who are desperate to escape the emptiness and loneliness of life are willing to believe direct or implied promises backed up by a title and an office or an institute and a board of directors. And so, fantasy follows fantasy until we come full circle back to the mirage of empty promises and testimonials, which look like an oasis in the desert of despair.

17

Diluted,
Polluted,
or Pure?

Although both the psychological way and the biblical way claim to lead people to mental-emotional-behavioral stability and positive changes in thought and behavior, they are actually quite different. The psychological way originates with man, utilizes man-made techniques, and ends with man. The biblical way originates with God, employs gifts and fruit of the Spirit, and leads a person to a greater awareness of God and of himself as created by God. The psychological way is based on manmade philosophies, mainly humanism, but the biblical way is based upon biblical principles.

The psychological way is a combination of techniques and theories, but the biblical way is a synthesis of love and truth. Jesus said, "I am the way, the truth, and the life" (John 14:6), and the apostle John defined God as

259

"love" (1 John 4:8). The psychological way involves changing standards and flexible morals. The biblical way follows the unchanging standard and authority of God's Word.

The psychological way has self at the center, while the biblical way is centered in Christ. The psychological way mainly attempts to treat the mind and emotions of a person apart from his body and spirit. The biblical way considers the whole man and transforms the mind, emotions, will, and behavior through bringing them into a right relationship to God. The psychological way attempts to change a person's thinking and behaving through the mind, will, and emotions alone. The biblical way changes a person's thinking, feeling, and behaving through his spirit.

The church would do well to develop this care of souls ministry and thus provide for the deeper needs of individuals, minister personally to those people who are suffering from mental-emotional stress, help those who are facing difficult situations, and even minister to those who are suffering from deep emotional disorders. Only one who ministers biblically can minister to the spiritual nature of an individual.

The biblical process through salvation and sanctification and the accompanying spiritual solutions are all that are necessary for establishing and maintaining mental-emotional-behavioral health and dealing with nonorganic problems of living. There is no need for both biblical and psychological solutions. There is no need to add psychotherapy to the biblical care of souls. Christians need simply and solely to rely on the Word of God and the work of the Holy Spirit and return the ministry of the care of souls to its proper place in the church. Dr. Thomas Szasz very clearly recommends that the responsibility for mental health care should be taken away from the professions and given to voluntary associations such as churches. He declared, "I would turn this whole business back to the ministers and priests and rabbis."[1]

One very difficult task, however, will be convincing Christians that there are not two equally good ways to solve problems of living—the biblical way and the psychological way. An even more difficult task will be convincing Christians that attempts to combine the psychological and the biblical only emasculates Christianity because of the inherent conflicting belief systems of the two. There is only one way for Christians and that is the biblical way.

We hope that we have revealed enough misconceptions, misunderstandings, and mistakes about psychotherapy to enable Christians to reject professional psychotherapy as a valid means of dealing with mental-emotional-behavioral problems.

Since the advent of psychotherapy, each generation has brought forth its psychotherapeutic innovators who have insisted upon the success of their systems. Dr. Jerome Frank says, "A historical overview of Western psychotherapy reveals that the dominant psychotherapeutic approach of an era reflects contemporary cultural attitudes and values."[2] In contrast, the Bible contains eternal truths about the human condition. God has given His Word, and it serves as a healing balm for all ages. God's Word does not change with the culture or the times.

Available evidence should discourage anyone's preference for psychotherapy over a biblical ministry that gives counsel and care to suffering souls. The biblical way always has been and continues to be the proper and successful way to deal with mental-emotional-behavioral problems. As we have demonstrated, the psychological way is questionable at best, detrimental at worst, and a spiritual counterfeit at least. We are not attacking the psychological way merely as a means of establishing the biblical way. As we have shown earlier, **professional psychotherapy should be condemned anyway**.

It is extraordinary that so many people have spent so much money for so many years on a system that has so little to give. After all the herculean effort of all the psychotherapies offered, purchased, and evaluated, and the billions of dollars changing hands, about all that may eventually be proved is this: on the average, given any problem, doing something about it is usually better than not doing anything at all.

The church does not need psychotherapy or its convoluted systems of false theories and fabrications offered as facts. Psychotherapy, from its very beginning, has been and still is detrimental to Christianity. It has dishonestly usurped the cure of souls ministry and it distorts any form of Christianity to which it attaches itself.

Amalgamation

Historically and philosophically many aspects of psychotherapy have been directly or indirectly antagonistic to Christianity, yet many believe that the two are complementary and that psychotherapy and Christianity are perfectly compatible as used simultaneously or separately under different circumstances.

The contemporary church has fastened its faith on psychotherapy and believes its claims beyond proof or justification. At the same time, the church has become suspicious and doubtful of the validity of biblical solutions to problems of living. The element of the self-fulfilling prophecy has transpired here. People have been rewarded according to their expectations. When one believes in psychotherapy and doubts the extent of the transforming power of Scripture, the psychological way appears more promising than the biblical way.

One of the largest referral systems to psychotherapy is the church. Pastors quite regularly refer Christians to psychotherapists, because they have been convinced that they themselves are not able to help such people and that only the professional has the expertise required for counseling a person in need. Such referrals to professional psychotherapists occur because Christians have been talked out of the curative power of God and His Word.

In most cases, pastors are referring their people to a system they know little about but have been convinced to accept as valid. Most pastors could not defend this system except by dredging up the defunct medical model or by leaning upon some unsupportable generalizations about the supposed effectiveness of psychotherapy. Most ministers could not even tell you the predominant psychotherapeutic orientation or the success or failure rate of the therapist to whom he sends his flock.

Through the guile of psychotherapy and the naiveté of the church, many have opted for the hollowness of psychotherapy more than the holiness of Christianity. An ever-increasing number of seminaries offer various programs to prepare people to practice professional psychotherapy as clinical psychologists, marriage and family counselors, and chaplains. Many seminaries and Christian colleges offer the services of psychiatrists, clinical psychologists, psychiatric social workers, and counselors to minister to the mental-emotional-behavioral needs of all. Psychotherapy is so universally acclaimed, accepted, and believed that one would think the church had received it as a vision from on high.

Many Christians think psychotherapy provides real truths about man and can therefore be trusted to help improve human behavior. The question is: which "truth" is true? There is not one Christian psychotherapeutic way. Christian psychotherapists follow a variety of the more than 400 available schools of thought. Psychotherapy, both outside and inside Christendom, provides a diversity of methods and belief systems. There is much the same confusion and contradiction of psychotherapeutic thought both in and out of Christendom. The Bible is eternal, but which psychotherapeutic systems are eternal? The Psalmist wrote, "The Lord bringeth the counsel of the heathen to nought: he maketh the devices of the people of none effect. The counsel of the Lord standeth for ever, the thoughts of his heart to all generations" (Psalm 33:10-11).

The Christian psychotherapist believes in combining the Bible with his favorite psychological theories and therapies. His faith is in a recipe that adds the ingredients from both. Even if the Christian psychotherapist uses the Bible, there is a danger. The person who finds a seeming compatibility between a psychological idea and a biblical truth becomes vulnerable to incorporating other ideas that may be contrary to Scripture. How much psychotherapeutic garbage has the Christian psychotherapist taken in and dispensed as a result of accepting therapeutic ideas that sound biblical? Psychotherapeutic techniques and theories should not be inflicted upon the Bible, nor should the Bible be forced to fit psychotherapy. True ministry to souls should rely on Scripture, while the Holy Spirit does the inner work.

It may be that some Christian psychotherapists' hidden reason for the lack of complete dependence upon Scripture is that this position might raise the whole question of charging fees for services. If the Bible is sufficient and caring for souls is a ministry of the church, what is the rationalization for charging a fee? If one can maintain the bankrupt medical model for using psychotherapy and defend professional training in psychotherapeutic techniques, charging a fee may appear justifiable. However, as we indicated earlier, we are opposed to professional psychotherapy and have recommended delicensing such individuals and stopping third-party payments.

The popularity and proliferation of psychotherapy in Christian circles have given it a validity and visibility it does not deserve. Psychotherapy is a system filled with many unproved theories and few facts. It is a ridiculous delusion to go on believing in the romance and ritual of psychotherapy, which is filled with speculative and spurious thought and often ends up killing one's confidence, confession, and convictions in Christianity.

The psychotherapeutic system usually centers on self and appeals to a sinful society. Too many for too long have been seduced by this orientation of self-centeredness, which produces only a pseudosolution for the soul. **The safest and sanest thing for Christians to do is to avoid psychotherapy and rely on a biblical ministry in the church.** Such a reversal would be a welcome relief from the woes of a system that is so subjective and so incapable of providing certainty or validity. Reestablishing the cure of souls and abandoning the psychotherapeutic domain would no doubt prove illuminating and spiritually invigorating.

Scripture, not psychotherapy, reveals the true condition and nature of humanity. The Bible contains sufficient information and counsel for maintaining mental-emotional-behavioral health and for ministering to problems of living. There may be psychotherapeutic systems that will help a person feel better or to indulge self without feeling guilty, but none has any eternal value.

Psychotherapy is the counterfeit currency of the world and a substitute for the healing balm of Gilead. Christian psychotherapy is a house divided against itself. How long shall Christians have one foot in the wilderness of the counterfeit cure of minds and one in the promised land of the biblical cure of souls?

Faith in What?

In all honesty, there is no research evidence for greater effectiveness of the psychological way over the biblical way. Faith leads people in one direction or the other. No one has proved outside of faith the superiority of either way. When a person chooses one way over the other, it merely constitutes a step of faith in one direction or the other. Psychotherapy is swathed in theories that are believed as fact by an *act of faith*. It is dishonest not to admit the element of faith and to insist that psychological theories are universal facts. Such theories rest on the same need for faith as religion does. They are wholly dependent on faith.

Some might argue that certain testimonials support the use of the psychological way, while others give testimonials that support the biblical way. However, if one overlooks the testimonials in either direction and demands hard evidence, the conclusion is that neither the psychological way nor the biblical way has final research proof of either superiority or greater effectiveness of one over the other. Each requires faith. The question is, are we going to place our faith and trust in the questionable systems devised by men or are we going to believe and trust the absolute truth in God's Word?

The psychological model has not proved itself as a superior substitute for the biblical model either theoretically or practically. The cure of minds malfunctioned from the very beginning and has floundered ever since. If psychoanalysis had done what it pretended to do at the beginning of the movement, people would never have had to invent more than 400 other therapies and thousands of techniques. The fact that so many different therapeutic systems are being tried and combined indicates that not much is really known for sure about the cause and cure of mental-emotional-behavioral disorders. Proposed causes and attempted cures are merely guesses as to how to deal with such problems.

Psychotherapy is like the naked monarch in the fable "The Emperor's New Clothes." It has proliferated itself and permeated our society for one hundred years. It has captured hearts and minds and turned the church away from the cure of souls. Like the emperor, psychotherapy stands proud and tall in its supposedly beautiful garments and few have dared whisper, "The emperor has no clothes!"

From Freud's unconscious determinants to Jung's archetypes to Maslow's hierarchy of needs to Rogers' positive self-regard to Harris's I'm OK-You're OK throughout the theory upon theory and ensuing eclecticism, the emperor is simply subjectivity garbed in the pseudo-sophistication of scientific sounding vocabulary and decorated with academic degrees and licenses. Psychotherapy nonetheless stands naked before the eyes of true science and research.

The emperor is naked and few have the vision or courage to speak up and say so. Few dare speak out because neither society nor the church dares question such a widely accepted activity that supposedly helps suffering souls. And so, all stand and look at the emperor and pretend that he is wearing fine apparel. They have pretended so long and so hard that they actually believe the emperor has on the most elegant clothes ever created. The illusion is so widely accepted that many people, both in and out of the church, do not want to deal with the facts of psychotherapy's nakedness and would rather believe a delusion than face reality.

Our primary objection to the use of psychotherapy and Christian psychology is not based merely on its confused state of self-contradiction or its phony scientific facade. Our primary objection is not even based on the attempts to explain human behavior through personal opinion presented as scientific theory. **Our greatest objection to psychotherapy and Christian psychology is that, without proof or justification, it has compromised the Word of God, the power of the cross, and the work of the Holy Spirit among Christians.**

One way out of the web of psychological myth and entrapment is to consider the following:

1. It is detrimental to add psychology to God's Word or to use psychology in place of the Bible.

2. The Christian psychologizer generally knows less about the Word and its application to problems of living than a pastor.

3. What the Christian psychologizer says about human relationships and problems of living is personal opinion rather than scientific fact.

4. Degrees, licenses, experience, and education in the field of counseling do not make the psychologizers experts on human behavior.

5. When the Christian psychologizer mentions God or His Word, he often does it to give more credibility to his opinions than to promote biblical understanding.

6. There is almost no psychological idea that cannot be made to sound biblical.

7. The Christian psychologizer often interprets Scripture from a psychological perspective rather than evaluating psychology from a biblical perspective.

8. What the psychologizer is saying is contrary to what numerous other psychologizers might say.

9. Case histories or successful examples are not generally representative of what normally happens.

10. Successes claimed have less to do with the counselor's psychological training, licenses, and experience than with factors in the client's own life.

11. Successes claimed in counseling could easily be matched by persons not receiving psychological counseling.

12. Successes in psychological counseling are often short-term.

13. For every success mentioned there are many failures.

14. If someone is improved or delivered from his problems, competent biblical ministry could have done better.

15. For every psychological solution suggested there is a better biblical solution available.

16. There is definitely a harm rate for every seemingly wonderful idea from the psychological systems of men.

There is absolutely no scientific justification for using psychological opinions and therapeutic techniques for understanding or treating the nonphysical realm of the soul and spirit. Such an intrusion violates the intention of Scripture and undermines the holy work of the Spirit. There is no biblical justification for pastors sending people outside the church to obtain psychological help.

Living Water

Psychotherapy has tried to maim the hand that holds the Sword of the Spirit and has made the church vulnerable in soul ministry by providing all sorts of substitute psychological ideas in place of genuine biblical solutions. Psychotherapy even offers all kinds of trinitarian psychotherapeutic models to draw people away from the Father, Son, and Holy Spirit.

God spoke through the prophet Jeremiah and said:

> Hath a nation changed their gods, which are yet no gods? but my people have changed their glory for that which doth not profit.
>
> Be astonished, O ye heavens, at this, and be horribly afraid, be ye very desolate, saith the Lord.
>
> For my people have committed two evils; they have forsaken me the fountain of living waters, and hewed them out cisterns, broken cisterns, that can hold no water (Jeremiah 2:11-13).

The psychological way is a broken cistern while the biblical way is the living water. The psychotherapists have filled their broken cisterns with the water from the four polluted streams of psychology.

The church has drunk this polluted water. In its attempts to provide mental-emotional-behavioral help, the church has turned to the world of psychotherapy, the very counterfeit that has undermined and nearly destroyed the biblical cure of souls ministry in the first place.

The church not only permitted the cure of minds to replace the cure of souls ministry without substantiation or proof, but has embraced psychotherapeutic theories, techniques, terminology, and theology in its blind desire to meet the needs of a suffering generation.

All mental-emotional-behavioral problems that have no organic base are best ministered unto by the Word of God and the mutual care in the Body of Christ. In addition, those with organic, biological problems can also be helped through such ministry in addition to medical treatment. God has asked in His Word, "Whom shall I send, and who will go for us?" (Isaiah 6:8). This is a call to serve and to minister.

How long shall Christians halt between the psychological way and the biblical way? Christians have a living God, the source of all life and healing. They have His living Word. His Word contains the balm of Gilead for the troubled soul. His Word ministers grace and restoration to the mind, the will, and the emotions. We pray that the Lord will fully restore the cure of souls ministry to the church. We pray that He will use pastors, elders, and other members of the Body of Christ who will confidently stand on the completeness of God's Word and minister under the anointing of God's Holy Spirit. We pray that all Christians will rely on God's principles outlined in His Word, serve as a priesthood of all believers, and minister God's love, grace, mercy, faithfulness, wisdom, and truth to those who are suffering from problems of living. We pray that many will voluntarily give their time to love, pray, and serve to lift the heavy burdens. We pray that believers will fulfill Paul's admonition:

> Brethren, if a man be overtaken in a fault, ye which are spiritual, restore such an one in the spirit of meekness; considering thyself, lest thou also be tempted. Bear one another's burdens, and so fulfill the law of Christ (Galatians 6:1-2).

The Lord has indeed promised more to His church than a Dead Sea. He has promised living water!

> In the last day, that great day of the feast, Jesus stood and cried, saying, If any man thirst, let him come unto me, and drink. He that believeth on me, as the scripture hath said, out of his belly shall flow rivers of living water (John 7:37-38).

Is not the Lord, the Creator of the universe, able to fulfill His promises? He has promised life and life abundant! Surely we can believe Him! His faithfulness is unto all generations!

> Ho, every one that thirsteth, come ye to the waters, and he that hath no money; come ye, buy and eat; yea, come, buy wine and milk without money and without price.
>
> Wherefore do ye spend money for that which is not bread? and your labour for that which satisfieth not? hearken diligently unto me, and eat ye that which is good, and let your soul delight itself in fatness.
>
> Incline your ear, and come unto me: hear, and your soul shall live. . . .
>
> For my thoughts are not your thoughts, neither are your ways my ways, saith the Lord.
>
> For as the heavens are higher than the earth, so are my ways higher than your ways, and my thoughts than your thoughts (Isaiah 55:1-3, 8, 9).

Ho, every one that thirsteth, come ye to the waters. . . .

End Notes

Chapter 1: The End of "Christian Psychology"

1. P. Sutherland and P. Poelstra, "Aspects of Integration," paper presented at the meeting of the Christian Association for Psychological Studies, Santa Barbara, CA, June 1976.
2. Richard Simon, "From the Editor," *Networker* (May/June 1991), p. 2.
3. APA Commission on Psychotherapies, *Psychotherapy Research: Methodological and Efficacy Issues* (Washington: American Psychiatric Association, 1982), p. 192.
4. Tana Dineen, *Manufacturing Victims* (Montreal: Robert Davies Publishing, 1996), p. 249.
5. *Ibid.*, pp. 18, 19.
6. Robyn Dawes, *House of Cards: Psychology and Psychotherapy Built on Myth* (New York: The Free Press/Macmillan, Inc., 1994), p. 12.
7. Jack G. Wiggins, Jr., "Would You Want Your Child To Be a Psychologist?" *American Psychologist* (June 1994), p. 486.
8. Steve Rabey, "Hurting Helpers," *Christianity Today* (September 16, 1996), pp. 76,77.
9. Dawes, *op. cit.,* p. 11.
10. Alvin Sanoff, "Psychiatry Runs into an Identity Crisis," *U.S. News and World Report* (October 9, 1978), p. 64.
11. Jerome Frank, quoted in Dineen, *op. cit.,* p. 194.
12. Jerome D. Frank, "An Overview of Psychotherapy" in *Overview of the Psychotherapies*, Gene Usdin, ed. (New York: Brunner/Mazel, 1975), p. 7.
13. Sharland Trotter, "Nader Group Releases First Consumer Guide to Psychotherapists," *APA Monitor* (December 1975), p. 11
14. Frank, "An Overview of Psychotherapy," *op. cit.,* p. 8.
15. Leo Rosten, "Unhappiness Is Not a Disease," *Reader's Digest* (July 1978), p. 176.
16. George Albee, quoted in "Psychology is Alive and Well," *Santa Barbara News-Press*, 23 August 1981, p. B-7.
17. Alan Stone, quoted in Lois Timnick, "Psychiatry's Focus Turns to Biology," *Los Angeles Times*, 21 July 1980, Part I, p. 21.
18. Allen E. Bergin and Sol L. Garfield, eds., *Handbook of Psychotherapy and Behavior Change*, Fourth Edition (New York: John Wiley & Sons, Inc., 1994), p. 6.
19. Morris Parloff, "Shopping for the Right Therapy," *Saturday Review* (February 21, 1976), p. 14.
20. Dineen, *op. cit.,* p. 20.
21. *Ibid.*, p. 20.
22. *Ibid.*, p. 309.
23. *Ibid.*, p. 166.
24. R. Christopher Barden and the National Association for Consumer Protection in Mental Health Practices, "The Truth and Responsibility in Mental Health Practices Act."
25. The National Association for Consumer Protection in Mental Health Practices Press Release, Office of the President, 4025 Quaker Lane

North, Plymouth, MN 55441, Phone 612-595-0566, FAX 612-595-0035, e-mail: rebarden@aol.com.

26. *Ibid.*
27. See list of Martin and Deidre Bobgan's books on final pages of present volume.
28. Excerpted from Martin and Deidre Bobgan, *Competent to Minister: The Biblical Care of Souls* (Santa Barbara, CA: EastGate Publishers, 1996), pp. 200-201.

Chapter 2: Science or Pseudoscience?

1. *Webster's New Collegiate Dictionary* (Springfield: G. & C. Merriam Company, 1974).
2. Roger Mills, "Psychology Goes Insane, Botches Role as Science," *The National Educator* (July 1980), p. 14.
3. Sigmund Koch, ed., *Psychology: A Study of a Science* (New York: McGraw-Hill, 1959-1963).
4. Sigmund Koch, "Psychology Cannot Be a Coherent Science," *Psychology Today* (Sept. 1969), p. 67.
5. *Ibid.*, p. 66.
6. *Ibid.*, p. 67.
7. Sigmund Koch, "The Image of Man in Encounter Groups," *The American Scholar*, 42 (Autumn 1973), p. 636.
8. Gordon Allport, *Pattern and Growth in Personality* (New York: Holt, Rinehart & Winston, Inc., 1961), pp. 8-9.
9. Bertrand Russell, *The Impact of Science on Society* (New York: Simon and Schuster, 1953), p. 18.
10. Carlo Lastrucci, *The Scientific Approach: Basic Principles of the Scientific Method* (Cambridge: Schenkman Publishing Co., Inc., 1967), p. 115.
11. Karl Popper, "Scientific Theory and Falsifiability" in *Perspectives in Philosophy*, Robert N. Beck, ed. (New York: Holt, Rinehart, Winston, 1975), p. 342.
12. *Ibid.*, p. 343.
13. *Ibid.*, p. 344.
14. *Ibid.*, p. 345.
15. *Ibid.*, p. 343.
16. *Ibid.*, p. 346.
17. Jerome Frank, "Therapeutic Factors in Psychotherapy," *American Journal of Psychotherapy*, 25 (1971), p. 356.
18. E. Fuller Torrey, *The Mind Game* (New York: Emerson Hall Publishers, Inc., 1972), p. 8.
19. Adolf Grünbaum, *The Foundations of Psychoanalysis: A Philosophical Critique* (Berkeley: University of California Press, 1984); Adolf Grünbaum, personal letter on file.
20. Robert Rosenthal, *Experimental Effects in Behavioral Research* (New York: Appleton-Century-Crofts, 1966), p. vii.
21. Koch, "Psychology Cannot Be a Coherent Science," *op. cit.*, p. 66.
22. Thomas S. Kuhn, *The Structure of Scientific Revolutions*, Third Edition (Chicago: The University of Chicago Press, 1996), p. 206.
23. T. Theocharis and M. Psimopoulos, "Where Science Has Gone Wrong," *Nature*, 329 (15 October 1987), p. 596.

24. John D. Barrow, *The World Within the World* (Oxford: Clarendon Press, 1988), p. 336.

25. Paul Feyerabend, *Against Method: Outline of an Anarchistic Theory of Knowledge* (London: New Left Books, 1975), p. 28.

26. Paul Feyerabend quoted in Theocharis and Psimopoulos, *op. cit.*, p. 596.

27. Linda Riebel, "Theory as Self-Portrait and the Ideal of Objectivity," *Journal of Humanistic Psychology* (Spring 1982), pp. 91-92.

28. Harvey Mindess, *Makers of Psychology: The Personal Factor* (New York: Insight Books, 1988), p. 15.

29. *Ibid.*, pp. 15-16.

30. *Ibid.*, p. 16.

31. *Ibid.*, p. 46.

32. *Ibid.*, p. 169.

33. Frank, *op. cit.*, p. 356.

34. Jerome Frank, "An Overview of Psychotherapy" in *Overview of the Psychotherapies*, Gene Usdin, ed. (New York: Brunner/Mazel, 1975), p. 19.

35. Robert M. Johnson, *A Logic Book*, Second Edition (Belmont, CA: Wadsworth Publishing Company, 1992), p. 256.

36. *Ibid.*, p. 258.

37. Thomas Szasz, *The Myth of Psychotherapy* (Garden City: Double-day/Anchor Press, 1978), pp. 182-183.

38. *Ibid.*, p. 7.

39. Thomas Szasz, *The Myth of Mental Illness* (New York: Harper & Row, 1974), p. 262.

40. *Ibid.*

41. Ronald Leifer, *In the Name of Mental Health* (New York: Science House, 1969), pp. 36-37.

42. *Ibid.*, p. 38.

43. E. Fuller Torrey, *The Death of Psychiatry* (Radnor: Chilton Book Company, 1974), p. 24.

44. Daniel Goleman, "An Eastern Toe in the Stream of Consciousness," *Psychology Today* (January 1981), p. 84.

45. Jacob Needleman, "Psychiatry and the Sacred" in *Consciousness: Brain, States of Awareness, and Mysticism*, Daniel Goleman and Richard Davidson, eds. (New York: Harper & Row, 1979), pp. 209-210.

46. *Ibid.*

47. *Brain/Mind* (December 1993), p. 6.

Chapter 3: Integration or Separation?

1. *Christianity Today* (September 16, 1996), p. 77.

2. Steve Rabey, "Hurting Helpers," *Christianity Today, ibid.*, p. 76.

3. John D. Moffat, "Is 'All Truth God's Truth'?" *The Christian Conscience* (May 1997), p. 27.

4. *Ibid.*, p. 28.

5. *Ibid.*

6. Bruce Demarest and Gordon Lewis, *Integrative Theology: Knowing Ultimate Reality the Living God*, Volume One (Grand Rapids: Zondervan Publishing House, 1987), p. 61.

7. *Ibid.*, pp. 238-241.

8. *Ibid.*, p. 60.
9. *Ibid.*, p. 65.
10. Cornelius Van Til, *An Introduction to Theology,* Volume One (Philadelphia: Westminster Theological Seminary, 1947), p. 69.
11. "The Minirth-Meier Clinic" Radio Program, P. O. Box 1925, Richardson, TX 75085, March 2, 1988.
12. Gary R. Collins, *Can You Trust Psychology?* (Downers Grove: Inter-Varsity Press, 1988), p. 52.
13. *Ibid.*, p. 19.
14. *Ibid.*
15. James D. Foster et al., "The Popularity of Integration Models, 1980-1985," *Journal of Psychology and Theology,* 16, 1 (1988), pp. 4, 8.
16. *Ibid.*, p. 8.
17. *Ibid.*
18. E. E. Griffith quoted in Everett L. Worthington, Jr., "Religious Counseling: A Review of Published Empirical Research," *Journal of Counseling and Development,* 64 (March 1986), p. 427.
19. Charles Tart, *Transpersonal Psychologies* (New York: Harper & Row, Publishers, 1975), p. 4.

Chapter 4: Does Psychotherapy Work?

1. Michael J. Lambert and Allen E. Bergin, "The Effectiveness of Psychotherapy" in *Handbook of Psychotherapy and Behavior Change,* Fourth Edition, Allen E. Bergin and Sol L. Garfield, eds. (New York: John Wiley & Sons, Inc., 1994), p. 176.
2. Hans H. Strupp, Suzanne W. Hadley, Beverly Gomes-Schwartz, *Psychotherapy for Better or Worse* (New York: Jason Aronson, Inc., 1977), p. 51.
3. *Ibid.*, p. 83.
4. Jeffrey Moussaieff Masson, *Against Therapy: Emotional Tyranny and the Myth of Psychological Healing* (New York: Atheneum, 1988), p. 252.
5. Terence W. Campbell, *Beware the Talking Cure: Psychotherapy May Be Hazardous To Your Mental Health* (Boca Raton: Upton Books, 1994), p. iii.
6. Hans J. Eysenck, "The Effects of Psychotherapy: An Evaluation," *Journal of Consulting Psychology,* 16 (1952), p. 322.
7. Hans J. Eysenck, "New Ways in Psychotherapy," *Psychology Today* (June 1967), p. 40.
8. C. B. Truax and R. R. Carkhuff, *Toward Effective Counseling and Psychotherapy: Training and Practice* (Chicago: Aldine, 1967), p. 5.
9. Lewis Carroll, *The Complete Alice* (Topsfield: Salem House Publishers, 1987), p. 30.
10. Lambert and Bergin, *op. cit.*, p. 156.
11. Allen E. Bergin and Sol L. Garfield, "Overview, Trends, and Future Issues," in *Handbook of Psychotherapy and Behavior Change,* Fourth Edition, *op. cit.*, p. 822.
12. Morris Parloff, "Psychotherapy and Research: An Anaclitic Depression," *Psychiatry* (November 1980), p. 287.
13. *Ibid.*, p. 288.
14. Morris Parloff, quoted in Sally Squires, "Should You Keep Your Therapist?" *American Health,* June 1986, p. 74.

15. Lambert and Bergin, *op. cit.*, p. 156.
16. Bergin and Garfield, *op. cit.*, p. 822.
17. Morris B. Parloff and Irene Elkin, "The NIMH Treatment of Depression Collaborative Research Program" in *History of Psychotherapy: A Century of Change*, Donald K. Freedheim, ed. (Washington, DC: American Psychological Association, 1992), p. 448.
18. J. D. Frank, quoted in Lambert and Bergin, *op. cit.*, p. 167.
19. Stanley Sue, Nolan Zane, and Kathleen Young, "Research on Psychotherapy with Culturally Diverse Populations" in *Handbook of Psychotherapy and Behavior Change*, Fourth Edition, *op. cit.*, pp. 809-810.
20. Allen E. Bergin and Michael J. Lambert, "The Evaluation of Therapeutic Outcomes" in *Handbook of Psychotherapy and Behavior Change*, Second Edition, Allen E. Bergin and Sol L. Garfield, eds. (New York: John Wiley & Sons, Inc., 1978), p. 180.
21. Allen Bergin, personal letter on file, June 7, 1988.
22. Allen E. Bergin, "Therapist-Induced Deterioration in Psychotherapy," BMA Audio Cassette/T-302 (New York: Guilford Publishers, Inc., 1979).
23. Truax and Mitchell quoted by Sol Garfield, "Psychotherapy Training and Outcome in Psychotherapy," BMA Audio Cassette/T-305 (New York: Guilford Publishers, Inc., 1979).
24. Bernie Zilbergeld, *The Shrinking of America* (Boston: Little, Brown and Company, 1983), p. 190.
25. Ruth G. Matarazzo, "Research on the Teaching and Learning of Psychotherapeutic Skills" in *Handbook of Psychotherapy and Behavior Change,* Allen E. Bergin and Sol L. Garfield, eds. (New York: John Wiley & Sons, Inc., 1971), p. 915.
26. Strupp, Hadley, Gomes-Schwartz, *op. cit.*, p. 66.
27. Richard L. Bednar and Jeffrey G. Shapiro, "Professional Research Commitment: A Symptom or a Syndrome," *Journal of Consulting and Clinical Psychology*, 34 (1970), pp. 323-326.
28. Stuart A. Kirk and Herb Kutchins, *The Selling of DSM: The Rhetoric of Science in Psychiatry* (New York: Aldine de Gruyter, 1992), p. 199.
29. *Diagnostic and Statistical Manual of Mental Disorders*, Fourth Edition (Washington: American Psychiatric Association), 1994.
30. Lambert and Bergin, "The Effectiveness of Psychotherapy," *op. cit.*, p. 161.
31. Bergin and Garfield, "Overview, Trends, and Future Issues," *op. cit.*, p. 825.
32. Robyn M. Dawes, *House of Cards: Psychology and Psychotherapy Built on Myth* (New York: The Free Press/Macmillan, Inc., 1994), p. 44.
33. David Myers, *The Inflated Self* (New York: The Seabury Press, 1980), p. 136.
34. Allen Fromme quoted in Elain Warren, "Most Neurotics Don't Need Therapy," *Los Angeles Herald Examiner*, 4 June 1981, p. C-6.
35. Myers, *op. cit.*, p. 136.
36. Arthur Shapiro interview by Martin Gross, *The Psychological Society* (New York: Random House, 1978), p. 230.

37. Leslie Prioleau, Martha Murdock, and Nathan Brody, "An Analysis of Psychotherapy Versus Placebo Studies," *The Behavioral and Brain Sciences* (June 1983), p. 284.

38. Arthur Shapiro, "Opening Comments" in *Psychotherapy Research*, Janet B. W. Williams and Robert L. Spitzer, eds. (New York: The Guilford Press, 1984), p. 106.

39. *Ibid.*, p. 107.

40. H. J. Eysenck, "The Outcome Problem in Psychotherapy: What Have We Learned? *Behavioural Research and Therapy*, 32, 5 (1994), p.490.

41. D. A. Shapiro quoted in *Placebo: Theory, Research, and Mechanisms*, Leonard White, Bernard Tursky and Gary E. Schwartz, eds. (New York: The Guilford Press, 1985), p. 204.

42. E. Fuller Torrey, "The Case for the Indigenous Therapist," *Archives of General Psychiatry*, 20 (March 1969), p. 367.

43. Jerome Frank, *Persuasion and Healing* (New York: Schocken Books, 1974), p. 167.

44. Allen Bergin, "Psychotherapy and Religious Values," *Journal of Consulting and Clinical Psychology*, 48, p. 98.

45. Lewis Thomas, "Medicine Without Science," *The Atlantic Monthly* (April 1981), p. 42.

46. Larry E. Beutler, Paulo P. P. Machado, and Susan Allstetter Neufeldt, "Therapist Variables" in *Handbook of Psychotherapy and Behavior Change*, Fourth Edition, *op. cit.*, p. 259.

47. Joseph Wortis, "General Discussion" in *Psychotherapy Research*, *op. cit.*, p. 394.

48. Beutler et al., *op. cit.*, p. 259.

49. Lambert and Bergin, "The Effectiveness of Psychotherapy," *op. cit.*, p. 177.

50. Bergin and Garfield, "Overview, Trends, and Future Issues," *op. cit.*, p. 822.

51. Hans H. Strupp and Kenneth I. Howard, "A Brief History of Psychotherapy Research" in *History of Psychotherapy: A Century of Change*, Donald K. Freedheim, ed. (Washington, DC: American Psychological Association, 1992), p. 314.

52. Dawes, *op. cit.*, p. 50.

53. *Ibid.*, p. 52.

54. *Ibid.*, p. 62.

55. *Ibid.*, p. 15.

56. *Ibid.*, p. 38.

57. *Ibid.*, p. 73.

58. *Ibid.*, p. 55.

59. *Ibid.*, p. 13.

60. Beutler et al., *op. cit.*, p. 259.

61. Keith Humphreys, "Clinical Psychologists as Psychotherapists," *American Psychologist*, 51 (March 1996), p. 190.

62. Hillel J. Einhorn and Robin M. Hogarth, "Confidence in Judgment: Persistence of the Illusion of Validity," *Psychological Review*, 85, 5 (1978), p. 395.

63. Dawes, *op. cit.*, p. 105.

64. *Ibid.*, pp. 26-27.

65. American Psychiatric Association, *Amicus Curiae* brief, *Tarasoff v. Regents of University of California*, 551 P.2d 334 (Cal. 1976).

66. Dawes, *op. cit.*, p. 101.
67. Arthur Janov, *The Primal Scream* (New York: Dell Publishing Co., Inc., 1970), p. 19.
68. Beutler et al., *op. cit.*, p. 249.
69. Dawes, *op. cit.*, pp. 101-102.
70. Jerome Frank, "Mental Health in a Fragmented Society: The Shattered Crystal Ball," *American Journal of Orthopsychiatry* (July 1979), p. 406.
71. H. J. Eysenck, "Meta-Analysis Squared—Does It Make Sense?" *American Psychologist* (February 1995), p. 111.
72. "Ambiguity Pervades Research on Effectiveness of Psychotherapy," *Brain/Mind Bulletin* (4 October 1982), p. 2.
73. Hans H. Strupp and Suzanne W. Hadley, "Specific vs. Nonspecific Factors in Psychotherapy," *Archives of General Psychiatry* (September 1979), p. 1126.
74. Hans Strupp, "The Tripartite Model and the *Consumer Reports* Study," *American Psychologist* (October 1996), p. 1021.
75. Martin Seligman, "The Effectiveness of Psychotherapy: The *Consumer Reports* Study," *American Psychologist* (December 1995), p. 969.
76. Neil S. Jacobson and Andrew Christiansen, "Studying the Effectiveness of Psychotherapy," *American Psychologist* (October 1996), p. 1033.
77. David E. Orlinsky, Klaus Grawe, and Barbara K. Parks, "Process and Outcome in Psychotherapy—Noch Einmal" in *Handbook of Psychotherapy and Behavior Change*, Fourth Edition, *op. cit.*, p. 365.
78. H. J. Eysenck, "Meta-Analysis Squared—Does It Make Sense?" *op. cit.*, p. 110.
79. H. J. Eysenck, "The Outcome Problem in Psychotherapy: What Have We Learned? *op. cit.*, p. 477.
80. American Psychiatric Association Commission on Psychotherapies, *Psychotherapy Research: Methodological and Efficacy Issues* (Washington: American Psychiatric Association, 1982), p. 228.
81. Donald R. Peterson, "The Reflective Educator," *American Psychologist* (December 1995), p. 976.
82. Dawes, *op. cit.*, p. 58.
83. *Ibid.*, p. 8.
84. *Ibid.*, p. 71.
85. *Ibid.*, p. 133.
86. *Ibid.*, p. 8.
87. Garth Wood, *The Myth of Neurosis* (New York: Harper & Row, 1986), p. 291.
88. "Mental Health: Does Therapy Help?" *Consumer Reports* (November 1995), pp. 734-739.
89. Tana Dineen, *Manufacturing Victims* (Montreal: Robert Davies, 1996), p. 176.
90. Seligman, *op. cit.*, pp. 965-974.
91. "Special Issue: Outcome Assessment of Psychotherapy," *American Psychologist* (October 1996).
92. Seligman, *op. cit.*, p. 966.

93. Timothy C. Brock, Melanie C. Green, Darcy A. Reich, and Lisa M. Evans, "The Consumer Reports Study of Psychotherapy: Invalid Is Invalid," *American Psychologist* (October 1996), p. 1083.

94. Jacobson and Christensen, *op. cit.*, p. 1031.

95. Neil Jacobson quoted in "Does Therapy Work," *Networker* (January/February 1996), p. 13.

96. Dineen, *op. cit.*, p. 174.

97. Martin E. Seligman,*"Science as an Ally of Practice,"* American Psychologist* (October 1996), p. 1075.

98. Zilbergeld, *op. cit.*, pp. 117-118.

99. Jerome Frank, *Persuasion and Healing* (New York: Schocken Books, 1974), p. 102.

100. Brock, Green et al., *op. cit.*, p. 1083.

101. Zilbergeld, *op. cit.*

102. Bernie Zilbergeld quoted in Don Stanley, "OK, So Maybe You Don't Need to See a Therapist," *Sacramento Bee*, 24 May 1983, p. B-4.

103. Dawes, *op. cit.*, p. 293.

104. Masson, *op. cit.*, p. xv.

105. Dawes, *op. cit.*, p. 198.

106. Thomas S. Szasz endorsement of *The Psychological Way / The Spiritual Way*, Bobgan and Bobgan (Minneapolis: Bethany House Publishers, 1979), back cover.

107. E. Fuller Torrey, *ibid.*, back cover.

108. Martin and Deidre Bobgan, *Competent to Minister: The Biblical Care of Souls* (Santa Barbara: EastGate Publishers, 1996).

189. O. Hobart Mowrer, *The Crisis in Psychiatry and Religion* (Princeton: D. Van Nostrand Co., Inc., 1961), p. 60.

Chapter 5: Rejection of the Living Water

1. Morris Parloff, "Shopping for the Right Therapy," *Saturday Review* (21 February 1976), p. 14.

2. Robert C. Fuller, *Mesmerism and the American Cure of Souls* (Philadelphia: University of Pennsylvania Press, 1982), p. 1.

3. *Ibid.*, p. 10.

4. *Ibid.*, p. 12

5. *Ibid.*, pp. 46-47.

6. *Ibid.*, p. 104.

7. Donald K. Freedheim, ed., *History of Psychotherapy: A Century of Change* (Washington, DC: American Psychological Association, 1992), p. 32.

8. *Ibid.*

9. Thomas Szasz, *The Myth of Psychotherapy* (Garden City: Doubleday/Anchor Press, 1978), p. 43.

10. Sigmund Freud, *The Future of an Illusion*, James Strachey, ed. and trans. (New York: W. W. Norton and Company, Inc., 1961), p. 43.

11. Thomas Szasz, *op. cit.*, p. 173.

12. George E. Atwood and Silvan S. Tomkins, "On the Subjectivity of Personality Theory," *Journal of the History of the Behavioral Sciences,* 12 (1976), p. 167.

13. Szasz, *op. cit.*, p. 139.

14. *Ibid.*, p. 146.

15. *Ibid.*, p. 140.

16. C. G. Jung, *Memories, Dreams, Reflections,* Aniela Jaffe, ed., Richard and Clara Winston, trans. (New York: Pantheon, 1963), p. 55.
17. Viktor Von Weizsaecker, "Reminiscences of Freud and Jung" in *Freud and the Twentieth Century,* B. Nelson, ed. (New York: Meridian, 1957), p. 72.
18. Jung, *Memories, Dreams, Reflections, op. cit.,* pp. 170-199.
19. Shirley Nicholson, *Shamanism* (Wheaton: The Theosophical Publishing House), p. 58.
20. *Ibid.,* p. 59.
21. Jacob Needleman, *A Sense of the Cosmos* (Garden City: Doubleday and Co., Inc., 1975), p. 107.
22. Arthur Burton, ed., *Encounter* (San Francisco: Jossey-Bass Inc., 1969), p. 11.
23. Szasz, *op. cit.,* p. 188.
24. *Ibid.,* pp. 104-105.
25. *Ibid.,* pp. 27-28.
26. *Ibid.,* p. 188.
27. Herbert Lazarus, *How to Get Your Money's Worth Out of Psychiatry* (Los Angeles: Sherbourne Press, Inc., 1973), p. 229.
28. Szasz, *op. cit.,* p. 32.
29. Julian Meltzoff and Melvin Kornreich, *Research in Psychotherapy* (New York: Atherton Press, Inc. 1970), p. 465.
30. Thomas Szasz, *The Myth of Psychotherapy, op cit.,* p. xvii.
31. Stephen J. Morse and Robert Watson, Jr., *Psychotherapies: A Comparative Casebook* (New York: Holt, Rinehart and Winston, 1977), p. 3.
32. John T. McNeill, *A History of the Cure of Souls* (New York: Harper & Row, 1951), p. vii.
33. Kenneth Cinnamon and Dave Farson, *Cults and Cons* (Chicago: Nelson Hall, 1979), cover.
34. Martin Gross, *The Psychological Society* (New York: Random House, 1978), p. 9.
35. Carl Rogers quoted in Allen Bergin, "Psychotherapy and Religious Values," *Journal of Consulting and Clinical Psychology,* 48, p. 101.
36. Bernie Zilbergeld, *The Shrinking of America* (Boston: Little, Brown and Company, 1983), p. 5.
37. Christopher Lasch, *The Culture of Narcissism* (New York: W.W. Norton & Company, Inc., 1979), p. 13.
38. Christopher Lasch, *Haven in a Heartless World* (New York: Basic Books, Inc., 1977), p. 98.
39. Szasz, *The Myth of Psychotherapy, op. cit.,* p. xviii.
40. *Ibid.,* p. xxiv.
41. *Ibid.,* p. 26.

Chapter 6: Polluted Streams

1. James C. Coleman and Constance L. Hammen, *Contemporary Psychology and Effective Behavior* (Glenview: Scott, Foresman and Company, 1974), p. 35.
2. Abraham Maslow, *Toward a Psychology of Being* (Princeton: D. Van Nostrand Company, Inc., 1962, 1968), pp. iii-iv.
3. Maureen O'Hara, "A New Age Reflection in the Magic Mirror of Science," *The Skeptical Inquirer,* 13 (Summer 1989), pp. 368-374.

4. Mary P. Koss and Julia Shiang, "Research on Brief Psychotherapy" in *Handbook of Psychotherapy and Behavior Change*, Fourth Edition, Allen E. Bergin and Sol L. Garfield, eds. (New York: John Wiley & Sons, Inc., 1994), p. 667.

5. Allen E. Bergin and Sol L. Garfield, "Introduction and Historical Overview" in *Handbook of Psychotherapy and Behavior Change*, Fourth Edition, *ibid.*, p. 6.

6. Lawrence J. Crabb, Jr., *Effective Biblical Counseling* (Grand Rapids: Zondervan Publishing House, 1977), p. 56.

Chapter 7: Sigmund Freud/Psychoanalysis

1. E. M. Thornton, *The Freudian Fallacy* (Garden City: The Dial Press, Doubleday and Company, 1984), p. ix.

2. John Horgan, "Why Freud Isn't Dead," *Scientific American* (December 1996), pp. 74-79.

3. *Ibid.*, p. 74.

4. *Ibid.*

5. Robert W. McCarley, "Where Dreams Come From: A New Theory," *Psychology Today* (December 1978), pp. 54-65, 141.

6. Ernest Hilgard, Richard Atkinson, Rita Atkinson, *Introduction to Psychology*, Seventh Edition (New York: Harcourt, Brace, Jovanovich, Inc., 1979), p. 168.

7. Terence Hines, *Pseudoscience and the Paranormal* (New York: Prometheus Books, 1988), p. 111.

8. Dr. J. Allan Hobson, "Dream Theory: A New View of the Brain-Mind," *The Harvard Medical School Mental Health Letter* (February 1989), p. 4.

9. *Ibid.*

10. *Ibid.*, p. 5.

11. Sigmund Freud, *Three Essays on the Theory of Sexuality* (1905) SE, Volume Seven (London: Hogarth Press, 1953), p. 226.

12. Thomas Szasz, *The Myth of Psychotherapy* (Garden City: Doubleday/Anchor Press, 1978), p. 133.

13. Alvin Sanoff, "Psychiatry Runs into an Identity Crisis," *U.S. News and World Report* (9 October 1978), p. 64.

14. E. Fuller Torrey, *The Death of Psychiatry* (Radnor: Chilton Book Company, 1974), p. 24.

15. Thornton, *op. cit.*

16. E. Fuller Torrey, *Freudian Fraud* (New York: HarperCollins Publishers, 1992).

17. Jim Swan, "Mater and Nannie...," *American Imago* (Spring 1974), p. 10.

18. *Ibid.*, p. 10.

19. *Ibid.*

20. Edward C. Whitmont, "Jungian Analysis Today," *Psychology Today* (December 1972), p. 70.

21. Sigmund Freud, *The Ego and the Id*, Joan Riviere, trans., James Strachey, ed. (New York: W. W. Norton and Company, Inc., 1960), p. 13.

22. Lewis Carroll, *Alice's Adventures in Wonderland* (1865).

23. Jerome Kagan, "The Parental Love Trap," *Psychology Today* (August 1978), p. 61.

24. Victor and Mildred Goertzel, *Cradles of Eminence* (Boston: Little, Brown and Company, 1962).
25. Samuel Yochelson and Stanton Samenow, The *Criminal Personality*, Volumes One and Two (New York: Jason Aronson, Inc., 1976, 1977).
26. Hilgard, Atkinson, Atkinson, *op. cit.*, p. 390.
27. *Ibid.*, 390-391.
28. *Ibid.*, p. 426.
29. *Ibid.*, p. 427.
30. Sigmund Freud, "Mourning and Melancholia" (1917) in *The Standard Edition of the Complete Psychological Works of Sigmund Freud*, Volume 14 of 24, James Strachey, Anna Freud, et al., trans. and ed. (London: Hogarth Press, 1953-1974), p. 248.
31. Sigmund Freud, "Formations Regarding the Two Principles of Mental Functioning," quoted in William Glasser, *Reality Therapy* (New York: Harper & Row, 1965), p. xix.
32. Sigmund Freud, "Sexuality in the Aetiology of the Neuroses" *(1898)* in *Collected Papers,* Volume One (New York: Basic Books, Inc., 1959), p. 220.
33. Sigmund Freud, *The Origins of Psychoanalysis: Letters, Drafts and Notes to Wilhelm Fliess* (1887-1902) (Garden City: Anchor Books, 1957), p. 67.
34. Benjamin Spock, *Baby and Child Care* (New York: Pocket Books, Inc., 1957).
35. Benjamin Spock, "How Not to Bring up a Bratty Child," *Redbook* (February 1974), p. 31.
36. *Ibid.*, p. 31.
37. *Ibid.*, p. 29.
38. *Ibid.*, p. 31.
39. Quoted in A. Haynal, *Controversies in Psychoanalytic Method* (New York: New York University Press, 1989), p. 32.
40. Jay Haley, *Strategies of Psychotherapy (*New York: Grune & Stratton, Inc., 1963), p. 82.

Chapter 8: Carl Jung/Analytic Psychology

1. C. G. Jung, *Memories, Dreams, Reflections*, Aniela Jaffe, ed., Richard and Clara Winston, trans. (New York: Pantheon, 1963), p. 109.
2. *Ibid.*, pp. 12-15.
3. *Ibid.*, p. 13.
4. *Ibid.*
5. *Ibid.*, p. 14.
6. *Ibid.*, p. 93.
7. *Ibid.*, p. 171.
8. C. G. Jung, *The Archetypes and the Collective Unconscious*, Second Edition, R.F.C. Hull, trans. (Princeton: Princeton University Press, 1969), p. 4.
9. Jung, *Memories, Dreams, Reflections, op. cit.*, p. 186.
10. Jung, *The Archetypes and the Collective Unconscious, op. cit.*, p. 226.
11. Jung, *Memories, Dreams, Reflections, op. cit.*, pp. 398-399.
12. Alfred M. Freedman, Harold I. Kaplan, Benjamin J. Sadock, *Modern Synopsis* of *Comprehensive Textbook of Psychiatry*, Second Edition (Baltimore: The Williams & Wilkins Co., 1976), pp. 303-304.

13. Calvin S. Hall and Gardner Lindzey, *Theories of Personality* (New York: John Wiley & Sons, Inc., 1957), p. 80.
14. Jung, *Memories, Dreams, Reflections, op. cit.*, p. 160.
15. Jung, *The Archetypes and the Collective Unconscious, op. cit.*, p. 7.
16. C. J. Jung, *Psychological Types* (Princeton: Princeton University Press, 1971, 1976), p. 330.
17. *Ibid.*, p. 342 ff.
18. The National Research Council, *In the Mind's Eye*, Daniel Druckman and Robert A. Bjork, eds. (Washington: National Academy Press, 1991), p. 96.
19. *Ibid.*, p. 99.
20. *Ibid.*, p. 101.
21. *Ibid.*
22. L. J. Cronbach and P. E. Meehl quoted by Jerry S. Wiggins, "Review of the Myers-Briggs Type Indicator" in *Tenth Mental Measurements Yearbook*, Jane Close Conoley and Jack J. Kramer, eds. (Lincoln: University of Nebraska Press, 1989), pp. 537-538.
23. Wiggins, *ibid.*, p. 538.
24. Jung, *Memories, Dreams, Reflections, op. cit.*, pp. 190-191.
25. *Ibid.*, p. 191.
26. *Ibid.*, p. 192.
27. *Ibid.*, p. 183.
28. *Ibid.*, p. 177.
29. *Ibid.*, p. 356.
30. *Ibid.*, p. 201.
31. *Ibid.*, p. 209.
32. C. G Jung, *On the Nature of the Psyche* (Princeton: Princeton University Press, 1960), p. 133.
33. *Webster's New World Dictionary of the English Language*, Second College Edition (New York: Simon & Schuster, Inc. 1984).
34. Jung, *Memories, Dreams, Reflections, op. cit.*, p. 196.
35. *Ibid.*, pp. 334-335.
36. Richard Noll, *The Jung Cult* (Princeton: Princeton University Press, 1994), p. 242.
37. *Ibid.*, p. 219.
38. *Ibid.*, p. 220.
39. "Spiritus contra Spiritum: The Bill Wilson/C. G. Jung Letters: The roots of the Society of Alcoholics Anonymous," *Parabola*, XII (May 1987), p. 68.
40. *Ibid.*, p. 69.
41. *Ibid.*, p. 71.
42. C. G. Jung quoted in Noll, *op. cit.*, p. 188.
43. Noll, *ibid.*, p. 291.
44. Erica Goode, "Spiritual Questing," *U.S. News & World Report* (7 December 1992), p. 64.
45. *Ibid.*, p. 68.

Chapter 9: Alfred Adler/Individual Psychology

1. B. H. Shulman, "Adlerian Psychotherapy," in *Encyclopedia of Psychology*, Raymond J. Corsini, ed. (New York: John Wiley and Sons, 1984), p. 18.

2. Walter Kaufmann, *Discovering the Mind*, Volume Three: *Freud versus Adler and Jung* (New York: McGraw-Hill Book Company, 1980), p. 177.

3. Calvin W. Hall and Gardner Lindzey, *Theories of Personality* (New York: John Wiley and Sons, Inc., 1957), pp. 120-123.

4. Alfred Adler, *The Practice and Theory of Individual Psychology* (1925), P. Radin, trans. (New York: Harcourt, Brace & Company, Inc., 1929), p. 6.

5. Alfred Adler, *What Life Should Mean to You* (1931), Alan Porter, ed. (New York: Capricorn Books, 1958), p. 59.

6. Kaufmann, *op. cit.*, pp. 178-179.

7. Alfred Adler, *What Life Could Mean to You* (1931), Colin Brett, trans. (Oxford: Oneworld Publications Ltd., 1992), p. 22.

8. Adler, *The Practice and Theory of Individual Psychology, op. cit.*, p. 3.

9. *Ibid.*, p. 4.

10. *Ibid.*

11. Alfred Adler, *Understanding Human Nature* (1927), Colin Brett, trans. (Oxford: Oneworld Publications Ltd., 1992), p. 104.

12. Adler, *What Life Should Mean to You, op. cit.*, p. 57.

13. *Ibid.*, p. 58.

14. Adler, *What Life Could Mean to You, op. cit.*, p. 61.

15. Adler, *What Life Should Mean to You, op. cit.*, p. 69.

16. *Ibid.*, p. 61.

17. Alfred Adler, *Understanding Human Nature* (1927), Walter Beran Wolfe, trans. (New York: Greenberg Publisher, 1946), p. 70.

18. Adler, *What Life Should Mean to You, op. cit.*, p. 51.

19. *Ibid.*, p. 52.

20. Kaufmann, *op. cit.*, p. 175.

21. Adler, *What Life Should Mean to You, op. cit.*, p. 49.

22. Adler, *The Practice and Theory of Individual Psychology, op. cit.*, p. 23.

23. Adler, *What Life Should Mean to You, op. cit.*, p. 50.

24. Adler, *What Life Could Mean to You, op. cit.*, p. 34.

25. *Ibid.*, p. 19.

26. Hall and Lindzey, *op. cit.*, p. 124.

27. *Ibid.*, p. 123.

28. *Ibid.*, pp. 123-125.

29. Adler, *Understanding Human Nature*, Wolfe, trans., *op. cit.*, p. 271.

30. Adler, *What Life Could Mean to You, op. cit.*, p. 43.

31. *Ibid.*

32. Adler, *Understanding Human Nature*, Brett, trans., *op. cit.*, p. 18.

33. Adler, *What Life Could Mean to You, op. cit.*, p. 24.

34. Adler, *Understanding Human Nature*, Brett, trans., *op. cit.*, p. 75.

35. Adler, *The Practice and Theory of Individual Psychology, op. cit.*, p. 10.

36. Adler, *What Life Could Mean to You, op. cit.*, pp. 22-23.

37. *Ibid.*, p. 36.

38. *Ibid.*, p. 223.

39. Adler, *Understanding Human Nature*, Wolfe, trans., *op. cit.*, p. 97.

40. Adler, *The Practice and Theory of Individual Psychology, op. cit.*, p. 22.

41. Adler, *What Life Could Mean to You, op. cit.*, p. 30.

42. *Ibid.*, p. 15.
43. *Ibid.*, p. 16.
44. *Ibid.*, p. 35.
45. Adler, *What Life Should Mean to You*, *op. cit.*, p. 58.
46. Shulman, *op. cit.*, p. 19.
47. Adler, *What Life Could Mean to You*, *op. cit.*, p. 22.
48. *Ibid.*, p. 28.
49. *Ibid.*, p. 72.
50. *Ibid.*, p. 71.
51. *Ibid.*, p. 28.
52. *Ibid.*, p. 72.
53. Adler, *Understanding Human Nature*, Brett, trans., *op. cit.*, p. 59.
54. Adler, *What Life Could Mean to You*, *op. cit.*, p. 90.
55. *Ibid.*, p. 91.
56. Alfred M. Freedman, Harold I. Kaplan, Benjamin J. Sadock, *Modern Synopsis of Comprehensive Textbook of Psychiatry*, Second Edition (Baltimore: The Williams & Wilkins Co., 1976), p. 278.
57. Dorothy E. Peven and Bernard H. Shulman, "Adlerian Therapy" in *Psychotherapist's Casebook: Theory and Technique in the Practice of Modern Therapies*, Irwin Kutash and Alexander Wolf, eds. (Northvale, NJ: Jason Aronson Inc., 1986), pp. 109, 118, 122.
58. Adler, *What Life Could Mean to You*, *op. cit.*, p. 24.
59. *Ibid.*, p. 51.
60. Adler, *The Practice and Theory of Individual Psychology*, *op. cit.*, p. 10.
61. Adler, *What Life Could Mean to You*, *op. cit.*, p. 23.
62. *Ibid.*, p. 21.
63. *Ibid.*, p. 31.
64. *Ibid.*, p. 31-32.
65. *Ibid.*, p. 22.
66. *Ibid.*
67. Hall and Lindzey, *op. cit.*, p. 125.
68. *Ibid.*, p. 124.

Chapter 10: Erich Fromm/Unconditional Love

1. Erich Fromm, *Man for Himself: An Inquiry into the Psychology of Ethics* (New York: Holt, Rinehart and Winston, 1947), p. 13.
2. Erich Fromm, *The Art of Loving* (1956) (New York: Bantam Books, Inc., 1963), p. 53.
3. *Ibid.*, p. 59.
4. *Ibid.*, p. 8.
5. Erich Fromm, *To Have or To Be?* (New York: Bantam Books, 1976), pp. 130-131.
6. *Ibid.*, p. 131.
7. Fromm, *The Art of Loving*, *op. cit.*, p. 104.
8. *Ibid.*, p. 34.
9. Fromm, *Man for Himself*, *op. cit.*, pp. 128-130.
10. Johannes Calvin, *Institutes of the Christian Religion*, Book III, Chapter 7, John Allen, trans. (Philadelphia: Presbyterian Board of Christian Education, 1928), p. 619, quoted by Erich Fromm, *Man for Himself*, *op. cit.*, pp. 119-120.
11. Fromm, *The Art of Loving*, *op. cit.*, pp. 59-60.

12. Fromm, *Man for Himself, op. cit.*, p. 147.

Chapter 11: Abraham Maslow/Need Psychology

1. William Coulson, "Maslow, Too, Was Misunderstood," *La Jolla Program*, XX (April, 1988), p. 1.
2. Colin Wilson, *New Pathways in Psychology: Maslow and the Post-Freudian Revolution* (London: Victor Gollancz Ltd., 1972), p. 129.
3. *Ibid.*, pp. 129, 144.
4. Abraham H. Maslow, *Toward a Psychology of Being*, Second Edition (Princeton, NJ: D. Van Nostrand Company, Inc., 1962, 1968), p. 206.
5. *Ibid.*, p. 206.
6. *Ibid.*, p. 198.
7. *Ibid.*, p. 199.
8. *Ibid.*, p. 5.
9. Abraham H. Maslow, *Motivation and Personality* (New York: Harper & Row, Publishers, 1954), p. 101.
10. Maslow, *Toward a Psychology of Being, op. cit.*, p. 5.
11. Maslow, *Motivation and Personality, op. cit.*, p. 83.
12. Abraham H. Maslow, *The Farther Reaches of Human Nature* (New York: The Viking Press, 1971), p. 274.
13. *Ibid.*, p. 275.
14. Maslow, *Motivation and Personality, op. cit.*, p. 102.
15. *Ibid.*, p. 89.
16. Maslow, *Toward a Psychology of Being, op. cit.*, p. 42.
17. Maslow, *Motivation and Personality, op. cit.*, p. 90.
18. *Ibid.*, p. 91.
19. *Ibid.*, p. 53.
20. *Ibid.*, pp. 91-92.
21. Maslow, *Toward a Psychology of Being, op. cit.*, p. 25.
22. Maslow, *Motivation and Personality, op. cit.*, p. 149.
23. Maslow, *Toward a Psychology of Being, op. cit.*, p. 201.
24. Wilson, *op. cit.*, p. 145.
25. Maslow, *Motivation and Personality, op. cit.*, p. 100.
26. Maslow, *Toward a Psychology of Being, op. cit.*, p. 204.
27. *Ibid.*
28. *Ibid.*, p. 3.
29. *Ibid.*, pp. 3-4.
30. *Ibid.*, p. 5.
31. *Ibid.*, p. 165.
32. *Ibid.*, p. 166.
33. *Ibid.*, p. 60.
34. Maslow, *Motivation and Personality, op. cit.*, p. 150.
35. Adrianne Aron, "Maslow's Other Child" in *Politics and Innocence*, Rollo May, Carl Rogers, Abraham Maslow et al., eds. (Dallas: Saybrook Publishers, 1986), p. 96.
36. *Ibid.*, p. 107.
37. *Ibid.*
38. Michael A. and Lise Wallach, *Psychology's Sanction for Selfishness: The Error of Egoism in Theory and Therapy* (San Francisco: W. H. Freeman and Company, 1983), p. 162.
39. Coulson, *op. cit.*, p. 2.

40. Abraham H. Maslow, *Motivation and Personality*, Second Edition (New York: Harper & Row, Publishers, 1970), pp. 237-238.
41. Maslow, *Toward a Psychology of Being, op. cit.*, p. iv.
42. *Ibid.*, p. 167.
43. *Ibid.*, p. 170.
44. Abraham H. Maslow, *Religions, Values, and Peak-Experiences* (New York: The Viking Press, 1964, 1970), p. 20.
45. *Ibid.*
46. *Ibid.*, p. 27.
47. *Ibid.*
48. Maslow, *The Farther Reaches of Human Nature, op. cit.*, p. 116.
49. Jonathan Adolph, "What Is New Age? *The 1988 Guide to New Age Living (New Age Journal)*, p. 12.

Chapter 12: Carl Rogers/Client-Centered Therapy

1. Jay Haley, *Strategies of Psychotherapy* (New York: Grune & Stratton, Inc., 1963), p. 71.
2. *Ibid.*, p. 82.
3. E. J. Murray, "A Content-Analysis Method for Studying Psychotherapy," *Psychological Monographs* 70 (13, Whole no. 420), 1956; C. B. Truax, "Reinforcement and Nonreinforcement in Rogerian Psychotherapy," *Journal of Abnormal Psychology* 71 (1966), pp. 1-9.
4. Calvin S. Hall and Gardner Lindzey, *Theories of Personality* (New York: John Wiley & Sons, 1957), p. 476.
5. Carl Rogers, *On Becoming a Person* (Boston: Houghton Mifflin, 1961), p. 8.
6. *Ibid.*
7. *Ibid.*
8. *Ibid.*
9. William Kirk Kilpatrick, *The Emperor's New Clothes* (Westchester, IL: Crossway Books, 1985), pp. 129-184.
10. Carl Rogers, "Some Personal Learnings about Interpersonal Relationships," 33 min. 16mm film developed by Dr. Charles K. Ferguson, University of California Extension Media Center, Berkeley, Calif., film #6785.
11. Carl Rogers in *Psychology: A Study of a Science,* Volume Three, Sigmund Koch, ed. (New York: McGraw-Hill, 1959), p. 209.
12. Hillel J. Einhorn and Robin M. Hogarth, "Confidence in Judgment: Persistence of the Illusion of Validity," *Psychological Review* 85, 5 (1978), p. 414.
13. Carl Rogers, Graduation Address, Sonoma State College, quoted in Kilpatrick, *op. cit.*, p. 162.
14. E. Brooks Holifield, *A History of Pastoral Care in America: From Salvation to Self-Realization* (Nashville: Abingdon Press, 1983), p. 303.
15. Jeannette DeWyze, "An Encounter with Bill Coulson," *Reader: San Diego's Weekly,* 16 (20 August 1987), pp. 1, 10-23.

Chapter 13: Albert Ellis/Rational Emotive Behavior Therapy

1. Albert Ellis, "The Essence of Rational Emotive Behavior Therapy (REBT): A Comprehensive Approach to Treatment," Institute for Rational Emotive Behavior Therapy brochure, 1994, p. 3.

2. Albert Ellis, *Humanistic Psychotherapy: The Rational-Emotive Approach* (New York: The Julian Press, Inc., 1973), p. 4.
3. Albert Ellis, *"The Case Against Religion: A Psychotherapist's View" and "The Case Against Religiosity"* (New York: The Institute for Rational Emotive Behavior Therapy), p. 6.
4. *Ibid.*, p. 8.
5. Ellis, *Humanistic Psychotherapy, op. cit.*, p. 2.
6. Albert Ellis, *Reason and Emotion* (New York: Lyle Stuart, 1962), p. 387.
7. *Ibid.*, p. 137.
8. Ellis, *Humanistic Psychotherapy, op. cit.*, p. 9.
9. *Ibid.*, p. 11.
10. *Ibid.*, p. 24.
11. *Ibid.*, pp. 156-157.
12. *Ibid.*, p. 17.
13. *Ibid.*, p. 11.
14. *Ibid.*, p. 5.
15. *Ibid.*, p. 154.
16. *Ibid.*, p. 2.
17. *Ibid.*, p. 12.
18. *Ibid.*, p. 28.
19. *Ibid.*, p. 13.
20. Ellis, *Reason and Emotion, op. cit.*, p. 181.
21. *Ibid.*, p. 113.
22. *Ibid.*, p. 182.
23. *Ibid.*, p. 181.
24. *Ibid.*, p. 183.
25. Albert Ellis, "Can Rational Counseling Be Christian?" *Christian Counseling Today,* 5, 1 (1997), pp. 13, 48-49.
26. *Ibid.*, p. 13.
27. Ellis, *Humanistic Psychotherapy, op. cit.*, p. 16.
28. Ellis, "Can Rational Counseling Be Christian?" *op. cit.*, p. 13.
29. *Ibid.*, p. 48.
30. *Ibid.*
31. Albert Ellis interview, "Why I Am a Secular Humanist," *Free Inquiry* (Summer 1997), p. 35.
32. *Ibid.*
33. *Ibid.*, p. 36.
34. *Ibid.*
35. *Ibid.*

Chapter 14: William Glasser/Reality Therapy

1. William Glasser, *Reality Therapy* (New York: Harper and Row, 1965), p. 44.
2. *Ibid.*, p. 53.
3. *Ibid.*, p. 6.
4. *Ibid.*
5. *Ibid.*, p. 13.
6. *Ibid.*, pp. 10-11.
7. *Ibid.*, p. 12.
8. *Ibid.*, p. 9.
9. *Ibid.*, p. 57.

Chapter 15: Thomas Harris/Transactional Analysis

1. Thomas Harris, *I'm OK—You're OK: A Practical Guide to Transactional Analysis* (New York: Harper and Row, 1967), p. 26.
2. *Ibid.*, p. 27.
3. *Ibid.*, p. 41.
4. *Ibid.*, pp. 43, 37.
5. *Ibid.*, p. 50.
6. *Ibid.*, p. 52.
7. *Ibid.*, p. 5.
8. *Ibid.*, p. 39.
9. *Ibid.*, p. 243.
10. *Ibid.*, p. 28.
11. Edmund Bolles, *Remembering and Forgetting* (New York: Walker and Company, 1988), p. 139.
12. *Ibid.*, p. xi.
13. Jean Piaget, *Plays, Dreams and Imitation in Childhood* (New York: Norton, 1962).
14. *Ibid.*
15. Elizabeth Loftus, *Memory: Surprising New Insights into How We Remember and Why We Forget* (Reading, MA: Addison-Wesley Publishing Company, 1980), p. 37.
16. Harris, *op. cit.*, p. 42.
17. *Ibid.*, p. 225-226.
18. *Ibid.*, p. 239.
19. *Ibid.*, p. 184.
20. *Ibid.*, p. 230.
21. *Ibid.*, p. 241.
22. *Ibid.*, p. 227.
23. *Ibid.*
24. *Ibid.*, p. 228.
25. *Ibid.*, pp. 230-231.

Chapter 16: Arthur Janov/Primal Scream Therapy

1. Eileen Keerdoja, "The 'Screaming Cure,'" *Newsweek* (July 10, 1978), p. 12.
2. Arthur Janov, *The Primal Scream* (New York: Dell Publishing Co., Inc., 1970).
3. Janov, *op. cit.*, pp. 28-29.
4. *Ibid.*, p. 20.
5. *Ibid.*, p. 154.
6. *Ibid.*, p. 134.
7. Leonard Berkowitz, "The Case for Bottling Up Rage," *Psychology Today* (July 1973), p. 28.
8. *Ibid.*, p. 31.
9. *Ibid.*

Chapter 17: Diluted, Polluted, or Pure?

1. Thomas Szasz, "Nobody Should Decide Who Goes to the Mental Hospital," *Co-Evolution Quarterly* (Summer 1978), p. 60.
2. Jerome Frank, "Therapeutic Factors in Psychotherapy," *American Journal of Psychotherapy,* 25 (1971), p. 360.

For a sample copy of a free newsletter about the intrusion of psychological counseling theories and therapies into Christianity, please write to:

PsychoHeresy Awareness Ministries
4137 Primavera Road
Santa Barbara, CA 93110

phone: 1-800-216-4696

e-mail: phbobgan@silcom.com

Web Site Address:
http://www.silcom.com/~phbobgan

OTHER BOOKS FROM EASTGATE

PsychoHeresy: The Psychological Seduction of Christianity by Martin and Deidre Bobgan exposes the fallacies and failures of psychological counseling theories and therapies for one purpose: to call the Church back to curing souls by means of the Word of God and the work of the Holy Spirit rather than by man-made means and opinions. Besides revealing the anti-Christian biases, internal contradictions, and documented failures of secular psychotherapy, *PsychoHeresy* examines various amalgamations of secular psychologies with Christianity and explodes firmly entrenched myths that undergird those unholy unions.

Christian Psychology's War On God's Word: The Victimization Of The Believer by Jim Owen is about the sufficiency of Christ and about how "Christian" psychology undermines believers' reliance on the Lord. Owen demonstrates how "Christian" psychology pathologizes sin and contradicts biblical doctrines of man. He further shows that "Christian" psychology treats people more as victims needing psychological intervention than sinners needing to repent. Owen beckons believers to turn to the all-sufficient Christ and to trust fully in His ever-present provisions, the power of His indwelling Holy Spirit, and the sure guidance of the inerrant Word of God.

Against Biblical Counseling: For the Bible by Martin and Deidre Bobgan is about the growing biblical counseling movement and urges Christians to return to biblically ordained ministries and mutual care in the Body of Christ. It is an analysis of what biblical counseling is, rather than what it pretends or even hopes to be. Its primary thrust is to call Christians back to the Bible and to biblically ordained ministries and mutual care in the Body of Christ, "For the perfecting of the saints, for the work of the ministry, for the edifying of the body of Christ" (Ephesians 4:12).

OTHER BOOKS FROM EASTGATE

Competent to Minister: The Biblical Care of Souls
by Martin and Deidre Bobgan encourages believers to
care for one another in the Body of Christ and demonstrates that God enables them to do so without incorporating the methods of the world. Contains much
practical information for developing personal care ministries within the local fellowship of believers. Topics
include overcoming obstacles to caring for souls, salvation and sanctification, caring for souls inside and out,
ministering mercy and truth, caring for one another
through conversation and practical helps, cautions to
heed in caring for souls. This book exposes the professional, psychological intimidation that has discouraged
Christians from ministering to one another during trials and temptations. It both encourages and reveals
how God equips believers to minister to one another.

***Four Temperaments, Astrology & Personality
Testing*** by the Bobgans answers such questions as:
Do the four temperaments give valid information? Are
there biblically or scientifically established temperament or personality types? Are personality inventories
and tests valid ways of finding out about people? How
are the four temperaments, astrology, and personality
testing connected? Personality types and tests are
examined from a biblical, historical, and research basis.

***12 Steps to Destruction: Codependency/Recovery
Heresies*** by the Bobgans provides information for
Christians about codependency/recovery teachings,
Alcoholics Anonymous, Twelve-Step groups, and addic-
tion treatment programs. All are examined from a biblical, historical, and research perspective. The book urges
believers to trust the sufficiency of Christ and the Word
of God instead of Twelve-Step and codependency/recov-
ery theories and therapies.